THE JOURNAL OF THE ASSOCIATION OF MOVING IMAGE ARCHIVISTS

IGIMAGE THE **MOVING**IMAGE THE **MOVING**IMAGE THE **MO**

SPRING 2022

T0345942

The Moving Image (ISSN 1532-3978) is published twice a year in spring and fall by the University of Minnesota Press, 111 Third Avenue South, Suite 290, Minneapolis, MN 55401-2520. http://www.upress.umn.edu

Published in cooperation with the Association of Moving Image Archivists (AMIA). Members of AMIA receive the journal as one of the benefits of membership. For further information about membership, contact the Association of Moving Image Archivists, 1313 North Vine Street, Hollywood, CA 90028 (or email amia@amianet.org or visit http://www.amianet.org).

Postmaster: Send address changes to *The Moving Image,* University of Minnesota Press, 111 Third Avenue South, Suite 290, Minneapolis, MN 55401-2520.

Inquiries and information about manuscript submissions should be sent to editor@themovingimage.org. All manuscripts should be submitted as a Microsoft Word email attachment, double-spaced throughout, using 12-point type with 1-inch margins, using the *Chicago Manual of Style,* 17th edition.

Review copies of DVDs or books should be sent to the AMIA office at 1313 North Vine Street, Hollywood, CA 90028, USA.

Please allow a minimum of 4 months for editorial consideration.

Address subscription orders, changes of address, and business correspondence (including requests for permission and advertising orders) to *The Moving Image,* University of Minnesota Press, 111 Third Avenue South, Suite 290, Minneapolis, MN 55401-2520.

Subscriptions: For our current subscription rates please see our website: http://www.upress.umn.edu. *The Moving Image* is a benefit of membership in the Association of Moving Image Archivists.

Digital subscriptions to *The Moving Image* are available online through the Project MUSE Journals Collection Program at https://muse.jhu.edu/.

Most images reproduced in *The Moving Image* are available to view in color in the electronic edition of *The Moving Image,* accessible via Project MUSE.

Founded in 1991, the **Association of Moving Image Archivists** is the world's largest professional association devoted to film, television, video, and digital image preservation. Dedicated to issues surrounding the safekeeping of visual history, this journal covers topics such as the role of moving image archives and collection in the writing of history, technical and practical articles on research and development in the field, in-depth examinations of specific preservation and restoration projects, and behind-the-scenes looks at the techniques used to preserve and restore our moving image heritage.

Heather Heckman *University of South Carolina*

Jan-Christopher Horak *JCH Archival Consulting*

Eric Hoyt *University of Wisconsin–Madison*

Luna Hupperetz *University of Amsterdam/Vrije Universiteit*

Jennifer Jenkins *University of Arizona*

Jimi Jones *University of Illinois*

Peter Kaufman *Intelligent TV*

Andrea Leigh *Library of Congress*

Bert Lyons *AVP*

Mike Mashon *Library of Congress*

Jan Müller *Regional Public Broadcasting Foundation (RPO)*

Charles Musser *Yale University*

Joshua Ng *Archives New Zealand Te Rua Mahara o te Kāwanatanga*

Kassandra O'Connell *Irish Film Institute*

Miriam Posner *University of California, Los Angeles*

Rick Prelinger *University of California, Santa Cruz*

Meredith Reese *LA Phil*

Lauren Sorensen *Whirl-i-Gig*

Katherine Spring *Wilfrid Laurier University*

Shelley Stamp *University of California, Santa Cruz*

Rachael Stoeltje *Indiana University*

Dan Streible *New York University*

Kara Van Malssen *AVP*

Haidee Wasson *Concordia University*

Mark Williams *Dartmouth University*

Tami Williams *University of Wisconsin–Milwaukee*

Joshua Yumibe *Michigan State University*

Patricia Zimmermann *Ithaca College*

REVIEWS

BOOK

DVD/BLU-RAY

CONFERENCE

Editor's Foreword

DEVIN ORGERON

We at *TMI* had hoped, as we were putting our back-to-back double issues (volumes 20 and 21) together, that our first step into 2022 would be a "post-Covid-19" issue. You know, a "normal" issue. This was even the name of the file I created as it was being assembled: "Normal Issue." I am not an archivist, and my file-naming conventions are idiosyncratic at best! This was back in September 2021. We were so hopeful.

Of course, issue 22.1 emerges to a still-confused and increasingly exhausted world: new Covid-19 variants, economic uncertainty, record gas prices, a war in Ukraine, Supreme Court leaks, mass shootings, the January 6th hearings, and a historic (for good and sad reasons) night at the Oscars. In the midst of all this, our little *TMI* machine, we can admit, slowed down. We had visions of 22.1 coming out early! Then we aimed for April. Then we agreed that sometime in the spring would be OK. And then we realized that it would eventually come out! We've learned to be flexible. And, thankfully, the wonderful contributors assembled here, all of whom were navigating all of this on their own terms and in their own time, were patient with us.

You will also probably notice that issue 22.2 has been released close to 22.1. It turns out that your *TMI* editor, during times of crisis, collects essays! I directed essays to readers, took them through the process, and then lost count. The short story is that, by the time I had awakened from my stupor, I had collected enough material (so many great essays, conversations, profiles, etc.) for *two* issues. Let's call them *two normal issues.*

So what does a "normal" issue of *TMI* look like? It's an interesting question and one I think the essays assembled here answer in a particularly bold and, we hope, energizing and inspirational fashion. We are very fond of our special issues (and several more are on the horizon: a special issue on "Borders and Boundaries" [23.1], a centennial celebration of 16mm [23.2], and an issue on "Government Film" [24.1] edited by our superlative reviews editor, Brian Real). But our journal and the organization behind it are exciting because of the diversity of ideas and perspectives, the range of obsessions and interests, that they support. A normal issue of *TMI* reflects this remarkably well. And it doesn't look like a normal issue of any other academic journal.

Issue 22.1 begins with **Angélica Gasparotto de Oliveira**'s "Pioneer Cinematographers of Brasília: Home Movies and Newsreels during the Construction of the New Capital of Brazil." I had the privilege of being on an AMIA panel (this seems like decades ago!) with Angélica where I heard a nascent version of this work and was moved by it. It is a captivating glimpse into a city's birth and film's unique role in it. It emerges to a world that finds Brazil, once again, facing an uncertain future.

Adam Charles Hart's "In Search of Bigfoot: Recovering George A. Romero's *Jacaranda Joe*" is the sort of feature *TMI* has always enjoyed running. It's a "discovery" piece—and one that will coincide brilliantly with our meeting in Pittsburgh, where we hope to screen the film. Hart's discovery also follows a unique critical thread that has implications for similar discoveries and asks readers to reconsider their thinking about unfinished work. You'll notice a fine image of Joe himself on the cover of this issue. Take it all in.

Luna Hupperetz's "Cineclub Vrijheidsfilms: Restoring a Militant Cinema Network" is also a discovery piece. It examines a recently discovered film, *Vrouwen van Suriname/Oema foe Sranan* (1978). But, perhaps more critically, it discovers the issues at stake in, as she phrases it, "go[ing] from a militant cinema to a 'militant archive.'" Hupperetz's article asks provocative questions and demonstrates a handle on the history that brings the reader right to the center of the action, and I think *TMI* readers will look forward to hearing more from this author.

Brian Real and **Teague Schneiter**'s "The 2020 AMIA Annual Salary and Demographics Survey of the Field: Findings and Future Directions" takes the conversation, for a moment, in a usefully practical direction, focusing on the economics of our professions. While some of the information here has been presented in other formats and has been circulating within the organization, it is, we think, the first time the journal has published these statistics and, we hope, not the last.

Our Features section closes strong with **Anthony L. Silvestri**'s "Photo Blocks, Sex Dollar Bills, and 'Useless' Packing Cushions: Kenneth Anger and the Kinsey Institute, 1947–2015." This a fascinating examination of Anger's understudied pursuits as an amateur researcher and collector. Providing a history of the Anger archives at the

Kinsey Institute, Silvestri's work leaves us with an understanding of Anger as archivist.

Our Collections section showcases a piece by **Martine Bouw** and **Anne Gant** called "Hard Drive Failures and Learning Curves: Results from Ingesting Twelve Years of Born-Digital Film at Eye Filmmuseum." Pieces like this one are especially useful, as they can provide powerful examples for individuals and institutions facing similar situations.

Victoria Duckett's "Covid Conversations" series continues with interviews with Mike Mashon and Haden Guest. Our thanks to Victoria for making our universally altered routines seem less isolated.

So there you have it—a jam-packed issue that will flow elegantly into issue 22.2. That's your weekend all sorted! Enjoy! And, as always, submit to *The Moving Image*.

Devin Orgeron is editor of *The Moving Image*, Professor Emeritus of Film and Media Studies at North Carolina State University, and chair of the Northeast Historic Film Summer Symposium, which takes place in late July in Bucksport, Maine. He is the author of *Road Movies* (2008) and editor of *Learning with the Lights Off* (2012).

PIONEER CINEMATOGRAPHERS OF BRASÍLIA

ANGÉLICA GASPAROTTO DE OLIVEIRA

Home Movies and Newsreels

during the Construction of

the New Capital of Brazil

Brasília was built by the pioneers in the central desert region of the country, and it was amid this idealized city, still under construction, that several cinematographers began to film what would be the first moving image records of the new capital of Brazil.[1] The Brazilian cinematographers moved to the Brasília region either to work on the construction or to register the peculiarities of those early years in the capital; foreigners, in turn, decided to venture into another country or came to work on the construction, having on several occasions curiosity in registering construction workers, also known as *candangos*.[2]

This article considers six pioneer cinematographers—Manuel Mendes, Fernando Rosendo, Dino Cazzola, Isaac Rozemberg, José Antônio Silva, and Sálvio Silva—who filmed the construction and initial years of the city of Brasília and who are mentioned in archival records, news reports, books, academic papers, scientific articles, and oral histories. I focus on these six because the first inhabitants of Brasília, both Brazilian and foreign, were discovered after extensive research about the cinematographers who had filmed and lived in the capital during its construction.

It is important to highlight that the 16mm films of the workers, in some cases, are the only existing records of specific events that occurred during that period because the press from other states only sometimes covered construction events. The images produced various perspectives of the city, which created a unique collection of film artifacts about the period.

Manuel Mendes described that the Rio de Janeiro and São Paulo press were not interested in reporting on work to which they were opposed, and Brasília newspapers did not exist by then; therefore most footage of the construction comes from the work of the cinematographers mentioned.

The aims of this article are to discuss the lives and cinematographic works by these early inhabitants related to the construction of Brasília and to present the history of the first films of this city. My hope is that this detailed examination will also stimulate interest in the preservation of these important collections and draw attention to the need to catalog and safeguard. These works, I argue, are among the best documentation we have of this important moment in Brazilian history.

I conducted research about the cinematographers' movies at the Federal District Public Archive (ArPDF) in Brasília, at the Brazilian Cinematheque of São Paulo,[3] at the National Archive of Rio de Janeiro,[4] and at the Cinematheque of the Museum of Modern Art (MAM),[5] also located in Rio, because they are the largest film archives in Brazil, and films from or about Brasília that were not kept in ArPDF were sent to these three institutions.[6]

It should be noted that Brasília still does not have its own cinematheque but instead has a refrigerated room to store films within ArPDF. These works are consequently found in passive preservation with an Excel database that does not adequately register the archives.[7] There is thus no information about the level of preservation of these collections at the Brazilian Cinematheque of São Paulo and whether they can be accessed or are only stored in refrigerated rooms.

Accessing these films today is very difficult, and there are no reports or records of what exactly they contain. What is known can be found in Mendes's biography, interviews, and the few titles located within documents donated to ArPDF or in the researched archives' databases.

Figure 1. Oscar Niemeyer *(first from left)* and Juscelino Kubitschek *(eighth from left).*

Figure 2. Oscar Niemeyer *(second from left)* and workers in front of Catetinho Palace. From the Federal District Public Archive.

THE NEW CAPITAL

In January 1956, Juscelino Kubitschek[8] was sworn in as president of Brazil and released a program that aimed to redemocratize and develop the country. Such a plan came to fruition in the construction of Brasília. Kubitschek's dream became real after approximately one thousand days, due to the uninterrupted work of technicians, *candangos,*[9] and machines he led himself.[10]

Kubitschek supported the capital's construction for two reasons: to move the Brazilian administration to the countryside, thus developing and revitalizing that area, and to remove the sociocultural and economic life concentrated on the coast.[11] The construction of the first structure, known as the Catetinho Palace,[12] began in October 1956, and in 1960, Brasília was inaugurated.

In 1964, however, a military coup took place in Brazil that brought about the dictatorship period, which would last twenty-one years. During this time, Kubitschek endured strong pressure from the military regime members and ended up dying in a car accident in 1976.[13]

Architect Oscar Niemeyer and engineer Lúcio Costa worked with Companhia Urbanizadora da Nova Capital do Brasil (Novacap)[14] following Kubitschek's plans and Novacap's president Israel Pinheiro, also the first governor of Brasília from 1961 to 1962.[15] Niemeyer, like Kubitschek, left Brazil after the 1964 coup. On several occasions, the architect was the victim of humiliating interrogations by the military police, who questioned him about his communist bias, in addition to having his office in Rio de Janeiro ransacked.

A great number of Niemeyer's highlighted international projects were inspired by his greatest project: the construction of Brasília. Costa's plan and Niemeyer's architecture resulted in the eye-catching administrative center of the new capital.

Those who had been part of Brasília's construction had a dream of modernity, including a rhetoric of democracy and the rise of a new, equal society. However, several dichotomies appeared throughout the city and its social development: the most remarkable one was the division into different neighborhoods of those who worked for the government and lived downtown and those who worked in construction—the latter were transferred to a city forty kilometers from Brasília.

PIONEERS

Shots of Brasília were not only produced spontaneously, as in the home movies[16] of pioneers like Manuel Mendes and Fernando Rosendo, but also by companies hired by

Figure 3. Worker in front of the Congress building. From the Federal District Public Archive.

Figure 4. Workers. From the Federal District Public Archive.

Novacap, such as PRODIC of Dino Cazzola, Organização Cinematográfica I. Rozemberg of Isaac Rozemberg, and Libertas Filme Produtora Cinematográfica of José Antônio and Sálvio Silva. Documentaries or newsreels produced by these companies were usually displayed before feature films in Brazilian cinemas, for advertising purposes and to disclose the steps in the construction process.[17]

MANUEL MENDES

Manuel Mendes came from Rio de Janeiro to Brasília in November 1957 as part of the second group of pioneers. He reported that Brasília was only a deserted and bucolic landscape where workers felt extremely alone. The document with the largest amount of information found on Mendes is his autobiography, which is dedicated "to the forgotten pioneers of Brasília, my witness and my gratitude."[18]

According to Mendes, as small shops and the improvised housing of pioneers arose, the city gained Western airs. Some years later, after the city was finished, Mendes looked for the two big sheds that had hosted the Novacap board of directors, "the construction brain of Brasília," and was deeply sorry when he heard that they had been destroyed. He considered that these big sheds were a historical relic of the construction and that many others had been destroyed—including signs, old paths, the National Bank agency, the city's first hospital—because "it seems we are in a big hurry of getting to the future and we forget or despise what has happened." Indeed, only Catetinho had been saved. In this statement, he referred specifically to Brazilians, but he himself did not forget: he did his best to register many scenes on film during the construction.

At that time, many institutes were in charge of sending workers to Brasília and providing them with aid and wages, such as the Instituto de Previdência e Assistência dos Servidores do Estado (IPASE). Some of these institutes, including IPASE, bought 16mm projectors for film sessions improvised in the workers' free time. Mendes ended up in charge of the projections because he had previously done similar work at a school in Rio de Janeiro, where he managed a cinema for children. Mendes became the film projectionist of the IPASE camp.

He reported that movies came from Rio de Janeiro, and then projectors and films were transported in a Jeep to the camp; the event coordination, program elaboration, and movie distribution were Mendes's responsibilities. He used to promote two sessions for employees, on Saturdays and Sundays, but, after some time, Mendes started projecting movies for other institutes, and his work tripled.

This pioneer thus became closer to cinema and closer to his coworkers. When the first soccer teams arose—which, like cinema, helped to break the monotony of spare time—the projectionist decided to become a camera operator and filmed some soccer matches, including one that took place at a party organized for workers by Mendes and his colleagues on Labor Day, May 1, 1958.

> Soccer teams representing several camps and even a Luziânia team took part in it. The initial kick was given by pioneer Father Raimundo from Colégio Dom Bosco. Amidst the supporters there was a worker playing the accordion and our friend Clério Gomes was blowing a trumpet, which I was not aware where he got it. It all gave me some scenes that I have recorded in 16mm.

However, at times, work would completely stop because of a lack of resources, and government debt started to increase as the city construction progressed, so Kubitschek decided to pay a visit to Brasília. Mendes quickly found himself holding a camera at the place where he would record the president's arrival. The helicopter that flew in carried a major and another person who was not Kubitschek—he had traveled by car to the same location, from another direction. Even though he had missed Kubitschek's arrival, Mendes recorded it all, even the president's speech, as soon as he found him.

As a city under development did not present a great risk concerning kidnappings and attacks against the president, Kubitschek moved on to other institutes and freely among workers, talking to them and giving them autographs, with no guards,

Figure 5. Juscelino Kubitschek arriving by Jeep to the Institute of Bankers. I found these photographs at the Public Archive, and they illustrate the facts as narrated by Mendes in his autobiography. Unfortunately, the photographer is unknown. From the Federal District Public Archive.

security team, or TV cameras. Mendes ended up being the press: he remained at the president's side throughout November 10, 1958, on which he reported, "After he noticed me always around him, with a heavy video camera, he hit my shoulder and laughing told me that I would probably be very tired."

Brasília became the focus of the world press a few days before its inauguration, on April 21, 1960. United Press International hired Mendes to create a short documentary titled *Como a cidade se prepara para a mudança* (How the city prepares for a change), in which he recorded trucks arriving with furniture, people organizing apartments, offices being set up, and interviews, among other footage. He also filmed a parade in Asa Sul (South Wing) on the day of Brasília's inauguration. A North American company heard about Mendes because he helped its team to develop pictures of U.S. President Eisenhower's visit to Brasília in February 1960.

Mendes's films are now found at ArPDF. One may identify in the archive's documents a list of movies that may be those the pioneer mentions in his autobiography, with the titles *Scenes of the Commemoration of Labor Day in 1958*; *Scenes of Juscelino in the Works of IPASE on 11/11/1958*;[19] *Scenes of a Soccer Tournament*; and *Founding Scenes at 208 South Wing by Rabello Company Who Dug the Big Corkscrew Sharks*. Also on the list are films about the construction work on the first apartments of the South Wing, helicopter flights, parties, and scenes of the IPASE warehouse.

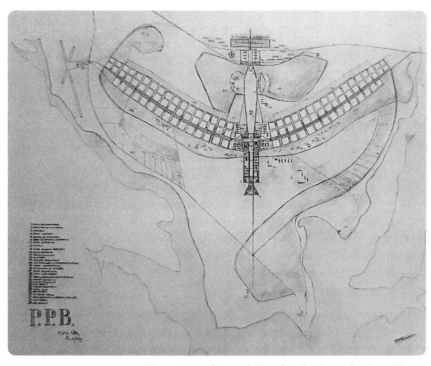

Figure 6. Brasília was designed in the shape of a plane. Thus the North and South are called "wings," coming from the center. From Fonseca, 2002.

Figure 7. Juscelino Kubitschek and Israel Pinheiro eating lunch in one of the institutes to celebrate. From the Federal District Public Archive.

FERNANDO DA GLÓRIA ROSENDO

Fernando da Glória Rosendo[20] disembarked in Brasília in 1956 to help build Palácio da Alvorada. For two years, he devoted himself to Niemeyer's project and to recording the life of *candangos,* authorities' visits to Brasília, and city construction.

In 2011, Rosendo was interviewed by the newspaper *Jornal Correio Braziliense,* and the article mentioned the images he had filmed of the construction of Brasília and where he had stored them. The historical value of the engineer's collection was noted when he reported, "For being in charge of Alvorada's work, I had the opportunity of witnessing all of Juscelino's [Kubitschek's] visits and of other personalities when the palace was being built. I registered almost all of them." He filmed the visit of Fidel Castro, Eisenhower, and many *candangos* with his Nikon Super 8mm camera. The strongest memories he kept were of workers with machetes strapped to their waists and also movie sessions that he promoted to entertain them.

Rosendo, like Mendes, presented movies sent from Rio de Janeiro. The first session stood out in the engineer's memory because, as he reported, "the laborers stood up and started touching the white sheet that I had stretched to use it as canvas. They wanted to see if the reproduced pictures had life."[21]

Rosendo was more interested in the anonymous characters of the construction, the *candangos,* who surprised him so much and proved memorable: "I was not a photographer or professional cinematographer. I was a curious man. And that people, with a different lifestyle from mine, always called my attention. This is why I filmed and photographed them."

In 2011, Rosendo, who at the time lived in Portugal, reported that he had half of the films with him abroad and had sent the other half to his daughter Ana Maria Rosendo, who still lives in Brasília.

Ana Maria Rosendo reported in 2011 that her father's films were still very well conserved in six duly identified cans, and she was advised to send the movies to Cinemateca Brasileira de São Paulo to keep them in an appropriate environment.

DINO CAZZOLA

Contardo Dino Cazzola[22] had already recorded the destruction caused by the Second World War in Italy and, when he moved to Brazil, he was excited to capture images that were opposed to his previous effort; this time, he would record the construction of a capital, rather than the destruction of war. Thus he founded Produções Dino Cazzola

Figure 8. Oscar Niemeyer and Fernando Rosedo in front of Palácio da Alvorada. From the Federal District Public Archive.

Figure 9. Juscelino Kubitschek and Fidel Castro's visit to Brasília. From the Federal District Public Archive.

Figure 10. Fernando Rosedo and Oscar Niemeyer inside Palácio da Alvorada. From the Federal District Public Archive.

Figure 11. Dino Cazzola
(right). From the Federal
District Public Archive.

Ltda (PRODIC) in Brasília to create advertising pieces for the state.[23]

Even though he created an extensive documentary record of the construction of Brasília, only three hundred hours of movies were preserved. In 2012, a documentary, *Dino Cazzola: A Filmography of Brasília,* was released and, during the research for its production, Cazzola's collection of content was finally discovered. Reels were found in the RJ National Archive: the can labels indicated the subjects of the films as the construction of the North–South axis, Brasília Cathedral construction, and Kubitschek walking on the city construction works, among other topics.

ArPDF databases list several documents regarding PRODIC that referred to advertising campaigns that had been produced through contracts with Novacap, with the following themes: educational campaign of Brasília's population; Tree Week; Axis Week; and a nameless campaign, presenting only its summary. The latter would be a black-and-white documentary with a thirty-minute duration and two copies in Kinescope, related to the planning and execution of construction works, about which the Italian cinematographer declared "that we understand it of great historical value as a record of Novacap's accomplishments, in a period of greater mobilization. . . . This collection could not be left unnoticed for the future."[24]

ISAAC ROZEMBERG

Isaac Rozemberg[25] was one of the most active cinematographers in Brazil, and he registered the economic, social, and cultural transformations of the country. A great part of these records was ordered through his company, Organização Cinematográfica I. Rozemberg, for advertising the government. In some of the films he made, Rozemberg was famous for his aerial images, long takes from many angles, and shot–reverse shot cutting.[26]

The cinematographer also worked directly with Kubitschek and made many records of his visits to Brasília. In 1974, two years before his death, Kubitschek wrote a friendly letter to Rozemberg asking for some of his footage because he was shooting a color film about the history of Brasília.

> The tape will last one hour in which I hope to leave a declaration of historical character that will serve for universities of Brazil and abroad. You understand the meaning of this filming for me. Modern technology allows me to eternalize a declaration on something I played the leading role in. Thus, History may also tell, following my version of the facts, that I know how much sacrifice, watch and hope men like us had to make to live intensely that wonderful and creating period of the Brazilian life. But for this videotape, I need a support from your cinematographic collection, past and present, about Brasília. . . . The recording will contain, in the presentation signs, the reference to the companies that collaborated with it.[27]

None of the researched collections presented information about the film recorded by Kubitschek, thus it is unknown whether it was concluded.

Currently Reizi Rozemberg is in charge of taking care of fifteen hundred rolls of her father's films stored at the National Archive and, in ten years, she managed to assemble fifty DVDs—in 2015, she coordinated the project Preservação da Série Fílmica Coisas do Brasil do Acervo I. Rozemberg [Preservation of the things of Brazil film series of I. Rozemberg's collection].[28] The project's first phase comprised the technical analysis, cataloging, cleaning, and reconditioning in new wrappers of 170 titles of the series with the purpose of locating the filmic material and building a database.

The series film list, currently in a preservation process, includes titles regarding Brasília during its construction, such as *Brasília, sonho que se fez realidade*; *Brasília 62*; *Contrastes do Brasil*; *Imenso, belo e grandioso* and *Nova mensagem*, in which Oscar Niemeyer presents the plan and model of the future presidential palace in Brasília.

The films were hitherto stored under temperature-proper conditions in the rooms of the Rio de Janeiro National Archive and the São Paulo Brazilian Cinematheque. These institutions reported that sixty-two titles were found in good condition, presenting

Figure 12. Photograph of Juscelino Kubitschek with a dedication to I. Rozemberg, which reads, "To the dearest friend and brave pioneer that in the dawn of Brasília came with me to the Planalto loneliness and, day after day, with dedication and idealism, helped build the new capital of Brazil . . . Brasília, April 3, 1960." From Reizi Rozemberg's personal collection.

Figure 13. Cineac Trianon, Rio de Janeiro. From Reizi Rozemberg's personal collection.

moderate damage, and seventy-three titles were found in a stage of advanced deterioration.

Movies about Brasília, including those of Rozemberg's authorship, not only were included in the UNESCO World Memory List, in December 2014, but his entire collection was also declared of public and social interest by the Conselho Nacional de Arquivos. Several printed documents associated with the cinematographer's name do exist, including the following criticism of the newspaper *A Manhã* (1953) at Cinemateca Brasileira:

> Rozemberg is a pioneer, a renovator. His completely dynamic and observatory camera, always careful at focusing on the smallest things, and used by someone who knows great resources of the seventh art brings us much of the things we are not aware of yet.[29]

In October 2019, Reizi reported that she was unable to raise money to restore her father's work. Reizi submitted another grant in Brazil for a project of digitization and recovery of Rozemberg's collection, but it has been canceled in the last government of Jair Bolsonaro, which ended in December 2022.

JOSÉ ANTÔNIO, SÁLVIO, AND SINÉSIO SILVA

Figure 14. Alvorada Palace during construction *(left)* and today. From the Federal District Public Archive.

José Antônio Silva[30] was the owner of Libertas Filme Production Company, which was later called Alvorada Filmes and SSS Produções. His two sons, Sálvio and Sinésio Silva, worked with their father at the production company.

> Cinematographers traveled to Nova Capital [New Capital], under construction, once or twice a month. The conditions of production, shooting performance, development and distribution were very precarious and work required a spirit of improvisation, accumulation of duties and creativity that are features of such period and cinema history in Brazil.[31]

Owing to his friendship with Israel Pinheiro, Silva was invited to film Brasília through an agreement with Libertas Filme, which produced, shot, and edited approximately twenty-four films between 1957 and 1960, from the beginning of construction until the inauguration of Brasília. These shoots contain records of visits of foreign authorities, the openings of monuments like Palácio da Alvorada, and remarkable events, such as the burial of engineer Bernardo Sayão[32] and Kubitschek's birthday in Brasília, both in 1959.[33]

During an interview he gave to Fundação Nacional Pró-Memória, Silva declared,

> I would sometimes ask to be taken to film and I would not be picked up. I only returned when a truck passed by me. It was very hard to find transportation at that time. Not even my friendship with Israel made things easier, because they did not actually have a transport. Sacrifice had to be done. I could only film Cidade Livre,[34] for instance, from its top. Israel did not want me to shoot

there. Feeling anxious to shoot Brasília, I was not even aware of the State. I was almost fired because of it. Now I am not aware of shoots in Brasília. Films speak by themselves. But it was profoundly exciting.[35]

Silva's son Sálvio also reported during the interview that he might have taken the first official shots of Brasília, through a contract with Novacap, but that the contract was noncommercial because they filmed and in return were provided with transportation, accommodation, and payment of the costs of developing and copying.

The first material to be filmed was the first Mass in Brasília. The only footage of this first Mass is from Libertas Filme because the other companies that were there did not know how to manage, during the filming, the excess light characteristic of the city and lost all their material.[36]

At some moments, the city was even shot from inside a bus. According to Sálvio, films were recorded with a lot of sacrifice, but "we continued until the opening, a very lovely spectacle. The most beautiful one that I have ever witnessed in my entire life." At one point, the cinematographer himself exhibited his films in many cities in Brazil to show the development of construction works in the city owing to the strong pressure by local governments and politicians of opposition parties against its construction. Sálvio reported that "nobody wanted to come to Brasília. But I enjoyed it. It was a very valid experience. I enjoyed making this job."[37]

At the end of Sálvio's life, he and his family went through serious financial difficulties. The cinematographer was in a wheelchair due to a stroke and, to help him, his wife, Kitita Távora Silva, tried to sell his films in 1987. There were nine short films in 35mm showing Kubitschek's birthday, the visit of a Japanese prince, and the opening of the U.S. Embassy, among other works produced by Novacap.[38]

CONCLUSION

In 2016, even though the researched collection was considered part of world heritage by UNESCO, during the search for cinematographic works related to Brasília's construction in ArPDF databases, the Brazilian Cinematheque of São Paulo, the National Archive of Rio de Janeiro, and the Cinematheque of MAM, I could not find results related to home movies or newsreels from the first years of the capital.

Nevertheless, according to information found in documents I accessed at ArPDF—donation terms and lists with movie titles—Mendes's films and Libertas Filme films were found to be stored in this institution. Films by Libertas Filme were transferred through a donation on March 6, 1991, by Maria Etelvina Távora Correia Silva. Mendes

Figure 15. *Left,* cinematographers film the Congress during its construction; *right,* the Congress in 2016. From the Federal District Public Archive and the author's personal collection.

donated his films to the institution on April 4, 2001. There were fifteen of his movies in 16mm, with images of Brasília dated 1958.

Rozemberg's films remained in the care of his daughter, who has been doing a great job at preserving them, as mentioned. The titles of his film collection were also not included in the databases of the researched institutions. Rosendo's films were not found in the researched databases or at ArPDF, where his name appears only in documents related to agreements for engineering works. The same is true of Cazzola's collection. Although many printed registers with titles of films produced by his company have been found, no film was located in the search among those indexed and/or digitized by the archive, with one exception: after watching some of the films digitized at ArPDF, by chance, one was found to have been produced by the Italian cinematographer during construction.

Thus there are originals or copies of the cinematographic works in at least two of the archives mentioned. Why, then, could I not find them in the 2016 databases?

Attention is drawn to the fact that users of archives, in search of films, require access to a database in which works are appropriately cataloged and indexed.

Few countries' capitals have little more than half a century of life. Both the home movies—which show homemade scenes of families' daily routines and cause viewers to wonder at the strangeness of people's dress, their haircuts, and car designs—and the newsreels, which were produced with a preestablished script, have a particular way of depicting, along with the daily lives of pioneers, scenes of a city planned to be the capital of Brazil in full construction mode.

Cinematographers who were interested in making such films, according to what was observed in documents found in the archives, had a great interest in recording the city's construction for posterity and in a way that would be accessible to future generations. However, records of hardworking films made in the 1950s and 1960s are now rarely accessible.

The grouping of films about Brasília's construction, diagnosis, and registration in databases, revealing its situation or allowing access to such works, is a great step toward the preservation of films that have so much to say not only about the history of Brazil's capital but also about its designers, founders, and first inhabitants.

Angélica Gasparotto de Oliveira holds a doctorate in cinema studies from the Department of Arts at the University of Bologna, where she developed a dissertation on the adaptation of traditional European film restoration laboratories to digital techniques. She holds a master's degree in information science from the Graduate Program in Information Science (PPGCinf) at the University of Brasília (UnB), with a thesis titled "Preservation of Film Collections in the Federal District."

NOTES

1. The city and monuments were designed by internationally renowned architect Oscar Niemeyer during the government of Juscelino Kubitschek (1956–61). For more information on this topic, see David Kendrick Underwood, *Oscar Niemeyer and the Architecture of Brazil* (New York: Rizzoli, 1994).

2. Workers who moved from other Brazilian states to build Brasília.

3. The Brazilian Cinematheque of São Paulo originated from a film club in 1946 and became one of the main cinematheques responsible for safeguarding films in Brazil. The São Paulo Film Club was created by Paulo Emílio Salles Gomes, a historian, film critic, professor, and author exiled in France during the government of Getúlio Vargas because of his constant activity in political manifestations considered dangerous to the public order. President Getúlio Vargas, who preceded Juscelino Kubitschek, commanded a dictatorial government (1951–54), which banished various artists and intellectuals.

According to Fausto Douglas Correa Júnior, Paulo Emílio Salles Gomes helped to build the International Federation of Film Archives (FIAF), which was certainly fundamental in the creation of cinematheques in Brazil and in FIAF's support to help maintain the Brazilian Cinematheque. For more information on this topic, see Fausto Douglas Correa Júnior, *A Cinemateca Brasileira: das luzes aos anos de chumbo,* 172 (São Paulo: Unesp, 2010).

4. The National Archive, created in 1838, before cinema existed, looks after the documentary heritage of the country. Even though the organization of a structure to preserve and store moving images is recent in the National Archive, in the 1980s, newsreels in serious risk of deterioration were transferred to the National Archive, which inspired a team to rapidly prepare themselves to conserve them. The institution was thus modernized and has not stopped receiving films since. Nevertheless, there are still few resources in Brazil for the enormous number of films, few specialized professionals, and even fewer institutions that can store them with certain security. For more information, see "Brasil. Ministério da Justiça. Arquivo Nacional," http://www.arquivonacional.gov.br/cgi/cgilua.exe/sys/start.htm?sid=1; and Clóvis Molinari Júnior, "Apresentação," *Revista Acervo* 16, no. 1 (2003): 4–8.

5. Cinematographic activities at MAM began in 1955 with exhibitions of films to the public. In 1957, the museum effectively had its own cinematheque to store and preserve films. More information is available at "Museu de Arte Moderna do Rio de Janeiro," http://mamrio.org.br/.

6. A. G. de Oliveira, "Preservação de acervos fílmicos no Distrito Federal" (master's thesis, Universidade de Brasília, 2013).

7. Clara de Andrade Alvim, Vera Americano Bueno, and Marco Antonio Guimarães, *Os cine-jornais sobre o período da construção de Brasília* (Brasília: Ministério da Cultura, 1983).

8. In the so-called Quarta República (Fourth Republic) between 1957 and 1960, the project that saw the creation of Brasília was instigated by President Kubitschek de Oliveira. For more on this topic, see Laurent Vidal, *De nova Lisboa à Brasília: l'invention d'une capitale, Xixe-Xxe siècles* (Paris: IHEAL, 2002).

9. Workers who moved from other Brazilian states to build Brasília.

10. Adirson Vasconcelos, *A epopéia da construção de Brasília* (privately published, 1989).

11. Adirson Vasconcelos, *A mudança da capital* (privately published, 1978).

12. The first structure of Brasília, the so-called *palácio de tábuas* (board palace), was used as the president's house; Vasconcelos, *A epopéia da construção de Brasília*, 66.

13. Luciene Aquino, "O peixe vivo fora da água fria," *Correio Braziliense: JK 20 anos depois*.

14. It was a company created to the means required to build the new capital. Documents created during the construction of Brasília—movies, photos, architectural plans—were kept at this institution.

15. *Jornal de Brasília*, April, May, and June 2002.

16. *Home movies*, in this context, means not only family movies but also amateur cinema as described by the Home Movies Association, http://home movies.it/.

17. De Oliveira, "Preservação de acervos fílmicos no Distrito Federal."

18. All the quotes in this section and most of the information on Mendes can be found in Manuel Mendes, *Meu testemunho de Brasília* (Brasília: Distrito Federal: Horizonte, 1979).

19. Mendes's biography reports that such a visit took place on November 10, but the film title described the visit as on November 11.

20. Portuguese engineer.

21. "Tesouros da construção de Brasília permanecem guardados," *Correio Braziliense*, February 7, 2011.

22. Born in the region of Lombardy, Italy, he arrived in Brazil in 1959 disguised as a Brazilian military officer without documents, helped by *pracinhas*, soldiers of the Brazilian Army he had met during the Second World War, when his city was destroyed.

23. "Oriundo na Belacap: trajetória de Dino Cazzola é revista em festival," *Carta Capital*, March 2012.

24. Novacap technical report 1.813, protocol 07767, Arquivo Pùblico do Distrito Federal, Brasília.

25. As Guilherme Cerqueira and Pâmela Pinto mentioned, Romanian cinematographer Rozemberg was born in 1913 and came to Brazil in 1927 to escape military recruitment. He also went to the United States, where he took courses at Eastmancolor Laboratories to learn how to film in color. During the same period, he worked at Hollywood studios and returned to Brazil in 1953. He passed away in 1983. Guilherme M. Cerqueira and Pâmela A. Pinto, "O Milagre do Maranhão: Uma Análise do Maranhão Novo Registrado pela Lente de Isaac Rosenberg," in *IV encontro nacional de história das mídias*, 1–15 (São Paulo: Rede Alcar, 2006).

26. Cerqueira and Pinto, 4.

27. Reizi Rozemberg's personal collection.

28. "Ministério da Cultura, Preservação da série fílmica Coisas do Brasil," https://pesquisa.in.gov.br/imprensa/servlet/INPDFViewer?jornal=1&pagina=1 1&data=27/09/2016&captchafield=firstAccess.

29. "Rosemberg no cinema brasileiro," *A Manhã*, March 1953, 7.

30. Born in Portugal in 1901.

31. Alvim et al., *Os cine-jornais sobre o período da construção de Brasília.*

32. Engineer responsible for the New Capital's infrastructure. He died on January 15, 1959, when a tree fell on him during the construction of Belém-Brasília road; see http://justilex.jusbrasil.com.br/noticias/597516/ha-50-anos -morria-bernardo-sayao-engenheiro-que-ajudou-a-construir-brasilia.

33. Tereza Eleutério de Sousa, "Technical Advice of the Permanent Archives Coordinator about the process number 151.000029/2015 which has as subject Technical Cooperation Agreement with Memorial JK," Arquivo Público do Distrito Federal, Brasília.

34. An area for commercial use only. Lots were granted through a lending system to encourage the arrival of traders to the region, and the place was free of taxes, thus the name Cidade Livre. Lots should have been returned to Novacap in 1959, which did not happen, considering that the old Cidade Livre corresponds to Núcleo Bandeirante, a satellite city of Brasília (Museu Vivo da Memória Candanga).

35. Alvim et al., *Os cine-jornais sobre o período da construção de Brasília.*

36. Alvim et al.

37. Alvim et al.

38. "Cinegrafista põe acervo sobre Brasília à venda," *Correio Braziliense,* September 25, 1987.

IN SEARCH OF BIGFOOT

ADAM CHARLES HART

Recovering George A. Romero's

Jacaranda Joe

In 2019, the University of Pittsburgh Library System (Pitt ULS) acquired

the archives of George A. Romero, the filmmaker still best known

for his debut feature, *Night of the Living Dead* (1968). Romero, born

in the Bronx, had come to Pittsburgh to attend Carnegie Tech (now Carnegie Mellon

University), making the Steel City his home and center of production for the bulk of his

filmmaking career. In the course of directing fifteen features (and writing, producing,

or codirecting several more), Romero more or less founded the feature film industry in

Pittsburgh, giving several generations of local filmmakers their start on his sets. He's

a revered figure among genre fans, with endless homages and rip-offs of his features

dotting the horror landscape for the past fifty years. He invented (or coinvented) the

modern zombie movie and will forever be associated with a subgenre that ascended to

the forefront of popular culture in the twenty-first century. His status within the industry

Figure 1. George Romero and his collaborators in the production company the Latent Image on the hills overlooking Pittsburgh, circa 1969. From Archives and Special Collections, University of Pittsburgh Library System.

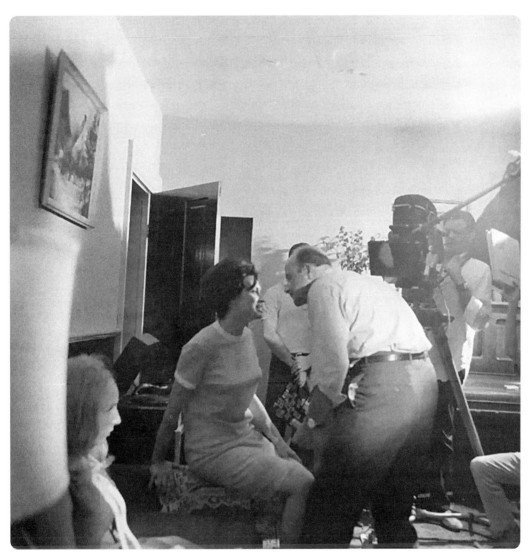

Figure 2. George Romero filming actors Karl Hardman, Marilyn Eastman, and Judith O'Dea for *Night of the Living Dead* (1968). From Archives and Special Collections, University of Pittsburgh Library System.

never remotely reflected this, but to find an equivalent level of influence and cultural penetration, you would likely have to look to the Spielbergs, the Zemeckises, and the Lucases of the world. For any filmmaker, that is a remarkable legacy.

And yet the George A. Romero Archival Collection at Pitt ULS suggests that Romero was a radically more expansive and prolific artist. The archive consists of fifty linear feet of paper materials, ten linear feet of AV materials, and one hard drive.[1] There are extensive collections of press clippings, promotional materials dating back to the 1960s, and small collections of legal documents (mostly contracts), correspondence, and photographs, as well as a handful of props. The collection comes from three sources: Romero's widow, Suzanne; his daughter Tina; and his late-career producer and business partner Peter Grunwald. Nearly all materials related to production or financing come from Grunwald, as the material Romero himself held on to over the decades is limited primarily to writing, storyboards, and other documents related to the creative development of his projects. Among other things, the archive shows us what was most important to Romero: his writing.

Scripts, stories, treatments, and fragments make up the vast majority of the collection. Out of the entire 102-box archive, 72 boxes are devoted to scripts and other writings. This includes written material for at least ninety-six distinct unfilmed projects[2] in addition to early drafts or treatments for radically different versions of films like *Martin* and *Dawn of the Dead*. And the collection has been growing. Pitt ULS continues to conduct research into unfilmed scripts, which has led to conversations with a number of Romero collaborators, nearly all of whom mention yet another project that is not represented in the archive. Pitt ULS has obtained drafts of two additional projects so far, but there is no indication of how many additional works might still survive in the attics and storage units of collaborators and other friends to whom he'd sent his writing for feedback.[3]

Suffice it to say that Romero was astonishingly prolific and that his filmography might be a poor representative of his artistic range and ambitions. The unfilmed writings in the archives belong to nearly every conceivable genre, from westerns *(Gunperson)* to an artsy, Bergmanesque medieval allegory *(Whine of the Faun)* to a sci-fi "space rock musical" conceived for the stage *(Hoffman: Through the Mansions of the Moon)* to a manic, wacky satire of TV news *(Whiz Kid)* to a whimsical children's fantasy film *(Moonshadows)*.

There is an obvious and understandable bias in film studies toward films that have actually gotten made. The reasons for this are many and manifest and don't need to be rehearsed here. And yet this tendency does limit our understanding of film artists of all stripes to projects for which they could secure funding, projects endorsed and supported by studios, by producers, by financiers. For a filmmaker like Romero, working independently in Pittsburgh for most of his career, more or less quarantined within low-budget horror, countless stars had to come into alignment for a project to make it to the screen. And the good fortune required for a project to be filmed does not reflect Romero's interests or passions, nor even the amount of time or energy put into developing a script. In very concrete ways, film studies' traditional approach to auteurism excludes many of the projects about which Romero was most passionate. It ignores years of writing and development, of some of Romero's finest *work*.

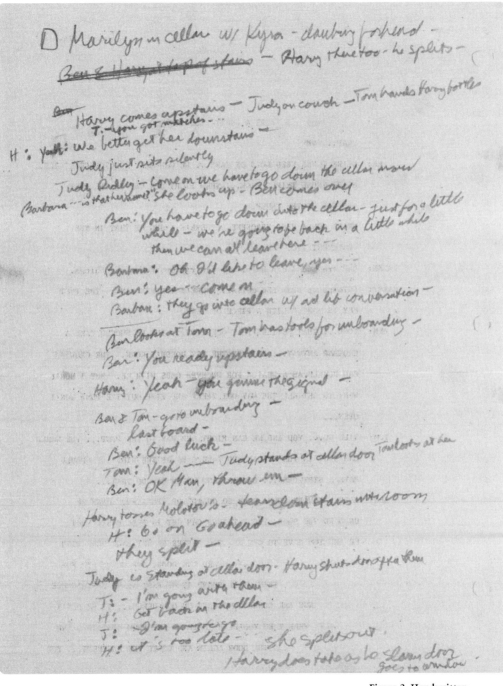

Figure 3. Handwritten script revisions for *Night of the Living Dead* (1968). From Archives and Special Collections, University of Pittsburgh Library System.

How radically would our conception of film history, or of auteurism, or even of cinematic artistry writ large, be altered if we at least took into account the total creative output—scripts and treatments and other work that did not lead to complete features—produced by the countless filmmakers who were excluded from studio resources or who were unable to access the enormous resources required to produce a film outside of Hollywood? Obviously, innumerable women filmmakers, filmmakers of color, queer filmmakers, political radicals, and others were excluded from film resources because they or their work were deemed unacceptable or unprofitable, filmmakers and aspiring filmmakers whose work writing and developing films that were never produced is not reflected in what we think of as their filmographies.

Romero provides an instructive and utterly fascinating case study because he had experienced enough commercial success to solicit *some* level of interest in his work throughout his career, which encouraged him to continue writing even when production funds were not forthcoming. And, of course, as a straight, cis-White man, he was able to retain some level of access to studios even when they declined actually to fund his films. But also, it bears repeating: Romero was *astonishingly* prolific. The giant pile of unfilmed material that he has left behind is not equivalent to speculation about possible directions in which his career may have veered under different circumstances: it is tangible artistic output, and if that output varies wildly in polish, at the very least, it merits *consideration* as part of Romero's oeuvre.

Nowhere is this more clear than with ideas that can be traced back over unfilmed projects, sometimes reaching back decades. *Martin* (1978), Romero's film about an awkward teen vampire, seems to have begun life as an abandoned novel about a dissatisfied middle-aged businessman.[4] *Day of the Dead* (1985) was originally conceived on an epic scale that his eventual budget could not support,[5] and a number of themes and plot details made their way into an unfilmed script called *Copperhead*, a *RoboCop*-like sci-fi film written in collaboration with Marvel Comics editor in chief Jim Shooter. The lineage of ideas that would eventually make their way into the 2007 film *Diary of the Dead* begins in the early 1970s, with an unfilmed project about bigfoot that would have starred at least one member of the Pittsburgh Steelers. That surprising lineage included the most unexpected discovery of the archive: a lost, almost completely unknown short film written and directed by Romero called *Jacaranda Joe*.

In June 1994, George Romero spent ten days at Valencia Community College in Florida, working with a crew of faculty and students to film a short script on 35mm and video. At the time of filming, Romero had plans to return for another shoot the following year to turn the short into a feature.[6] The sole news item about the production explains that the film "is an experiment. In the faux documentary, a Geraldo Rivera–like TV talk show host investigates an encounter with the alleged monster on a hunting show. Romero wants to know if audiences can be scared by a documentary format, if they can be frightened when they don't know much about the story's characters."[7] The film introduces a number of elements that aren't fully realized, evidently set up to continue the story in potential future installments that would never come to be. An edit of *Jacaranda Joe* on VHS—a blank tape with a handwritten label—was discovered in the Pitt archive, along with a script and storyboards and a handful of production documents. An identical, higher-resolution DigiBeta video was recovered from the film's first assistant director, Michael Sellers. This edit runs seventeen minutes, with no titles or credits, but this is the most complete version of the film in existence. The nature of Valencia's program at the time meant that all students involved in the production graduated almost immediately after Romero completed filming. It was only through the persistence of already-former students Bobby Gibis and George Rizkallah throughout the subsequent summer that any version of the film was completed.[8] The film had no public screenings until March 2022, when Pitt ULS held a virtual screening of the film over Zoom. It will eventually be made available to watch through Pitt's library catalog.

In 2021, with help from crew member Elizabeth Tobln Kurtz, we located the nine extant reels of 35mm film from the shoot, saved from the trash years ago by current Valencia faculty member Bruce Wood. The reels, which have been preserved and digitized by the archives, include three positive prints, all of them severely warped, as well as six pristine reels of original camera negatives. These negatives compose the full 35mm camera footage contained in the seventeen-minute film. (The VHS workprint also includes short sequences shot on 16mm film, but we presume that footage to be lost.)

Jacaranda Joe has its roots in a project that Romero tried unsuccessfully to get off the ground in the mid-1970s, a bigfoot movie that would have starred at least one member of the Super Bowl–winning Pittsburgh Steelers called *The Footage,* which riffs on two treatments for a project called *Enemies* about protohuman societies that he had written several years earlier. But key ideas from *Jacaranda Joe* would be translated into a spec script that Romero had written in 2004 as the pilot for a proposed *Night of the Living Dead* television series.[9] He would continue developing that script and then, after the somewhat disappointing box office of 2005's *Land of the Dead,* would pick it up again, revise it, and film it as the "found footage" film *Diary of the Dead.*

In an envelope marked "old writings," there were a number of undated short stories, fragments, and film treatments that Romero wrote in the late 1960s or early 1970s. These include two versions of a short treatment for a film called *Enemies.* The likely earlier version (which is untitled) is shorter and plays out like a scarcely elaborated segment of *2001: A Space Odyssey* in which two tribes of prehuman apes fight over territory.[10] In the longer version, which retains some character names and the basic narrative framework, Romero digs deeper into the psyches of his protohuman characters and into the workings of their society. There is a clear fascination in this second version with these creatures as a version of human society without the corruptions of modernity.[11]

During this period, Romero met with American International Pictures (AIP) about potentially producing a sequel to *Night,* already dubbed *Dawn of the Dead.*[12] No film came from that meeting, but the feedback was crucial for Romero's efforts over the next few years. According to a letter written by Romero contained within the archive, AIP seems to have expressed interest in producing it, but with conditions. It was at that time looking to capitalize on *Night*'s success among Black audiences and rewrite *Dawn* for an all-Black cast, with a superstar athlete in the lead. Romero had begun work on *The Winners,* a series of TV documentaries profiling sports stars. The first installment, directed by Romero, had recently been broadcast nationally, and its subject, O. J. Simpson, was perhaps the only current athlete popular enough to open a movie. Simpson had been considered as the star for an all-Black *Dawn of the Dead* but, according to the letter, was not available. (Romero would later claim that he did not work with AIP because he "didn't think it needed to be produced that big."[13])

AIP did not end up producing *Dawn,* but the idea of attaching a high-profile athlete as a means of getting a feature financed clearly stuck with Romero. Through *The Winners,* Romero had worked with a number of Pittsburgh athletes, especially from the Steelers. And if star running back Franco Harris wasn't quite famous enough to open a movie made even on the margins of Hollywood, he might be enough of a draw for the purposes of Romero's ultra-indie low-budget productions. So Romero devised two projects as vehicles for Harris and other Steelers players.

One was a wild spoof of 1950s creature features called *Monster Movie.* In the introduction to this brief treatment, Romero claims that "it is anticipated that Franco Harris, of the Pittsburgh Steelers will play the role of Bruno in Monster Movie, and that other members of the Steeler team and of other NFL teams will appear in cameo roles." "A la *MASH,*" the proposed film would mix campy slapstick humor with "absolute, gut-shattering realism, and the fright sequences will be unmitigated with humor."[14] In the treatment, an alien crash-lands in the Pennsylvania hills and inadvertently stumbles onto a college campus where a dance has brought together a band, the ROTC, and both professional and college football players, with "peaceniks" and "rednecks" and other assorted groups from on and off campus making an appearance. The alien, searching for parts to repair its crashed ship, stumbles across Bruno's girlfriend, Janelady, and "falls

Figure 4. Actor Bill Cross as talk show host Remington Pierce in *Jacaranda Joe* (1994). Courtesy of Sanibel Films. From Archives and Special Collections, University of Pittsburgh Library System.

instantly in love" with her, grabbing her and running off into the night. The story hews largely to the goofy tone established by its premise, ultimately culminating in Bruno and the pro football players getting the band to play to accompany them as they use "every dirty trick in the book" to befuddle the alien and get the upper hand enough to back it into quicksand. But there is one sequence that stands out as "gut-shattering." The sheriff and his posse unleash a "red-neck barrage of firepower" on the alien, injuring it but firing directly into the "Hari Krishnas and Jesus Freaks" marching for peace. The alien creature uses its body to protect Janelady from bullets, and while the posse continues to chase without pause, the creature is appalled at the slaughter that surrounds it.[15]

The other project was more fully developed, including multiple drafts of treatments, character designs, and makeup tests.[16] The archive contains a letter addressed to a potential funder indicating that Harris had agreed to star.[17] Romero titled the proposed

Figure 5. Archivists Stephen Haines and Miriam Meislik inspecting the 35mm film print of the original camera footage of *Jacaranda Joe* (1994).

film *The Footage*. There are three drafts in the archive, with substantial varia-tions. The common story is about a TV show that follows a football star paired with professional hunters for a wilderness expedition. The group stumbles onto a bigfoot community and earns the wrath of the creatures, who cor-rectly see the humans as threats. In a four-page treatment kept in an envelope labeled "Big Foot Franco Version," the hero is "Johnny Shaw, a Star NFL quaterback [*sic*] who is just beginning a career as a country and western recording artist."[18] In a twelve-page screenplay fragment, the hero is "Johnny Wilson, a Black man; star Quarterback for the NFL. He has never been hunting in his life, but his Manager has decided that the image would be good for Wilson who is just launching his career as an actor."[19] The longest draft is a thirty-seven-page screenplay, printed on "Communicators Pittsburgh" stationery. In this version, the hero is Jerry Shaw, a quarterback with a lifetime of hunting experience.[20]

In the four-page treatment, Romero makes clear his emotional investment in the characters: "We cannot sympathize with the red-neck hunting experts nor with most of the television types, who rape the environment and chase women constantly."[21] Johnny Shaw is here being "exploited as though he were a retail product" and manipulated by everyone around him, including his girlfriend. Shaw, wandering through the forest on his own, "discovers a creature which is ape-like in appearance, but obviously intelligent. It is about the size of a ten year old human child, and its articulation of sounds is quite sophisticated for an animal." Shaw discovers that it is wounded and brings it back to camp, chased by the adults of "the society of Yetti. The Big Foot of the Northern Rockies."[22]

As in *Monster Movie,* the hunters' immediate response is to "instinctively open fire on the giant creatures" and to then chase after them to "search and destroy."[23] And as with *Night,* the bulk of the film is devoted to increasingly frantic arguments among the humans about both what to do with the baby (and who gets to profit) and what to do with the footage recorded by the TV crew—all while the bigfoot community coordinates attacks. In the Communicators draft, the slimy, anti-Semitic producer tries to force the camera operator to give him the film, but the operator understands that the producer selling the film would ensure the almost immediate destruction of the bigfoot community. Jerry wants to set the baby free but does not prevail until the adult bigfeet destroy most of the crew. He has a moment of connection with the bigfoot community in which the creatures accept him and he recognizes the emotion they all feel for their child: "They go to the old male . . . he seems as old as time itself . . . they help him to his feet . . . they bring him to Jerry . . . what eyes . . . they are filled with sadness . . . a single tear comes down his face . . . all at once he stands alone, proud . . . the others kneel . . . it's almost . . . a spiritual thing . . . almost like being in the presence of a living God . . . Jerry is overcome with emotion . . . what should he do? . . . the old one bows his head toward Jerry . . . Jerry looks up into his eyes . . . the silence is awesome . . . Jerry kneels before him in the manner of the others and bows his head . . . he places his hand on Jerry's head . . . there is a beautiful sound in unison from the others, like a bass chord from an organ. Jerry faints and slumps to the floor."[24]

The producer, insistent throughout that he was the owner of the baby and of the footage, has protected himself from further attacks by holding the baby at gunpoint. Shooting his gun into the air while the adults watch, he sees they comprehend its danger and puts the gun to the baby's head. In the end, Jerry dies helping the adults rescue the baby and confront the producer:

> Richard looks up . . . four bigfeet are towering over him . . . he drops the gun . . .
> he cowers in a kneeling position . . . the bigfeet rip open the cage . . . there is a
> tremendous reunion scene. [. . .] Dawn—helicopter . . . lands. Two armed rangers
> [. . .] come into the clearing. Richard is in the cage . . . hands on bars . . . he has
> gone insane . . . he is screaming . . . the sounds are almost identical to those
> of the baby bigfoot.[25]

In that version, the camera operator buries his film in a secret location so as not to let
it be exploited without him—it will be, he says, "the achievement of my life." He dies,
shot by a crew member, as he attempts to dig it up and run off. He dies "film cans in his
arms and a soft smile on his face."[26]

In the four-page treatment, Johnny pleads with the producer to release the baby,
but when he does not, an adult bigfoot "swats at him virtually severing his head." Johnny
survives and communicates to the adult bigfeet that they will need to leave the area to
avoid being discovered while showing them how to use the remaining guns. It ends with
the creatures digging up the film cans and presenting them to Johnny, who opens the
cans to expose them to light: "The creatures, who do not understand the process take it
as a celebration. They hurl the footage into the air as though it were party streamers."[27]

If *Enemies* showed a tentative fascination with nonhuman societies, with how
a civilization can be structured outside of human hierarchies, then with *The Footage,*
the bigfeet in the woods are presented as a nearly utopian alternative to modern human civilization. The corruption of modern life is represented not just by humans but by
filmmakers, the destructive power of the camera directly equated with that of the guns
wielded by the trigger-happy hunters.[28] This would have been a proto–"found footage"
film in which the footage is never developed and thus never seen by anyone. When
Romero returned to this idea two decades later, consumer-grade video had become
commonplace and recorded images spread much more quickly and freely.

For his film at Valencia in 1994, Romero transposed *The Footage* to a quintes-
sentially 1990s setting: a *Geraldo*-like talk show called *Remington.* In it, sleazy host
Remington Pierce—in between hitting on a much younger blonde in the audience—and
his guests opine on the controversies, disagreements, and arguments that have popped
up after a local TV crew caught on camera the briefest of glimpses in the Florida swamps
of what appears to be a bigfoot-like creature, nicknamed "Jacaranda Joe." That crew was
shooting a National Rifle Association–sponsored show in which "celebrities from the
worlds of sports and entertainment are taken on a safari to remote parts of the country
where they try to bag themselves a trophy on camera." The fateful episode's celebrity

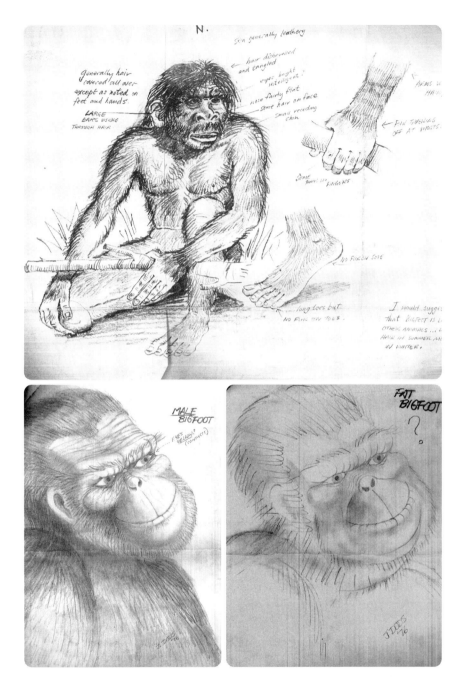

Figure 6. Creature designs
for the unmade feature film
The Footage, circa 1976.
From Archives and Special
Collections, University of
Pittsburgh Library System.

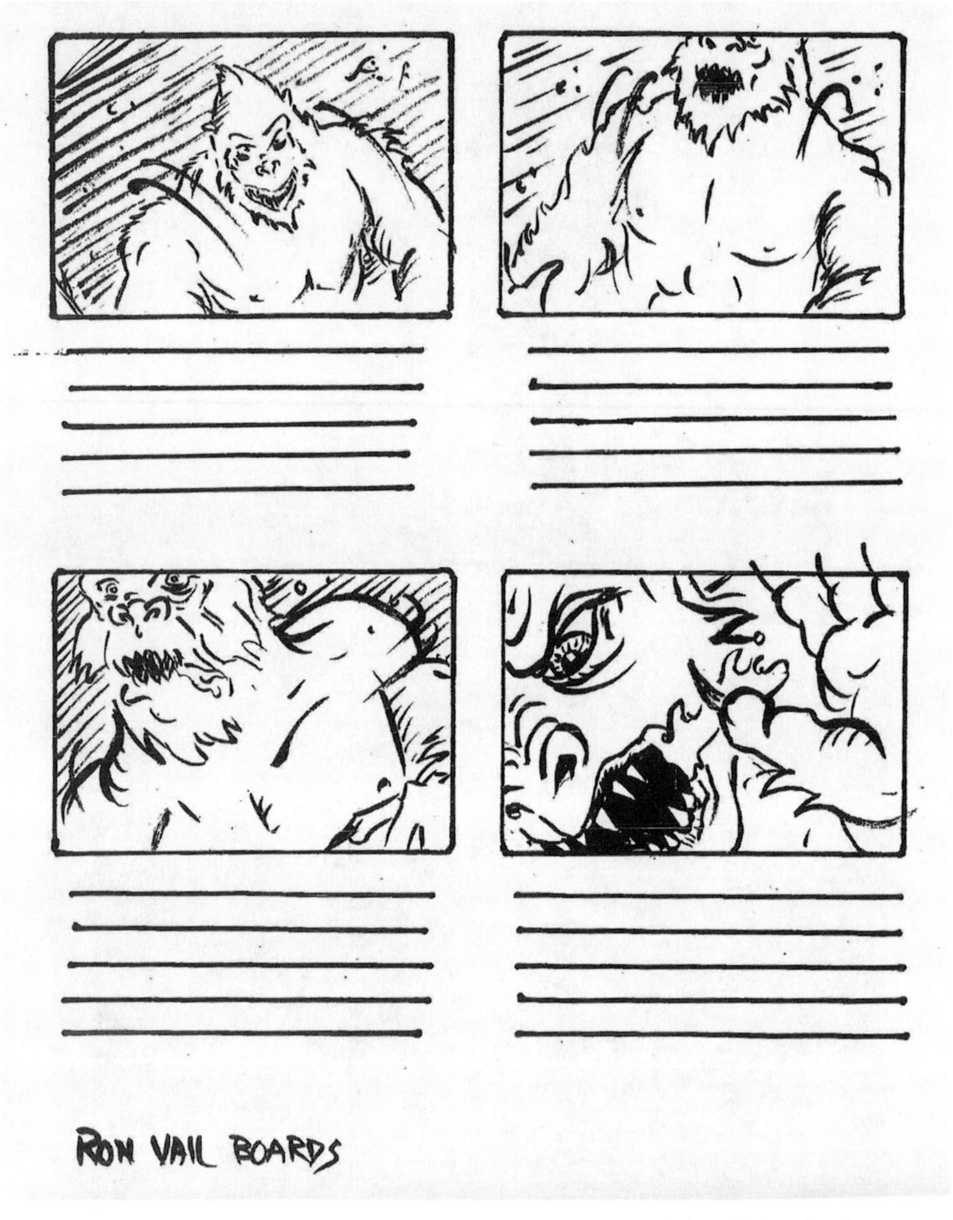

RON VAIL BOARDS

Figure 7. Storyboard illustrations by Valencia Community College film student Ron Vail for *Jacaranda Joe* (1994). From Archives and Special Collections, University of Pittsburgh Library System.

Figure 8. Creature design by Rick Gonzales for *Jacaranda Joe* (1994). From Archives and Special Collections, University of Pittsburgh Library System.

host is NBA superstar Jesse "Thunderball" Wilson—the switch from football to basketball seemingly made only to set up a joke about how "the only Bigfoot I know is Kareem." We see the images of Joe twice: during the panel discussion and then, at the very end, in slow motion, giving us the first clear look at Joe himself. The short ends with Remington teasing the next segment, seemingly inviting the then-planned continuation of the film.

As in *The Footage*, the humans seem, whether by malice, greed, or mere curiosity, intent on destroying the creature. Seen on video shot on location, massive crowds have flocked to the site and the surrounding area. Vendors line the streets of the closest town selling T-shirts and souvenirs. Bands of hunters have started roaming the area in search of the world's most exotic hunting trophy. Whether or not anyone succeeds in finding Joe—if the video is not a hoax—its habitat is being quickly destroyed by tourists.

The first guest on *Remington* is not a hunter or the TV crew but Benjamine Tall Trees, of the Miccosukee tribe.[29] Benjamine's role is undoubtedly clichéd, but he also voices a strong critique of the violence and indifference of White society.[30] A White hunter starts a shouting match with Benjamine, angry that he has to purchase a hunting license and still cannot shoot endangered species, while Indigenous people are "allowed" to kill panthers with impunity. Benjamine replies forcefully that he does not use a gun and that "more panthers are killed by rental cars than by Native Americans!" He goes further, asking White society to respect the laws of *his* community, just as his tribe has respected theirs.[31]

In both *The Footage* and *Jacaranda Joe,* Romero uses the diegetic camera to distinguish between an opportunistic and cruel modern society, which he associates with filmmaking, and a more natural society in the wilderness. In *The Footage*, that is the bigfeet. In *Joe*, that is Joe himself and the Seminole tribe that Romero not unproblematically aligns with him. What is important for Romero is that Benjamine and his people represent a rejection of White society; they signify an alternative tradition that is older and more stereotypically "natural."

The following year, Romero revisited *Jacaranda Joe* for a short "pitch" that he titled *Jacaranda,* promising that *Jacaranda* will do "for horror what *This Is Spinal Tap* did for the music business"—with the caveat that it is "going for scares rather than laughs."[32] In this version, the creature has already killed three people and injured two others, "one of the bodies so badly mangled the man's mother wouldn't recognize him."[33] While filming the ESPN hunting show *Call of the Wild* just outside a small town in the Everglades called Jacaranda, a video crew is attacked by a creature, the whole ordeal being captured on tape. Word has gotten out and Jacaranda has turned into a madhouse, drawing people from all over the country wanting to catch a glimpse of the creature, to study it, to shoot it, and to exploit the hell out of the crowds. Rumors fly that it's a hoax, or perhaps a bear or some other less exotic animal.

Remington builds his show around the slow reveal of the ESPN footage (which has, presumably, not yet been widely seen), interspersed with interviews and discussions, until he reveals that he will be taking a helicopter into the Everglades, into the precise spot where the attack originally occurred: "He's out to prove there's nothing in there except gators and birds. And he's going to do it on live tv." His hubris will prove to be fatal.

On location, the creature stalks and kills the members of his crew one by one, the whole thing being broadcast live and gaining steam as "the highest rated show in the history of television."[34] Remington is not among the survivors as the broadcast and the movie offer a final thought about something "Remington should have known at the start": "Man is encroaching on too many places like the Everglades. It only stands to reason that sooner or later nature would strike back."[35]

The feature pitch fixes a basic structural problem of the short, in which the only "action" taking place in the present is a panel discussion. But relocating to the swamp right after showing the original footage, the film (and the show) brings the action into the present tense. The final word belongs to the camera operator, who takes over the broadcast after the creature kills Remington.

Romero would never complete that feature-length script, but some of those ideas would be repurposed for *Diary of the Dead*. Romero explained the project in the *Night* pilot script that became *Diary*:

> The entire series will be photographed by subjective cameras, some in the hands of professional newscasters, most in the hands of amateur videographers, who will be our principal characters. Objective angles will occasionally be seen, but only through the lenses of surveillance or security cameras mounted on the walls of various buildings. There will be no musical score. Dialogue will closely follow what is scripted, but actors will be asked to paraphrase or ad lib. The reader will find that the characters curse occasionally (you probably would too, in their circumstances) but please note that the script's [*sic*] will be adjusted to suit whatever broadcast or cable standards are required.
>
> Our intention is to explore the zombie mythology from its starting point in a way that hasn't been seen before . . . to provide an air of heightened realism (a la The Blair Witch Project), which will automatically increase tensions, and will serve to involve viewers in the overall experience.[36]

As much as this was clearly, explicitly inspired by *The Blair Witch Project,* it was also directly inspired by his previous collaboration with Valencia on *Jacaranda Joe,*[37] casting film students as its heroes. Romero himself had never taken a single film class, though there was clearly something autobiographical in the initial setup of young filmmakers on the set of their first monster movie. He had, however, worked very closely with film students at Valencia on a proto–found footage film, with the hope of securing funding for a feature-length version—which makes his impulse to film it there all the more logical.

In the interim between Romero writing that pilot script and deciding to revise it for his follow-up with *Land,* a great deal had changed about the landscape of amateur video, and that would entirely direct his reshaping of the script and story. YouTube was launched in 2005, and it took less than a year to become a major cultural force. Suddenly, anyone with a camera phone could share a video with the entire world, and already a number of those videos exceeded the number of viewers for a major studio production like *Land.* In that, Romero found inspiration. The script for *Diary* would take most of the structure of the pilot script and add in a few action-/gore-oriented set pieces, including the entire final section set in the enormous family mansion of one of the film students, but it would also contextualize the student filmmakers within the new urgency of social media.

In all these projects, the camera is a marker of the corruptions of modernity, both symbolizing and enacting inhumane engagements with those around us, as it is throughout his work. It brings the masses of hunters, vendors, filmmakers, and tourists to the town of Jacaranda seeking to profit off the discovery. It allows a young filmmaker to treat his friends like characters in a script as they run for their lives. It turns the rarest of cryptozoological discoveries into a money-making scheme. It makes us less empathetic, less human.

Adam Charles Hart is the author of *Monstrous Forms: Moving Image Horror across Media* (2019) and the forthcoming *The Living Camera: The History, Theory, and Politics of Handheld Cinematography* and *Raising the Dead: The Work of George A. Romero.* As a visiting researcher at the University of Pittsburgh Library System, he helped process the George A. Romero Archival Collection. He is currently a project curator at the Media Burn Archive.

NOTES

My deepest thanks to the University of Pittsburgh Library System's Horror Studies Collection coordinator Ben Rubin, as well as to Miriam Meislik, Steven Haines, Michael Gornick, Elizabeth Tobin Kurtz, Robert Gibis, George Rizkallah, Michael Sellers, and Bruce Wood. The finding aid can be found online at https://digital.library.pitt.edu/islandora/object/pitt%3AUS-PPiU -SC201903/viewer. Unless otherwise noted, all archival materials come from the George A. Romero Archival Collection, 1962–2017, SC.2019.03, Archives and Special Collections, University of Pittsburgh Library System.

1. Much of the material on the hard drive duplicates scripts and video footage that exist in other forms within the archive, but at least three scripts appear to be unique projects. As Romero would sometimes reuse titles or change titles between drafts, each file will need to be evaluated. There is also room for disagreement about whether different drafts are part of a singular project. For example, the vampire project *Blood* has been categorized as an early version of *Martin* but may have been regarded as a separate film entirely by Romero. Similarly, Romero wrote a treatment for a *Night of the Living Dead* TV series in 1997 that has almost no similarities to the pilot script that he wrote in 2004 discussed in this article. For this reason, although I will attempt to be as precise as possible, the numbers will often need to be estimates.

2. This number includes ideas that were entirely original conceptions, collaborations with other writers, or adaptations—sometimes radical revisions—of previously existing material. Eighteen additional scripts are credited exclusively to other writers, including longtime collaborators like Stephen King but also Emmy-winning comedy writer Lee Kalcheim, who authored a script titled *Friends* in 1984 but has no knowledge of why or how Romero would have obtained two copies of it. Kalcheim, email correspondence with the author, November 11, 2020.

3. Projects for which Pitt has no drafts or other documentation include the late 1980s script *Twilight of the Dead*, the early 2000s *The Diamond Dead*, and an early 1980s script titled *Mayday*. The latter project was a script written by Paul Larsen adapting the novel by Thomas H. Block, on which Romero was not credited but for which he had contributed substantial feedback.

4. George A. Romero, Untitled Story or Treatment begins "The Parkway East was...," apparent early draft of *Martin*, undated, box 1, folder 11.

5. George A. Romero, *Day of the Dead* synopsis, 1979, box 6, folder 1.

6. According to Romero, he had hoped to find studio backing before returning to film the rest of the film, as he wanted to release the film theatrically. Catherine Hinman, "Horror Flick Master Involves VCC Students in Latest Effort," *Orlando Sentinel*, June 16, 1994, https://www.orlandosentinel.com/news/os -xpm-1994-06-16-9406160632-story.html.

7. Hinman.

8. Confirmed by first assistant director Michael Sellers and editor George Rizkallah. Adam Charles Hart, Benjamin T. Rubin, George Rizkallah, Michael Sellers, and Elizabeth Tobin Kurtz, "George A. Romero's Jacaranda

Joe: Screening and Discussion," University of Pittsburgh Library System, Archives and Special Collections, April 12, 2022.

9. According to *Empire*, Romero began the script that became *Diary of the Dead* "nearly a decade" before *Diary*'s 2008 release, returning to it after *Land of the Dead* "tanked." His intention was to make the film with "a cast of unknowns at a film school in Florida," clearly referring to Valencia. Damon Wise, "Dead Again," *Empire*, March 2008, 85–86.

10. George A. Romero, *Enemies [Untitled]* treatment, undated, box 32, folder 13.

11. George A. Romero, *Enemies* treatment, undated, box 32, folder 14.

12. George A. Romero to Richard Rubinstein, April 9, 1974, box 54, folder 12. This letter also includes a handwritten script fragment revising early versions of *Dawn* to include a larger cast.

13. Ed Bland, "'Living Dead' Sequel Opens Here April 13," *Pittsburgh Press*, April 1, 1979, N1.

14. George A. Romero, *Monster Movie* story synopsis, undated, box 40, folder 13: 1. This would not be the last time Romero would write a *M*A*S*H*-inspired monster spoof. In 1996, he would write a brief treatment for a film called *Monster MASH*, in which a group of creatures traveled around the world administering emergency medicine to fellow monsters.

15. Romero, *Monster Movie*, 7. Romero would make another attempt to direct a spoof of alien invasion movies at the end of the 1970s, with *Shoo-Be-Doo-Be-Moon*—written by Romero's longtime friend and collaborator Rudy Ricci—one of several projects Romero tried to get made immediately after the success of *Dawn of the Dead.* He would return to alien invasions in the mid-1980s with the more serious, action-forward Wells adaptation *War of the Worlds.*

16. The authorship of one of these drafts is uncertain. There is a scribbled note on the front page that reads, as far as I can tell, "First rough draft. Original screenplay by Walton Cook." Whether that indicates this draft was written by Cook or whether it was an adaptation of Cook's screenplay written by Romero is difficult to parse, but it appears to be written in Romero's customary style and voice. Another draft fragment by Romero credits the "original story" to Cook and Gornick. George A. Romero, *The Footage [Bigfoot]* original draft, undated, box 34, folder 1. Referred to below as *"The Footage* (Communicators Draft)." Neither Cook nor Gornick, however, has any memory of contributing to the project. Cook, telephone conversation with the author, December 14, 2021; Gornick, email correspondence with the author, December 15, 2021.

17. George A. Romero to Susan Gaydos, June 4, 1976, box 69, folder 11. Michael Gornick has suggested that the Steelers' then-quarterback Terry Bradshaw had been discussed for another role. Gornick, email correspondence with the author, December 15, 2021.

18. George A. Romero, *The Footage [Bigfoot]* "Franco Version," undated, box 34, folder 3: 1. Referred to below as *"The Footage* (Franco Version)."

19. Romero, *The Footage [Bigfoot]* original draft, undated, box 34, folder 1: 2.

20. Romero, *The Footage* (Communicators Draft), 13.

21. Romero, *The Footage* (Franco Version), 1.

22. Romero, 2.

23. Romero, 2.

24. Romero, *The Footage* (Communicators Draft), 32. The liberal use of ellipses is a near-universal constant in Romero's writings, such that it has helped to identify the authorship of a handful of unsigned texts in the archive.

25. Romero, 37.

26. Romero, 36.

27. Romero, *The Footage* (Franco Version), 4.

28. This approach to film as a destructive force can be traced back to the very beginning of Romero's artistic life, when he appeared in Pittsburgh's first production of Jack Gelber's *The Connection* at age twenty. In that play, documentarians filming the lives of heroin addicts are portrayed as plainly opportunistic and exploitative.

29. Romero would reuse this name in 1995–96 for one of the heroes in a script called *The Golem.* George A. Romero, *The Golem,* multiple drafts, box 36, folders 3–7.

30. The archive contains a letter from a then-unknown Owl Goingback, who was considered for the part of Benjamine, that points out several inaccuracies in the script's depiction of Seminole customs. Goingback, now a celebrated novelist, would work with Romero around the turn of the millennium, with Romero interested in developing one of Goingback's books into a feature film. Owl Goingback to George A. Romero, undated, box 59, folder 3.

31. The Communicators draft of *The Footage* has a substantial discussion about the positives and negatives of hunting for nature conservation. Romero, *The Footage* (Communicators Draft), 13–15.

32. Romero, "NEW PROJECTS SYNOPSES.docx," March 4, 1995, digital file, 23.

33. Romero, 17.

34. Romero, 25.

35. Romero, 26.

36. George A. Romero, "*Night of the Living Dead: The TV Series* Note 1," undated, digital file, SC20190303_HD7–1a_NoTLD_TV_Note1.

37. There are further connections to *The Blair Witch Project.* One of the producers of that film, Gregg Hale, was a student at Valencia Community College. He had graduated before Romero's production at the school, but he continued to have close relationships with students and faculty at the school. Nobody who would work on *Blair Witch* had worked on *Jacaranda Joe,* none of the primary *Blair Witch* creators ever saw Romero's short, and there was no direct collaboration between Romero and the *Blair Witch* filmmakers. But there would be enough overlap between Hale's circles and collaborators in the mid-1990s and Romero's student crew that it is difficult not to speculate about some, perhaps unconscious, relationship between *Joe* and *Blair Witch,* an intangible influence that is then explicitly returned with *Diary.*

CINECLUB VRIJHEIDSFILMS

LUNA HUPPERETZ

Restoring a Militant

Cinema Network

What Cineclub shows is not always
"science" but certainly never "fiction":
reality is at the core of "their" political
filmmakers, agitatoric, protesting,
documentary, alike to Felix Greene (his
newest film *Cuba*), argumentative like
Joris Ivens (*Borinage* and *Laos*).

—ELLEN WALLER, *NRC HANDELSBLAD*

(TRANSLATION BY THE AUTHOR)

AMSTERDAM, JUNE 17, 1981. "FILM STAYS OFF THE TUBE. The IKON is not obliged to broadcast the film Vrouwen van Suriname, produced by Cineclub and the National Organization of Surinamese in the Netherlands (LOSON)."[1] The documentary film *Vrouwen van Suriname* (1978) was acquired by the Dutch public left-wing broadcasting company IKON in February 1980, shortly after the military coup in Suriname. A year later, despite a reedit of the film, IKON argued that the political situation in Suriname had changed so drastically that the film would no longer represent Surinamese society correctly, and therefore the film should not screen on television.[2] The activist collectives that produced this critical mid-length documentary on Dutch (neo)colonialism understood this rejection to be political censorship. Filmmaker At van Praag stated that "it is in the interest of the Surinam people that finally the evil actions of Dutch government and Dutch companies are to be exposed."[3] More than forty years later, this article aims to demonstrate the relevance of the "film that stayed off the tube" as part of an effort to restore a militant cinema network.

Vrouwen van Suriname was rediscovered in 2019 within the context of an archival research project aimed at disclosing the 16mm film distribution collection of Cineclub Vrijheidsfilms, situated at the International Institute for Social History. The goal of this article is to reconstruct the Dutch noncommercial film circuit in which Cineclub distributed, programmed, and produced films and, in doing so, align this local movement with the international movement of militant cinema. Describing the status of the Cineclub collection and providing a more detailed analysis of the film Vrouwen van Suriname will lead us to the contemporary issue on archival challenges related to the disclosing of a militant archive: how do you reanimate or recontextualize a film practice based on community grassroots initiatives, taking into consideration the realities of film preservation in mainstream heritage institutions? As I will show in the following pages, the challenges faced in the Vrouwen van Suriname project represent a story of interdependence that exists between local activist networks and the institutional network of the heritage sector.

The film Vrouwen van Suriname/Oema foe Sranan[4] portrays the life of four women who, through personal stories, tell a history of Dutch colonialism, neocolonialism, and discrimination in Suriname and the Netherlands. Suriname, a republic situated in the northeastern part of South America, was colonized by the Dutch in 1667, when Suriname became an independent state. As a result of almost four hundred years of Dutch slave trade, colonialism, and imperialism, the country consists of an ethnically mixed and segregated population, including Indigenous inhabitants, Creoles, Hindustani, Maroons, Javanese, and Chinese.

The cinematic involvement of Cineclub and LOSON (Landelijke Organisatie van Surinamers in Nederland) in capturing this colonial history should be viewed within the larger context of militant cinema, a global development defined by two cinematic movements from the 1960s: Tercer Cine/Third Cinema in Argentina and Cinéma Militant in France.[5] However, before examining these topics' movements in greater depth, we need to turn to a more detailed explanation of the film Vrouwen van Suriname and the activist organizations of Cineclub Vrijheidsfilms and LOSON. The film was produced in light of a political struggle, as a sign of solidarity between Surinamese and Dutch people conveying a collective message on the sociopolitical affairs in Suriname. Fierce critiques of decades of colonial rule are brought to the viewer through the stories of Sonja, Sylvie, Somai, and Jetty, which encompass symbols of resistance in contexts ranging from farmer protests to squatting, neighborhood theater associations, and political campaigns. As members of the neighborhood committees of the Progressive Women's Union, the main characters symbolize the socialist ideals of an independent and progressive Suriname. The film also brings to the fore the neocolonial Dutch and American exploitation of Suriname's resources by shooting the Dutch Shell-Billiton and American Suralco bauxite companies. Furthermore, the historical image of Surinamese female resistance is empowered by the story of the Maroon figures Flora and Séry, who are visualized in the film by citations of an excerpt of Anton de Kom's *We Slaves of Suriname* (1934).[6] In addition to capturing a revolutionary movement in Surinamese history, the film contains value in pointing out the experience of Surinamese exiles. The film follows Sonja Boekstaaf, a LOSON activist and squatter in Amsterdam, who decides to return to Suriname after having lived in the Netherlands for three and a half years.[7]

HISTORY OF CINECLUB

The initiator of Cineclub Vrijheidsfilms was filmmaker and political activist At van Praag (1940–86). Through Cineclub, he created an activist film collective that worked as a producer, distributor, and exhibitor of political and subversive film in the Netherlands from 1966 until 1986. Cineclub started out mainly by programming films in Amsterdam for politically engaged film audiences. In 1968, owing to increasing interest from film clubs, students, and activists situated in other Dutch cities, the Cineclub Coordination Centre (CCC) was established in Amsterdam.[8] Rather than focusing solely on one-time or two-time events, Cineclub established a sustainable network of cine-clubs spread out over different towns in the Netherlands, such as Utrecht, Rotterdam, Groningen, the Hague, Haarlem, and Arnhem, as well as smaller university towns, such as Hengelo and Wageningen, that were also taking part.[9] CCC wanted to improve the efficiency of what had become the three main activities of Cineclub: the international import of political films, subtitle translations, and the national distribution of the films.

Part of its distribution efforts have now resulted in a collection entailing 135 film productions ranging from Latin American guerrilla movements in Cuba and Argentina to Western activist collectives like Newsreel (United States) and Cinegiornali liberi (Italy) to the Black Panther Movement, communist propaganda from the People's Army of Vietnam, and Cineclub's own productions. These films were considered as contributing to Cineclub's slogan "For better information,"[10] as its understanding of providing "better information" anticipated radical change.[11] This slogan reveals a distrust of Western official broadcasters that had grown since the sanitized coverage of the Vietnam War on American television.

Cineclub's films—containing socialist, anticolonial, antiracist, or environmental objectives—were considered as a tool to fight against the struggle that imperialism and capitalism brought about. The political objectives of Cineclub were linked to New Left activism:[12] the voice-overs, intertitles, and editing of these films all worked toward the ideological framing of the film's topic. As such, militant cinema rejected the idea of documentary realism. By stressing the power of cinema to neutralize modes of representation, militant and Third Cinema focused on laying bare the manipulative cinematic techniques of representation.[13] Through postproduction, militant film gained a new aesthetics of repetition, slow motion, and freeze frames that aimed to make visible the modes of representation used in media. An example of this is found in the short film *Now* (Santiago Álvarez, 1965), which rhythmically mixed photographs of police violence with a civil rights song.[14]

The incorporation of this film into Cineclub's film programs serves as an example of how antiracist statements in the United States turned into symbols for worldwide liberation and solidarity.[15] *Now* was programmed during the early years of Cineclub, when it arranged midnight film programs in independent cinemas, focused on themes or regions, for example, "fight for independence in Latin America," "dictatorship in Chile," or "apartheid in South Africa." Over the course of time, Cineclub established a strong network of partners consisting of community centers, (international) film festivals, schools, and various activist committees that enabled the manifestations, exhibitions, demonstrations, and thematic film programs.[16]

The early death of van Praag in 1986 occurred at a time when Cineclub was in the midst of a digital transition, as Cineclub invested in a scanning machine that transferred 16mm or 35mm film to (U-matic) video. Through this service, it managed to eliminate its debts, which had started to accumulate since the early 1970s owing to large investments in film productions and a decrease in funding. Although Cineclub functioned as a collective, van Praag was the driving force behind the organization, and his unfortunate death resulted in the end of Cineclub.

What stems from the film print and paper collection at International Institute of Social History (IISH) is that Cineclub has played a vital role in the development of a Dutch noncommercial, activist film circuit through the inclusion of political films from countries that had recently gained independence or were still fighting for liberation between 1966 and 1986.[17] Prior to Cineclub, the Dutch noncommercial film circuit was shaped by Filmliga (1927–33), which exhibited (socialist) art films mainly from the Soviet Union, France, and Germany. Both film clubs had to establish their own networks of filmmakers, distributors, exhibitors, and members, as their films of interest were not suitable for commercial film theaters. However, a crucial difference exists in their intentions: Filmliga's noncommercial film was understood as an experimental art form with political implications; for Cineclub, noncommercial film served as an activist tool that moved away from artistic practice, as its main purpose was to inform and mobilize the masses for an anticapitalist and antiracist struggle.

A MILITANT CINEMA

The aesthetic form of militant cinema was shaped by the tools within financial reach: lightweight film cameras and projectors; relatively cheap, 16mm film gauge; and portable sound recording equipment. Ideologically, this new mode of filmmaking fulfilled a counterinformational role, raising themes like social inequality, as seen in *Viva Portugal* (Christiane Gerhards and Malte Rauch, 1975) or *Angela Davis: Portrait of a Revolutionary* (Yolande DuLuart, 1972); natural resources, as with *Dead Earth* (Leonard M. Henny, 1970); environmental pollution, as in *Lieber heute aktiv als morgen radioaktiv* (Nina Gladitz, 1976); or capitalist exploitation of cities, like with *Tolmers: Beginning or End* (Philip Thompson, 1974), and neocolonialism, as with *La hora de los hornos* (Grupo de Cine Liberación, 1968).[18]

      The European exhibition and distribution of this last film, *La hora de los hornos* (The hour of the furnaces), is seen as a pivot for the interaction between the Third Cinema movement of Latin American political film and the European Cinéma Militant.[19] The manifesto written prior to the film, titled "Towards a Third Cinema" (1969), defined a cinema that criticized and rebelled against the formal and intentional qualities of Hollywood (First Cinema) and the European "auteur cinema," exemplified by the French *nouvelle vague* (Second Cinema). Gaining experience from the reception and various screening settings of this film, Solanas and Getino formulated their second manifesto "Militant Cinema: An Internal Category of Third Cinema" (1971),[20] which treated Third Cinema as a method of direct intervention, stressing the importance of the context in which the film is viewed. As explained in their notion of the *film act,* a film screening was considered a "pretext for dialogue," activating spectators to come to action and fight against cases of oppression. This is a tradition that has been inherited by Cineclub Vrijheidsfilms in its militant practices of production, distribution, and exhibition. Cineclub's screenings were initially an act of defiance against the dominant film circuit in the Netherlands, which was shaped by the Dutch Cinema Association's commercial monopoly of all the Dutch cinemas and the Board of Film Examiners' subsequent censorship of theatrical screenings of politically subversive films.[21] To exemplify this briefly, the rejection of the

Dutch short film *Omdat mijn fiets daar stond* (*Because My Bike Stood There*; Louis van Gasteren, 1966), which was announced on April 8, 1966, gave rise to the accumulated frustration of various Dutch filmmakers and cinephiles regarding the authority of the Board of Film Examiners (Centrale Commissie voor de Filmkeuring). Van Gasteren's critical stance toward the Dutch police caused the 16mm short film to be described as "manipulative and causing to undermine the authorities."[22]

The film's rejection was a direct trigger for the founding of Cineclub Vrijheids-films on December 12, 1966, at the student-run Filmtheater Kriterion in Amsterdam.[23] Cineclub constructed a membership-based cine-club, which allowed it to screen *Because My Bike Stood There* in a semipublic screening setting. Memberships could be purchased right at the entrance of the show, which served as an inventive way to bypass the Dutch censorship laws that would withhold or withdraw political films from public circulation in Dutch cinema. The first membership ticket was *f*1.75,[24] and once one obtained this annual membership, the next ticket was available at a discount for only *f*1.25[25] per screening.[26] In June 1968, the total number of memberships was estimated at eighteen thousand.[27]

Since its start, Cineclub had strong connections with the many (inter)na-tional action groups that came into existence in the late 1960s and early 1970s (e.g., Dutch Palestine Committee/NPK, Anti-Apartheid Committee/Azania-comité, Actiongroup against City Redevelopment/Aktiegroep Nieuwmarkt, National Organization of Suri-namese in the Netherlands/LOSON), as these organizations often helped to arrange film titles for distribution and promoted their film programs.[28] Aside from these connections, distribution "customers," who rented 16mm films from Cineclub, and Cineclub "members" who visited the cine-club's weekly organized screenings were found through community centers, film clubs, schools, universities, and squatted cultural venues.[29]

LOSON

Apart from representing the interdependence between local activist networks and institutional networks, the realization of *Vrouwen van Suriname* also touched on the involvement of both Surinamese and Dutch organizations in producing this film. It is important to look at the involvement of LOSON and the Democratic People's Front (DVF) of the Communist Party of Suriname. When the film crew visited Suriname in the summers of 1976 and 1977, the local DVF advised the film crew and helped to arrange meetings with individuals and organizations.[30] Three of the main characters in the film (Silvie, Jetty, and Somai) were members of the neighborhood committees of the Progressive Women's Union.[31]

Figure 1. Still from *Vrouwen van Suriname*. *On the left*: Jetty Meurzing, one of the four women in the film. *On the right*: Rita Rahman, initiator and chairperson of the Progressive Women Union.

In addition to these political figures that stress the collaborative quality of the film with Suriname, the collaboration between Cineclub and LOSON, a Surinamese organization based in the Netherlands, was of crucial importance for both the production and successive distribution of the film in the Netherlands. As the Dutch branch of DVF, LOSON supported the workers' and independence movement in Suriname and advocated for social progress of Surinamese migrants in the Netherlands and solidarity between the Surinamese and the Dutch. Henk Lalji, a LOSON member who lived in Amsterdam, collaborated with At van Praag in script writing and the first recordings for the documentary, which were made in the Netherlands between 1974 and 1975. As a result, Lalji visited Suriname in 1976 to conduct interviews and to shoot and eventually also edit the film. Two years later, LOSON member, actress, and singer Nadia Tilon wrote and recorded the narrating text in the Surinamese language Sranantongo and selected the soundtrack for the film.[32] In the 1970s, the formal Dutch-based educational system of Suriname still repressed the use of Sranantongo, or "Surinamese Tongue." As such, the film is thought to be the first documentary in the language given the prominent use of this lingua franca, which can be considered an anticolonial statement. Another such aspect is the inclusion of a variety of Surinamese music genres, ranging from battle to traditional folk songs and from nationalistic songs to popular music, some of which capture the spirit and culture of leftist politics in Suriname.[33]

The production of *Vrouwen van Suriname* coincided with a period in which Surinamese and Dutch activists were squatting buildings in Amsterdam as a means of exerting pressure on unfair housing policies and the dispersal policy toward Surinamese migrants.[34] Various of these demonstrations and squatting actions were documented by Cineclub starting in 1973. Thus, in addition to documenting what they called "Het Onbekende Suriname," or "the Unknown Suriname," the film sheds light on the hostile Dutch climate of racism and the subsequent resistance through solidarity events, demonstrations, and squatting in the Netherlands. In the 1970s and 1980s, through the Cineclub and LOSON network, this film was screened in various schools, social academies, and community centers that were located in neighborhoods with many Surinamese migrants at that time, such as De Pijp in Amsterdam. A reconstruction of the local exhibition practices was partially enabled through the Cineclub paper archive at IISH but also through interviews with Juanita Lalji, former activist at LOSON and distributor of *Vrouwen van Suriname*. Lalji traveled across the Netherlands with the film, provoking discussions and debate after screenings. The exhibition of this film in the Netherlands provided insights into the socioeconomic and political situation of Suriname, countering a general (colonial) ignorance in the Netherlands regarding the motivations of Surinamese migrating to the Netherlands. Because its films could not be distributed without the presence of a questionnaire on the screening details—either attached to the rental contract or brought by the representative of Cineclub—relevant insights on the reception of the films from the Cineclub collection could still be found. This demand for results by the filmmakers and distributors is a significant aspect of militant cinema, considering the movement's aim to affect viewers by inciting action.

THE SHAPING AND DISCLOSING OF A COLLECTION OF "ORPHAN FILMS"

When planning to screen *Vrouwen van Suriname* in 2019 in correspondence with IISH and LOSON, we discovered that no high-resolution digitized copy of the film existed and that the most suitable print was degraded and discolored. As such, with the aim of presenting the film and its history to new audiences, we encountered various archival challenges. The first challenge concerned the history of the collection. A couple of Cineclub productions' original negatives were once found in a dump of the bankrupt Dutch Film Laboratory and stored at IISH in 1986.[35]

As the original negatives for *Vrouwen van Suriname* have not yet been found,

there might be a chance that these negatives also ended up in this dump, but we cannot say this with certainty. Years later, a couple of found prints were merged with the previously mentioned collection: international distribution titles, unedited film tapes, photos, sound tapes,

Figure 2. Filmmakers At van Praag and Henk Lalji (last name misspelled in the embedded label) and camera operator Hans Schellinkhout filming in Suriname, 1976.

and a paper archive nearly eleven meters in length. In 2003, this collection, which until then was stored in the old Cineclub office and studio, a squatted factory nominated for demolition, was acquired by one of the largest labor and social history archives in the world: IISH in Amsterdam.

As analog projection gradually disappears from the cinema screen, accessibility of celluloid archives becomes an enormous issue. In the Netherlands, the expertise and equipment necessary for the study of analog film are now concentrated within a few professional institutions, such as the Eye Filmmuseum or the Netherlands Institute for Sound and Vision. Between 1989 and 2000, the Film and Science Foundation was situated

... en dan ontmoet je bekenden ...

we maakten liedjes over de kraakaktie

Sonja vlak voor haar terugkeer naar Sranan.

Figure 3. Sonja Boekstaaf in Amsterdam, photo exhibition from *Vrouwen van Suriname*, undated. Archief Cineclub, inventory no. 484-485, International Institute of Social History, Amsterdam.

Figure 4. Ticket for the hundredth screening of *Vrouwen van Suriname*, September 29, 1979. Archief Cineclub, inventory no. 484-485, International Institute of Social History, Amsterdam.

in the same building as IISH. As such, IISH occasionally transferred its 16mm and 35mm stock directly to the Film and Science Foundation due to a lack of in-house capability. However, when the Film and Science Foundation departed in 2000 to merge with other audiovisual organizations to form what is now the Netherlands Institute for Sound and Vision, no more expertise or equipment from the neighboring institution was present to initialize certain IISH audiovisual collections. As a result, the Cineclub film collection, which was acquired by IISH in 2003, had remained unstudied for almost twenty years. This has led Floris Paalman, a lecturer in the preservation and presentation of the moving image at the University of Amsterdam (UvA), to identify the Cineclub archive as a collection of "orphan films," defined as "a motion picture abandoned by its owner or caretaker." Aside from the accessibility issue, the "orphan" status is a result of the film collection's interdisciplinary content, which, according to some, is related to social justice movements, whereas for others, owing to its cinematic content, it is related to film historical movements such as direct or radical cinema. The fact is that the collection covers both histories and thus becomes difficult to fit into existing established audiovisual collections that are categorized along certain lines.

To tackle the aforementioned accessibility issue, the media studies department

Figure 5. Open-air action prior to the hundredth screening of *Vrouwen van Suriname* in the De Pijp neighborhood of Amsterdam, September 29, 1979. Color slide, COLL00544, International Institute of Social History, Amsterdam.

of UvA, Eye Filmmuseum, and IISH initiated the collaborative project of disclosing the Cineclub collection. In checking the physical state of the films, we looked not just for physical issues (such as mold, scratches, color degradation, and splices) but for material specificities that provide insights into the local appropriation practices of Cineclub (e.g., intertitles, Dutch translations in subtitles, or local action groups involved in exhibiting the film). As an example, one of the 16mm copies of *Vrouwen van Suriname* included material of solidarity actions against the Billiton/Royal Dutch Shell—a (tin) mining company situated in La Vigilantia (Paramaribo District, Suriname). During the Orphan Film Symposium in Vienna in May 2019, as a reflection on the pilot project on disclosing the Cineclub film collection, Rommy Albers (Eye), Simona Monizza (Eye), and Floris Paalman (UvA) had identified "four main types of appropriation practices": (1) the translation texts made by Cineclub, (2) the modification of film material through cutting and editing in existing distribution productions, (3) Cineclub's programming, and (4) the making of its own film productions.[36] These kinds of local appropriations are

in line with the *film act* notion, which is "required for a specific type of reading of the film, in a specific setting that would stimulate active spectatorship."[37]

Figure 6. A visit at the Eye Collection Center with filmmaker Henk Lalji and restorer Simona Monizza, December 4, 2020. Photograph by Ananta Khemradj.

ARCHIVAL STRATEGY

In November 2020, after the screening of *Vrouwen van Suriname* in Cinema Kriterion, IISH and Eye announced the digital restoration of the 16mm film print.[38] The revival of the film *Vrouwen van Suriname* happened in close collaboration with former members of LOSON. As such, the interdependency between the mainstream archival institutions (IISH and Eye) and the individual actors and grassroots initiatives, such as LOSON, is stressed. Restoring this militant film demands a restitution of the network of actors that were involved in producing, distributing, and exhibiting the film in the 1970s and 1980s. The rerelease of *Vrouwen van Suriname* feeds into a new sociopolitical debate on Surinamese and Dutch collective memory: with the restoration and digitization of the film, the organization of intergenerational and intercultural discussions will offer new insights into the cultural and historical value of the film. This historical and political document that has been hiding in the archive for more than forty years not only allows for discussion of a forgotten revolutionary era but should also engender consideration of how the discovery of this archive tells us something about contemporary archival practices that focus on exchanges between individual actors, grassroots community-based initiatives, and mainstream heritage institutions.

CONCLUSION

In the café of the student-run cinema Kriterion in Amsterdam one evening in September 2020, Surinamese battle songs were spinning on the vinyl turntables, and the *Wrokoman,* a radical socialist Surinamese newspaper from the 1970s, lay open on the tables among excited chatter from a Surinamese Dutch community. As much of the wider Cineclub collection remains unavailable for presentation today, demonstrating the possibilities in an engaged context is essential for establishing the value of the material and influencing the future direction of the collection. Thanks to the engagement of grassroots community-based initiatives, militant cinema programming practices were explained and applied, and as such, the urgency of preservation of this "orphan" archive was advocated through the projection of a damaged 16mm film gauge. Similar to Cineclub's continual remaking, reframing, and repositioning of militant film, working with this "militant archive" nowadays requires reconstructing and repositioning its content and context. Presenting the film in the context of the group's activism, but also in light of the current preservation politics, this project brings together a shattered network of activists and a new generation of cultural programmers, curators, and archivists. In doing so, one is confronted with archival constraints and the complexity of operating on various levels of heritage preservation. The success of this project depends on the ability of the archival institutions to implement suggestions from those actors who have created the history that is now being restored. Vice versa, the expertise of mainstream heritage institutions should be given the trust to accurately restore a political document, working within well-thought-out preservation ethics. Aside from the two parties being crucial for the favorable outcome of this project, reaching out to old and new communities is necessary for the reanimation and recontextualization of a militant cinema network. As such, a "militant archive" could serve as a strategy that continues the long-standing conversations on a film's preservation and contemporary value.

The restored documentary film Vrouwen van Suriname/Oema foe Sranan *(1978) was screened at the Eye International Conference 2022, Global Audiovisual Archiving: Exchange of Knowledge and Practices. For more information, see* http://oemafoesranan.org.

Luna Hupperetz graduated as an MA student in Curating Art and Cultures (University of Amsterdam) in September 2020. With her thesis on the Cineclub Vrijheidsfilms archive, she aimed to shape a recollection of the Dutch activist 16mm film distribution and screening circuit between 1966 and 1986. She has directed the short introductory film *A Battle Restored,* which portrays the history of the making of the film *Oema foe Sranan* in light of the current restoration of the 16mm film print *Oema foe Sranan* executed by Eye Filmmuseum. Currently she is involved with the international heritage research project focused on archiving and distributing *Oema foe Sranan* in Suriname in collaboration with the National Archive of Suriname.

NOTES

1. "FILM BLIJFT VAN DE BUIS Rechtbank steunt weigering IKON," *De Volkskrant*, June 17, 1981, https://resolver.kb.nl/resolve?urn=ABCDDD:0108 79877:mpeg21:p006 (translation by the author).

2. "Cineclub wil via kort geding film op tv brengen," *Parool*, June 14, 1981, https://resolver.kb.nl/resolve?urn=ABCDDD:010847206:mpeg21:a0063 (translation by the author).

3. "Cineclub wil via kort geding film op tv brengen."

4. Eye has cataloged the film with the Dutch title *Vrouwen van Suriname*; the alternative Sranantongo title was *Oema foe Sranan*. Both titles are translated to "Women of Suriname."

5. In recent years, the original manifestos have been translated and contextualized by film scholars. See Mariano Mestman, "Third Cinema/Militant Cinema: At the Origins of the Argentinian Experience (1968–1971)," *Third Text* 25, no. 1 (2011): 29–40, and Paul Douglas Grant, *Cinéma Militant: Political Filmmaking and May 1968* (London: Wallflower Press, 2016).

6. In May 2020, Anton de Kom was included in the Dutch historical canon as an important resistance fighter; earlier that year, his book *We Slaves of Suriname* was reissued. The book became a bestseller in the Netherlands, eighty-six years after its publication.

7. With approximately 350,000 Surinamese (first, second, and third generation) living in the Netherlands currently, the emigration story of Sonja contains relevant sensibilities in regard to Surinamese exiles.

8. Leo Molenaar, "Cineclub Coördinatiecentrum: een nieuw geluid?," *Critisch Filmforum* 7, no. 8 (1968): 150–51.

9. "Cineclub Arnhem telt nu bijna 3000 leden, in het hele land tezamen tegen de 18.000," *Het Vrije Volk*, June 18, 1968; "Ook buiten Amsterdam komen Cine-Clubs. Niet moeilijk meer om 'verboden films' te zien," *Trouw*, March 12, 1968, http://resolver.kb.nl/resolve?urn=ABCDDD:010814032:mpe g21:p005 (translation by the author).

10. "Voor een betere voorlichting," slogan stated in *Cineclub Bulletin*, 1972.

11. In 1967, from a similar skepticism, a group of independent filmmakers in New York formed the Newsreel collective; see http://newsreel.us/.

12. The New Left is a broad political movement in the Global North that wanted to separate and distinguish itself from the "old" traditional left-wing parties of social democrats and Marxist–Leninist organizations by empowering demands of social justice through activism. See John Hess, "Notes on U.S. Radical Film, 1967–80," in *Jump Cut: Hollywood, Politics and Counter Cinema*, ed. Peter Steven, 134–50 (Toronto: Between the Lines, 1985).

13. In the manifesto "Towards a Third Cinema" (1969), Argentine filmmakers and politicians Fernando Solanas and Octavio Getino first of all stressed the intentions, aesthetics, and format of Third Cinema. Solanas and Getino, who earlier that year had founded the Grupo Cine Liberación, developed a cinematic movement of collective authorship that rejected the established U.S. movie industry format.

14. Bert Hogenkamp, *De documentaire film, 1945–1965: de bloei van een* *filmgenre in Nederland* [The documentary film, 1945–1965: The bloom of a film genre in the Netherlands] (Rotterdam: Uitgeverij 010, 2003), 233–35; Frank Kessler, "Because His Bike Stood There: Visual Documents, Visible Evidence and the Discourse of Documentary," *VIEW* 7, no. 13 (2018): 55–59.

15. Samantha Christiansen and Zachary A. Scarlett, eds., *The Third World in the Global 1960s* (New York: Berghahn Books, 2012), 4.

16. In the many correspondences with filmmakers and other distribution companies, Cineclub received photos and flyers that accompanied the film's topic.

17. Mariano Mestman, "Tracing the Winding Road of *The Hour of the Furnaces in the First World*," in *A Trail of Fire for Political Cinema: The Hour of the Furnaces Fifty Years Later*, ed. Javier Campo and Pérez-Blanco Humberto (Bristol, U.K.: Intellect, 2019), 9.

18. Luna Hupperetz, "The Militant Film Circuit of Cineclub Vrijheidsfilms: Reconstructing a Dutch Multi-sited Cinema History in Light of the Cineclub Paper Archive" (MA thesis, University of Amsterdam, 2020); Joris van Laarhoven, "Pan! Nederlandse film als socialistisch wapen. Een verkennend onderzoek naar Cineclub Vrijheidsfilms" [Pan! Dutch film as a socialist weapon. An exploratory research into Cineclub Freedom Films] (MA thesis, Universiteit Utrecht, 2013).

19. Hupperetz, "Militant Film Circuit"; van Laarhoven, "Pan!"

20. This article was only published in English in 2011 by Jonathan Buchsbaum and Mariano Mestman for the magazine *Third Text*.

21. De Nederlandse Bioscoop Bond (NBB) is a trade organization with which all cinema exhibitors and film suppliers (distributors) have been affiliated since 1921. Film producers joined NBB in 1937. The uniqueness of this organization was determined by federal regulations that required members to trade only with each other. This cartel-like organization decided what happened in the field of film in the Netherlands, what the public was shown, and which feature films were made. See Céline Linssen, Tom Gunning, and Hans Schoots, *Het gaat om de film! Een nieuwe geschiedenis van de Nederlandsche Filmliga 1927–1933* [It's about the film! A new history of the Dutch Filmliga 1927–1933] (Amsterdam: Lubberhuizen, 1999).

22. Patricia Pisters, *Filming for the Future: The Work of Louis van Gasteren* (Amsterdam: Amsterdam University Press, 2015), 104.

23. This was decided on April 8, 1966; see Kessler, "Because His Bike Stood There."

24. The value of *f* 1.75 from the year 1967 was €0.80, with a "purchasing power" of €4.36 in 2019. "Value of the Guilder versus Euro," https://iisg .amsterdam/en/research/projects/hpw/calculate.php.

25. The value of *f* 1.25 from the year 1967 was €0.60, with a "purchasing power" of €3.11 in 2019. "Value of the Guilder versus Euro."

26. Van Laarhoven, "Pan!," 155; film program announcement in *Het Parool*, December 6, 1967.

27. "Cineclub Arnhem telt nu bijna 3000 leden"; "Advertentie," *Het vrije volk: democratisch-socialistisch dagblad*, June 18, 1968, 20, http://resolver .kb.nl/resolve?urn=ddd:010956646:mpeg21:p020.

28. Van Laarhoven, "Pan!," 81.

29. Van Laarhoven, 90.

30. Henk Lalji, email correspondence with the author, January 11, 2022.

31. Rita Rahman, email correspondence with the author, December 23, 2021.

32. For more information on Nadia Tilon's activist history, see Annelore van Gool, "Het links Surinaams activisme van de jaren zeventig en tachtig in Nederland" [Left-wing Surinamese activism in the 1970s and 1980s in the Netherlands], https://werkgroepcaraibischeletteren.nl/het-links-surinaams -activisme-van-de-jaren-zeventig-en-tachtig-in-nederland/.

33. These songs were produced by OPO, Trio Tropical, Lieve Hugo, Kawina Band, and Gaje Dja Gaje Dja, to name a few bands or choirs that supported Suriname's independence and cultural plurality.

34. The housing corporations had difficulties finding occupants for newly built flats in the southeast of Amsterdam, but the newly arriving families were not allowed to rent these flats because of racist housing policies. LO-SON, as well as other squatting movements in the city of Amsterdam, such as the Nieuwmarkt squatters, supported the occupation of these buildings. See Lucy Cotter, ed., *Wendelien van Oldenborgh: Cinema Olanda* (Ostfildern, Germany: Hatje Cantz, 2017).

35. According to Charles Braam, it was the original negative of Cineclub's first production, the *Maagdenhuis Film* (1969), that was saved by a colleague from IISH in the late 1980s. Braam, personal interview with (and translated by) the author, November 18, 2019.

36. Floris Paalman, Rommy Albers, and Simona Monizza, "Cineclub Amsterdam Freedom Films at the International Institute of Social History," paper presented at the NYU Orphan Film Symposium, Vienna, June 6–8, 2019.

37. Fernando Solanas and Octavio Getino, "Militant Cinema: An Internal Category of Third Cinema (Argentina, 1971)," trans. Jonathan Buchsbaum and Mariano Mestman, *Third Text* 25, no. 1 (2011): 52–53.

38. In "Archiving the Legacy of Women in Film: Collaborations and Networks," December 2021, curator Simona Monizza highlights the project around *Vrouwen van Suriname*.

THE 2020 AMIA ANNUAL SALARY AND DEMOGRAPHICS SURVEY OF THE FIELD

BRIAN REAL AND TEAGUE SCHNEITER

Findings and Future Dircctions

The Association of Moving Image Archivists (AMIA) is a professional nonprofit organization dedicated to supporting established and aspiring professionals in the field of audio-visual preservation and access. AMIA has been interested in issues of salary fairness and diversity since its founding in 1990, but in 2016, the organization's leadership made structural changes and allocated additional resources to take more direct and intentional action to promote positive change across the profession.

In 2019, recognizing that good data are necessary precursors to effective advocacy, AMIA collaborated with the National Film Preservation Board's Diversity Task Force (NFPB DTF) to gather data on age, race and ethnicity, ability, sexual identity, level of education, years of professional experience, and other intersectional factors to examine how they might affect salary, employment, and professional advancement. In addition, AMIA launched a series of roundtables about advocacy concerns at its annual conferences in 2018 and 2019. The results of the survey and roundtables, as well as the findings from the NFPB DTF final report, showed significant concerns for the field, including but not limited to inadequate racial and ethnic representation and high student loan debt loads relative to participants' salaries. To work toward increasing equity, promoting fair labor practices, and encouraging professional sustainability fieldwide, the organization saw a need for ongoing data collection and analysis and decided to continue such research each year as the AMIA Annual Salary and Demographics Survey of the Field. The first follow-up in this ongoing longitudinal research project was launched in December 2020. Executing the survey at this time meant that questions about workplace situations co-incided with the ongoing Covid-19 pandemic.

This analysis primarily presents data from the 2020 AMIA Annual Salary and Demographics Survey of the Field, and the reader should assume that information comes from that study, unless the text explicitly states otherwise. However, for purposes of comparison, the authors have also included data from its 2019 predecessor survey at various points. In some instances where results from the most recent data collection cycle are surprising, showing demographic trends in the field of audiovisual archiving differing from the general population, the 2019 data appear to confirm that this is not due to sampling error or other survey bias. Additionally, there are some discrepancies between the 2019 and 2020 samples that show possible impacts of Covid-19 on younger persons' representation in the field and their interactions with AMIA and other profes-sional organizations.

Some of the findings that follow may seem discouraging, because it is clear that the makeup of the audiovisual heritage field does not match the diversity of the general population in the United States and beyond, but AMIA is dedicated to finding ways to allow this profession to be shaped by a full array of voices, experiences, and perspectives. Significant barriers to entry must be addressed, and the financial costs of education and training to enter the field for some may even negate the benefits that come with an eventual career in the audiovisual heritage community. These issues can only be surmounted through open discussion and a willingness to take decisive action to promote positive change.

BACKGROUND TO THE STUDY

The AMIA Annual Salary and Demographics Survey of the Field was influenced by broader professional trends in libraries, archives, and museums, along with discussions by AMIA's membership and leadership. Other organizations, such as the American Library Association (ALA) and Society of American Archivists (SAA), have conducted studies of these issues and are in the process of developing policies to allow professionals to advocate for fair salaries and to promote more diversity among library and archives staff.

Diversity and Salary Issues in Libraries, Archives, and Museums

ALA collected data on the field of librarianship in 2009–10 for the most recent iteration of its Diversity Counts study, which was published in 2012.[1] The organization found that 88 percent of librarians with master of library science (MLS) or master of library and information science (MLIS) degrees were non-Latino White.[2] Additionally, 83 percent of librarians with relevant graduate degrees were women, and 73 percent were White women. These figures improve somewhat for paraprofessionals or librarians who do not hold an MLS or MLIS degree, as about 73 percent of persons in that group are non-Latinx White. To put this in perspective, according to 2019 estimates from the U.S. Census Bureau, 76.3 percent of the U.S. population identifies as White, and 60.1 percent of the total population identifies as non-Hispanic, non-Latinx White.[3]

The authors of this study do not consider gender disparity favoring women in the library, archives, and museum professions to be a problem in itself. However, considering trends in the United States and other nations of women being paid less than men for the same work, a profession perceived as having a gender bias toward women carries the risk of lower salaries in general. SAA's Women Archivists Section (WArS) chose to address this problem head-on through the 2017 Women Archivists Section Salary Survey.[4] This study "was developed in response to [SAA] member interest in salary data about the archives profession and, in particular, in data about women archivists across intersectional identities."[5] The authors' findings suggested that women and Black,

Indigenous, and other Persons of Color (BIPOC) did receive less pay and have less access to opportunity within the field. However, perhaps the most significant finding is that the field of archives is overwhelmingly White—87.7 percent of respondents identified as such—meaning that SAA should take an active role in recruiting diverse persons to the profession and promoting equitable treatment of employees in a way that will promote retention.[6] To work against these inequities, SAA has taken numerous actions that include cultural diversity scholarships and other recruitment initiatives; salary transparency, so that people in the field know what other persons in comparable positions are paid; refusing to post positions to its LISTSERV or website without salary and benefit details; and more. As discussed later, AMIA has also been taking similar actions to promote diversity and salary transparency in the subfield of audiovisual archives.

AMIA's Advocacy for Diversity and Salary Fairness

AMIA has taken numerous actions to promote diversity, equity, and inclusion (DEI) over the years, but in 2016, AMIA began the process of structural changes that would allow the organization to place a greater emphasis on these matters. A statement on DEI was drafted and opened to the full membership for comment before adoption by the board of directors. A major step was made in the recommendation of AMIA's Diversity Committee of the Membership to dissolve itself and fold its objectives into the core work of the board of directors and other parts of the organization's senior leadership and expanding operations. In 2017, the board hired management consultant and DEI expert DeEtta Jones to work with the board in managing organizational change, offered training for committee and project leadership, and led conference sessions on DEI and organizational change. Members of the AMIA Board of Directors are required to complete a series of webinars in cultural competency. AMIA has also hosted several cultural competency webinars for its members in areas like disability consciousness raising, disability and audiovisual archives access, and mentorship training, along with webinars on areas of cultural sensitivity, such as a session on stewardship of Indigenous materials and another on transcribing Black narratives. Moving forward, AMIA plans to offer more webinars in similar areas for free to the organizational membership.

In 2018, AMIA transitioned its Advocacy Committee to the Advocacy Committee of the Board (ACOB). The primary difference between these two bodies is that the first consisted of AMIA members who volunteered for the committee discussing advocacy issues within the field, while members of the new committee were appointed by the AMIA Board of Directors and intended to be instrumental in developing AMIA's policy agenda, especially in the areas of promoting DEI and advocating for better working conditions in the audiovisual archives field for all.

In 2019, NFPB funded a study on DEI in the audiovisual archives field, initiated by NFPB DTF and chaired by Dr. Jacqueline Stewart, who is now chair of the NFPB Board of Directors. This first fieldwide assessment of key indicators on cultural equity and inclusion within the profession emerged out of a growing awareness that more understanding was needed of the deep structural issues preventing full participation in the audiovisual heritage community by all. Dr. Stewart provided oversight, and Teague Schneiter, an accomplished audiovisual archivist who was then a member of the AMIA Board of Directors, was hired as an independent contractor to collect qualitative and quantitative data for this study. To begin open conversations with the community, Schneiter and Stewart held three in-person open forum meetings in New York, Los Angeles, and Washington, D.C., along with an online multiregion session via Zoom. This allowed them to obtain a baseline understanding of concerns in the field. Schneiter and Stewart followed this up with ten online focus groups where colleagues of different affinities shared experiences navigating the field. This included BIPOC-led sessions; student-led sessions; regional forums; topical discussions, such as a conversation about visible and invisible disabilities; and more. To protect anonymity of the participants, none of the focus groups or forums was recorded, allowing the approximately 190 persons who took part in these events to speak freely about challenges they experienced and opportunities they saw for the field to do better.

Working with the AMIA Board of Directors and staff members, Schneiter and Stewart used the information gained from the open forums and focus groups and drew inspiration from the 2017 Women Archivists Section Salary Survey to develop the first fieldwide survey of salary and demographics in the audiovisual archives profession. AMIA managing director Laura Rooney provided logistical support, allowing this to launch in June 2019. This survey found similar issues in the field to what WArS and SAA had discovered through their 2017 study but also uncovered problems that were distinct to the area of media preservation and confirmed others that had been initially identified through the forums and focus groups. Salaries for entry-level media archivists are low when compared to costs of living, and the fact that many of the jobs in the field are clustered around three of the most expensive housing markets in the country (Los Angeles, New York, and Washington, D.C.) makes this particularly acute. High levels of student debt for persons entering the field compounded these concerns.

To ensure that this first fieldwide survey effort of reporting realities of the field was made a part of AMIA operations and done so under institutional review board (IRB) oversight, Teague Schneiter approached Dr. Brian Real, a library and information science educator with a background in survey research, to work on a revised version of the survey in 2020. The immediate impetus for this study, now officially named the

AMIA Annual Salary and Demographics Survey of the Field, was to follow up on specific trends in the earlier survey, especially to verify how much the field needs to improve to be truly representative of the wide array of people, cultures, and collections that ensure a healthy and thriving profession globally. A secondary objective was to capture information about the state of the profession during the Covid-19 pandemic and determine if AMIA needed to engage in any short-term interventions to meet the needs of its constituency.

METHODOLOGY

The 2019 survey and its associated focus groups were funded by a grant from NFPB DTF and administered by Teague Schneiter, who worked on this as an independent contractor at a flat rate for the full report. She contributed some of her own time to the project as well. This survey was launched through the SurveyMonkey software platform. The 2020 survey was not directly funded by any organization, but the lead author of this study and coordinator of that survey cycle, Real, did receive compensation for his research time as part of his salary for his faculty position at Southern Connecticut State University. Additionally, he used some university resources, such as its institutional license for the Qualtrics survey platform, which he used for data collection in the 2020 study.

Schneiter worked with ACOB to create the questions for the 2019 NFPB DTF Survey of the Field, using some of the concepts from the 2017 Women Archivists Section Salary Survey and other survey resources, such as the SAA census, as a point of departure. Real oversaw the revisions for the 2020 survey, working with Schneiter and ACOB to address concerns they developed during the previous survey and using his own past work as a quantitative researcher to refine questions for easier analysis. Additionally, Real worked with his partners to add several free-text entry questions to gather qualitative comments that could be useful in designing the next iteration of the survey.

The authors collaborated with AMIA staff and ACOB members to publicize each survey through AMIA's various communication channels and social media and during conference sessions. The survey was also sent through the email lists and social media accounts of SAA, the Association of Recorded Sound Collections, and several other allied groups. In both the 2019 and 2020 surveys, people working in audiovisual archives or in library positions primarily focusing on moving image and audio materials, regardless of whether these were analog or digital, were asked to participate, as were students studying for these types of careers. The surveys did not collect participant names or the names of their workplaces, allowing for more open responses on somewhat sensitive topics. It did, however, include a question about the cities where participants worked.

Participants were able to skip any question, and in many instances, no response was a valid answer. As such, the authors determined most of the percentages that follow by dividing the total number of responses by the total number of survey participants. However, for questions where available responses covered all possible responses, the authors determined percentages by using the total number of responses to the individual question as the divisor.

Real submitted the 2020 study to his university's IRB for its review and approval. IRB determined that the survey posed minimal risk to participants due to all responses being anonymous, exempting it from further review. Although the 2019 survey did not undergo a similar review, that study had a similar methodology and the same level of anonymity.

FINDINGS

A total of 477 persons replied to the 2020 iteration of the survey. Three hundred ninety-five of these responses came from persons who work in the United States, composing 83.2 percent of the sample, while an additional thirty-seven responses (7.75 percent) came from Canada. Only two participants worked in Mexico, and no other responses came from other North American countries. Twenty-five responses (5.2 percent) came from Europe, while the combined response rate for Oceania, Asia, Africa, and South America was less than 4 percent of the sample. By comparison, the 2019 survey received 545 responses, with 74.5 percent of these persons being from the United States. There has not been a full census of the audiovisual archives field, and as a result, it is impossible to say how strong the two response rates actually are. However, AMIA usually has between 925 and 950 members, while 631 people registered for the organization's fall 2020 conference.

As Figure 1 shows, almost half (46.5 percent) of the persons from the United States who responded to the 2020 survey worked in or within ten miles of five major metropolitan markets. Los Angeles had the strongest representation of any major city, as 20.7 percent of U.S.-based respondents were located in that area, while 11.4 percent were in New York City, 7.1 percent worked in or near Washington, D.C., 3.8 percent worked in the greater Chicago area, and 3.5 percent worked in or near San Francisco.

Age, Gender Identity, Sexual Orientation, and Disability

Both survey cycles had six categories for age groups, but because there were no responses from persons older than seventy-five years of age in either year, the authors are able to report on five groupings, as displayed in Figure 2. The smallest of these was

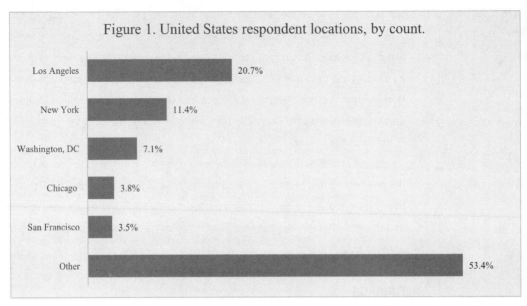

Figure 1. U.S. respondent locations, by count.

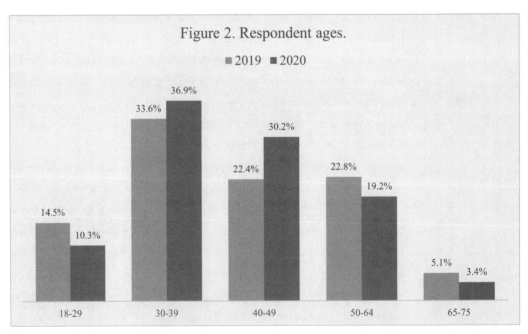

Figure 2. Respondent ages.

the sixty-five to seventy-five group, at just 5.1 percent of the total sample in 2019 and 3.4 percent in 2020. This is unsurprising because that is effectively retirement age. Persons in their thirties constituted the largest portion of the sample, at 33.6 percent in 2019 and 36.9 percent in 2020. However, there are some notable discrepancies between the two cycles of the survey for other categories. Fourteen and a half percent of respondents in 2019 were under thirty, but this dropped to 10.3 percent in 2020. Meanwhile, only 22.4 percent of respondents were in the forty to forty-nine group in 2019, but this increased to 30.2 percent in 2020.

Figure 3 shows participant responses to questions about gender identity. Of respondents, 61.2 percent identified as women in 2019, and 61.6 percent did so in 2020, showing little change between the two years. By comparison, men accounted for 36.2 percent of respondents in 2019 and 33.8 percent in 2020. This follows the general trend that women are better represented in cultural heritage fields like libraries, archives, and museums than men. Meanwhile, the authors saw a notable climb in persons who identified as nonbinary between the two surveys, increasing from 0.6 percent in 2019 to 2.9 percent in 2020. Participants who identified as transgender also increased from 0.4 percent in 2019 to a full percentage point in 2020. It is difficult to establish a firm baseline for how much of the overall U.S. population is nonbinary or transgender, because the U.S. census does not collect data on this and there have also been problems of oppressive practices and cultural stigmas against such persons, often limiting their openness about their identity. However, more people being willing to identify as who they are is a good thing, and the shift in these figures may reflect societal progress on openness about people's identity.

Figure 4 shows that in response to a 2020 question about sexual orientation, 68.8 percent of participants identified as heterosexual, 5.1 percent as homosexual, 9.6 percent as bisexual, 7.6 percent as queer, and 1.2 percent as asexual. Of participants, 7.6 percent chose the option "prefer not to say," meaning that their sexual orientation is unclear. The combined percentage for individuals who selected an option other than heterosexual or "prefer not to say" was 23.5 percent. The 2019 survey asked a similar question about sexual orientation that had three possible responses. In that instance, 72.7 percent of respondents reported that they were heterosexual, 23.2 percent selected LGBTQIA+, and 9.7 percent chose "prefer not to say." As such, a similar number of participants each year reported that they were not straight.

The U.S. census does not collect data on sexual orientation, so it can be difficult to establish a baseline for diversity in this area. However, Gallup has conducted polls about this since 2012, and in February 2021, the organization estimated that

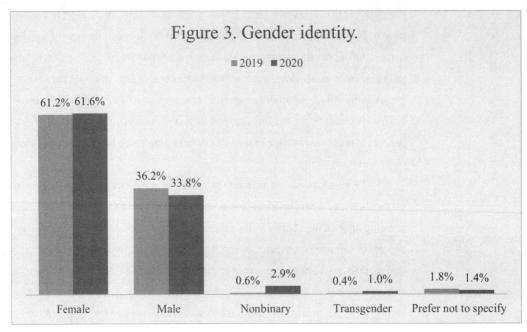

Figure 3. Gender identity.

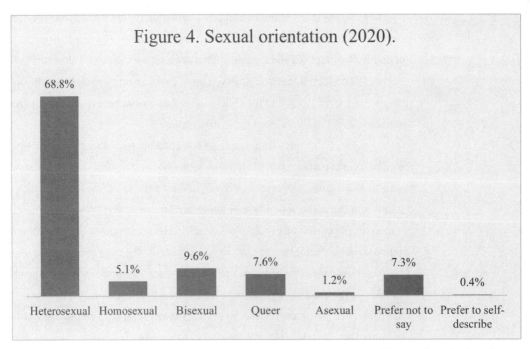

Figure 4. Sexual orientation (2020).

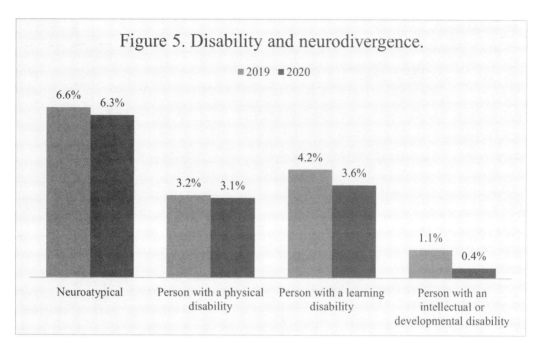

Figure 5. Disability and neurodivergence.

5.6 percent of the population is LGBT, to use Gallup's preferred acronym and grouping.[7] The fact that nearly one-fourth of AMIA survey respondents in 2019 and 2020 made a selection other than straight or "prefer not to say" almost certainly makes the audiovisual archives community more representative and inclusive of LGBTQIA+ persons than the general population.

Participants were allowed to select more than one option for the question about disabilities and neurodivergence. Figure 5 shows that in 2020, 6.3 percent of respondents identified as neuroatypical, 3.1 percent responded that they had a physical disability, 3.6 percent noted that they had a learning disability, and 0.4 percent identified as having an intellectual or developmental disability. The frequency of reporting for all of these categories decreased slightly when compared to 2019, suggesting that this is an area to monitor in future survey cycles. According to the Centers for Disease Control and Prevention, 13.9 percent of Americans reported having some form of mobility disability (i.e., serious difficulty walking or climbing stairs), 5.9 percent identify as deaf or hard of hearing, and 4.6 percent reported that they are blind or vision impaired.[8] As such, the fact that only 3.1 percent of respondents reported having any form of physical disability shows that the audiovisual heritage field needs to do more to be equitable and inclusive in this area.

Race and Ethnicity

Of survey respondents, 82.0 percent selected White as their race or ethnicity in 2019, and 81.6 percent did so in 2020 (Table 1). Considering that the survey had a number of responses from Canada, Europe, Oceania, and other geographic areas that have less racial diversity, one might hope that the situation may improve when looking at data only for the United States. However, this is not the case; Table 2 shows that 82.6 percent of U.S.-based respondents selected "White" as an option for their race or ethnicity in 2020.

Table 1. Race and ethnicity, all respondents, 2020

	Count	Percentage
White	400	82.0
Latino, Latina, or Latinx	23	4.7
Asian (East Asian, South Asian, Central Asian, Southeast Asian)	25	5.1
Black or African American	11	2.3
American Indian, Alaska Native, or Indigenous	5	1.0
Middle Eastern or North African	5	1.0
Native Hawaiian or Pacific Islander	2	0.4
Multiracial	17	3.5
Total	488	100

Table 2. Race and ethnicity, United States, 2020

	Count	Percentage
White	336	82.6
Latino, Latina, or Latinx	22	5.4
Asian (East Asian, South Asian, Central Asian, Southeast Asian)	14	3.4
Black or African American	11	2.7
American Indian, Alaska Native, or Indigenous	5	1.2
Middle Eastern or North African	4	1.0
Native Hawaiian or Pacific Islander	2	0.5
Multiracial	13	3.2
Total	407	100

There were some instances in which respondents who identified as "White" for the 2020 survey also made other selections. This includes ten instances of persons who identified as "Latino, Latina, or Latinx" and six instances of persons who identified as "multiracial" also selecting "White." However, this does little to mitigate the simple fact that the audiovisual archives field is not a profession that is ethnically or racially diverse. Of the persons within the United States who responded to the question about their race or ethnicity, 80.8 percent selected "White" without making any other selection. This White domination of the field, alongside other data about the low participation among certain groups, such as tribal and Indigenous professionals, shows that much work needs to be done.

Geography did have an impact on race and ethnic measures, as 73.9 percent of respondents from the five metropolitan areas with the highest response rates—Los Angeles, New York, Washington, D.C., Chicago, and San Francisco—selected "White" as their race or ethnicity with no secondary option in addition to this. By comparison, this was the case for 85.8 percent of respondents in the United States who were outside of these urban areas. However, much of this was driven by the two largest clusters of respondents, as 70.7 percent of participants from the greater Los Angeles area and 68.8 percent of those in New York City reported as "White" with no other race or ethnicity selected. The greater Washington, D.C., area lagged on diversity measures, since 82.1 percent of participants selected "White" as their only response to race or ethnicity, while Chicago fared worse, with 93.3 percent reporting as such.

Fields of Employment and Leadership

Survey respondents were able to select from a wide range of categories to describe their place of employment. These were not mutually exclusive, meaning that participants could select more than one category for their workplace. Table 3 shows these results in an unedited manner, which provides a broad view but does not lend itself to easy analysis. However, two trends related to race and ethnicity are worth noting. Of respondents, 36.1 percent reported that they worked in colleges or universities.[9] Of these individuals, 79.7 percent selected "White" as their race or ethnicity with no other option selected. Similarly, 15.9 percent of respondents work in government, and 82.9 percent of these persons identify only as White. In other words, academia and government are two of the largest employment categories for the audiovisual archives field, and ethnic and racial diversity in these areas is as lacking as it is for the profession as a whole. These two target areas should be considered for improvement initiatives.

Table 3. Types of organization or employment, 2020

Organization/employment type	Count
College or university–archives	131
College or university–libraries	94
College or university–academic department	41
Studio or streaming service	30
Corporate (for profit)	34
Commercial broadcasting	16
Nonprofit broadcasting/public media	35
Government (federal, state, or local/county/municipal)	76
Special collections	89
Stock footage house	10
Museum	53
Public library system	21
Law–legal firms or courts	1
Law–policing and law enforcement	1
Law librarianship	1
Medicine and health–professional practice	1
Medical and health librarianship	2
Nonprofit	113
Historical society	17
Religious organization	14
Consultant or freelance	22
Tribal government agency	1
Tribal cultural heritage agency	1
Professional archivist organization	12
Accrediting body organization	1
Nonarchivist position with limited archives-related responsibilities	11
Service or product supplier to the field	13
Self-employed	26

As detailed in Table 4, almost half (48.6 percent) of the respondents have some form of supervisory role in their organizations, while 18.7 percent are part of their organizational leadership. The authors found that race and ethnicity had no significant impact on the likelihood of someone having supervisory duties or being part of organizational leadership. However, gender identity seems to be more of an issue. Nonbinary persons were less likely to have supervisory or leadership duties, but transgender persons were more likely to have such roles than the overall sample. Considering that persons from these categories represent a small portion of the sample, though, it is not possible to conclude that these trends are part of any negative or positive bias. Meanwhile, women and men are about equally as likely to perform supervisory duties, as 52.9 percent and 51.0 percent of persons from these categories, respectively, reported as such. A greater concern is the fact that men are almost 10 percent more likely to be part of their organizational leadership than women, as 24.5 percent of men reported this versus just 15.6 percent of women. Longevity in one's career has something of a positive impact on this, as 20.2 percent of women who had ten years or more of experience in the audiovisual heritage field were part of their organizational leadership, but this also increased slightly to 29.1 percent for men.

Table 4. Survey participants in supervisory positions

	Supervisory duties		Organizational leadership	
	Count	Percentage	Count	Percentage
Female	125	52.9	41	15.6
Male	75	51.0	36	24.5
Nonbinary	5	35.7	1	7.1
Transgender	3	75.0	2	50.0
Total	208	48.6	80	18.7

Education and Student Loan Debt

Of 2019 and 2020 survey respondents, 95.5 percent and 97.8 percent, respectively, hold a bachelor's degree or higher (Figure 6). It is clear that a master's degree is often considered a prerequisite to employment in the audiovisual archives field, as 67.1 percent of respondents reported this as their highest degree obtained in 2019, and 73.4 percent did so in 2020. This 6.3 percent increase between the two surveys shows something of a concerning trend, as the percentage of respondents with only a high school diploma decreased from 2.2 percent in 2019 to 1.5 percent in 2020, the percentage of those with an associate's degree as their highest formal education achieved declined from 1.8 percent to 0.6 percent, and the percentage of those whose formal education ended with a bachelor's degree decreased from 20.3 percent to 18.9 percent. It is unclear whether this is due to some form of discrepancy in the data collection between the two surveys or if such individuals are not as actively involved in the profession as they were before Covid-19.

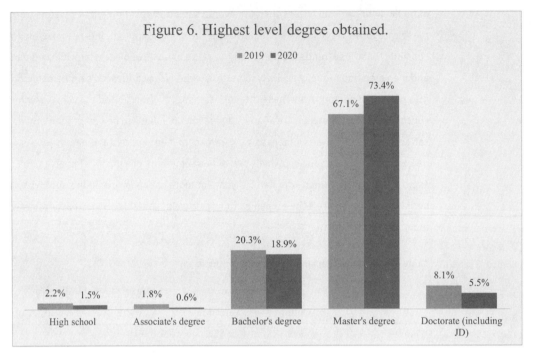

Figure 6. Highest degree level obtained.

Participants were able to enter the areas of study for their education into a free-text box. This question did not ask participants to identify the education level of the relevant degree (e.g., undergraduate, graduate) but instead only the subject. The purpose of this was to collect data that can be used to create a more refined quantitative question for the next iteration of the survey. The fact that participants could enter any text they deemed appropriate makes it difficult to provide exact figures for subject trends, so the analysis that follows is less precise than the rest of the findings. More than one-third of the participants who answered this question mentioned "library" or "information" as a degree subject, while approximately one-tenth of respondents mentioned archives without library or information science, often as part of a history or public history program. Just under 20 percent specified a non-MLIS film preservation degree or certificate, such as the George Eastman Museum's graduate certificate in film preservation, the moving image archives and preservation master's degree at New York University, preservation and presentation of the moving image at the University of Amsterdam, or the master's degree in moving image archives studies at the University of California, Los Angeles, which has recently been discontinued in favor of an MLIS concentration. Meanwhile, approximately one-quarter of participants who responded to this question had some form of degree in film and media studies or film production,

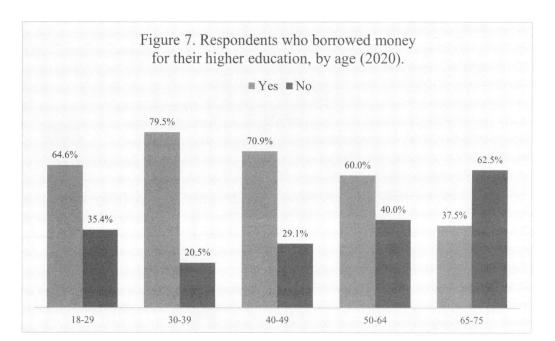

Figure 7. Respondents who borrowed money for their higher education, by age, 2020.

but approximately one-third of these people also had an MLIS or specialized film preservation degree.

Of participants who selected "White" as their only choice for race or ethnicity, 80.1 percent held a graduate degree in 2020, versus 81.1 percent for the sample as a whole. As such, race and ethnicity appear to have no significant impact on education level in the audiovisual archives field. This does not eliminate the possibility that education may be connected to the lack of ethnic and racial diversity in the field in other ways, though, as barriers to educational access may keep people out of a profession that requires a graduate degree for many positions.

Meanwhile, Figure 7 shows that 70.1 percent of survey respondents said they had borrowed money to finance their post–high school education, while 29.9 percent of respondents said they did not do so. Persons in the thirty to thirty-nine age group were the most likely to have borrowed funds for this purpose, as 79.5 percent of respondents said as such, while persons in the forty to forty-nine age group were the second most likely to do this, at 70.9 percent. Only 37.5 percent of persons in the sixty-five to seventy-five age bracket borrowed money to finance their higher education, making this the only group for which a majority did not do so. This is despite all but one of these sixteen persons having a college degree, including eight with master's degrees and three with doctorates. Meanwhile, 60.0 percent of the persons in the fifty to sixty-four age group borrowed money for their education.

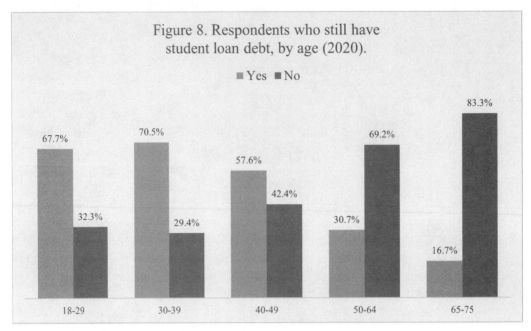

Figure 8. Respondents who still have student loan debt, by age (2020).

Respondents under the age of thirty appear to be something of an outlier in this study, as 64.5 percent of these persons borrowed money to finance their education, making them 14.9 percent less likely to have done so than persons in their thirties. If not for the inclusion of this group, there would be a steady trend of younger respondents being more likely to have financed their education through loans, as persons in the thirty to thirty-nine age group were more than twice as likely to have done so than those who were aged sixty-five or older. It is impossible to make a clear determination as to why persons younger than thirty years defy this trend, but this will be something to watch with future iterations of the survey.

Figure 8. Respondents who still have student loan debt, by age, 2020.

Figure 8 shows how many people who borrowed money for their education still hold debt. Just over two-thirds (67.7 percent) of persons under the age of thirty have outstanding student loans, but this increases to 70.5 percent for persons in their thirties, once again showing a trend among the youngest participants that defies expectations. Beyond this, debt loads decrease as persons get older, but 57.6 percent of participants in their forties still reported owing student loan debt. This only dropped to under half of participants with the fifty to sixty-four age group, as 30.7 percent reported that they are still paying for their higher education, before further declining to 16.7 percent for persons aged sixty-five or older.

On that note, Figure 9 contains responses from only the portion of survey respondents who still hold student loan debt, which constitutes 39.4 percent of the

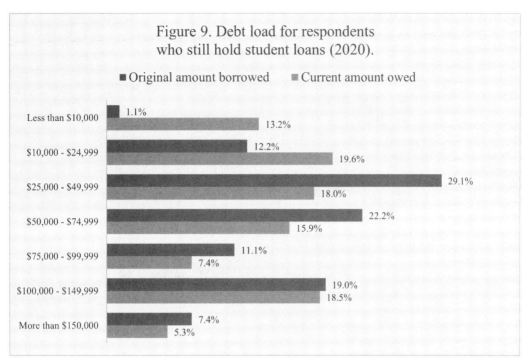

Figure 9. Debt load for respondents who still hold student loans (2020).

■ Original amount borrowed   ■ Current amount owed

Less than $10,000	1.1% / 13.2%
$10,000 - $24,999	12.2% / 19.6%
$25,000 - $49,999	29.1% / 18.0%
$50,000 - $74,999	22.2% / 15.9%
$75,000 - $99,999	11.1% / 7.4%
$100,000 - $149,999	19.0% / 18.5%
More than $150,000	7.4% / 5.3%

Figure 9. Debt load for respondents who still hold student loans, 2020.

total survey sample. For the most part, this is at least somewhat encouraging. As an example, just 1.1 percent of persons who still hold debt borrowed less than $10,000 for their education, yet 13.2 percent currently owe that amount. The only way that the number of people owing that amount could have increased is through participants paying down their debt. Likewise, one-third (33.3 percent) of respondents who have debt reported initially borrowing more than $50,000 and less than $100,000, and this has now declined to 23.3 percent owing in that range. However, a notable concern is that 26.4 percent of respondents who reported that they borrowed money to finance their higher education took out loans in excess of $100,000, while 23.8 percent of persons who still have loans owe more than this amount, showing a decline of just 2.6 percent. Put another way, 9.9 percent of total survey respondents currently owe more than $100,000 in student loans. Of the forty-seven individuals who owe more than six figures in student loans, only seven have PhDs, while forty have a master's degree as their highest level of education achieved.

Salaries, Benefits, and Professional Development

There are some notable discrepancies between salaries in the 2019 and 2020 data sets, as displayed in Figure 10. The largest single portion of survey participants make between $55,000 and $75,000 per year, but this increased from 28.3 percent of respondents in

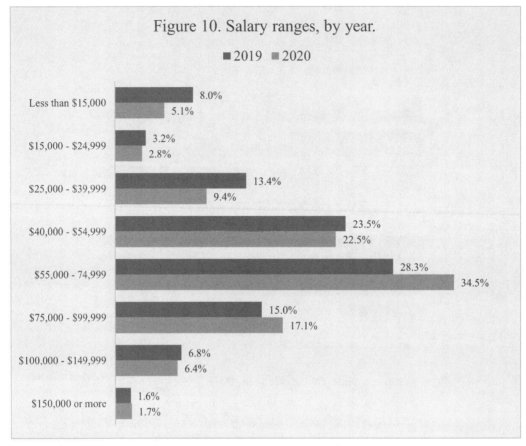

Figure 10. Salary ranges, by year.

2019 to 34.5 percent in 2020. Meanwhile, 24.6 percent of respondents in 2019 made less than $40,000, but in 2020, that dropped to 17.3 percent. A genuine increase in average salaries in the audiovisual archives field would be a cause for celebration, but it seems unlikely that this is the reason for these differences, especially during the financial uncertainty caused by the Covid-19 pandemic. As discussed later in this analysis, these discrepancies are most likely the result of differences between the two samples that may stem from slight variances in recruitment methods or differences in active participation in the survey and the field as a whole for persons with lower salaries between the two years.

Focusing only on the 2020 data, as Figure 11 shows, salaries do vary to some degree in relation to race or ethnicity. Of persons who did not select "White" as one of their options, 21.0 percent made $25,000 or less per year, versus just 5.5 percent of participants who selected White as one of their options. That is certainly alarming, but conversely, 14.1 percent of persons of color in the sample reported making more than $100,000 per year, versus about half that (7.4 percent) for participants who selected

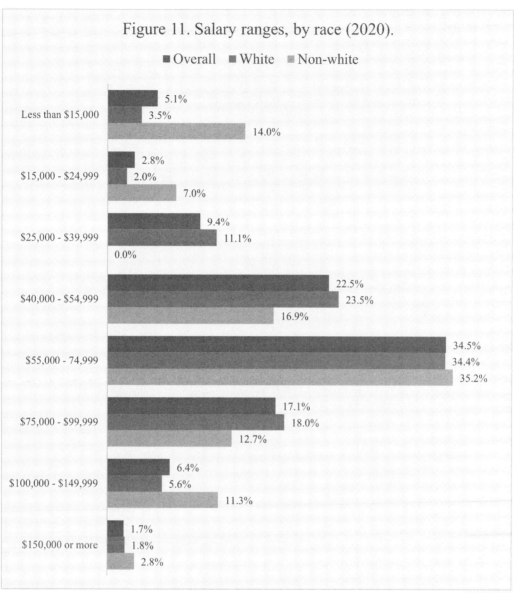

Figure 11. Salary ranges, by race (2020).

■ Overall ■ White ■ Non-white

Less than $15,000
5.1%
3.5%
14.0%

$15,000 - $24,999
2.8%
2.0%
7.0%

$25,000 - $39,999
9.4%
11.1%
0.0%

$40,000 - $54,999
22.5%
23.5%
16.9%

$55,000 - 74,999
34.5%
34.4%
35.2%

$75,000 - $99,999
17.1%
18.0%
12.7%

$100,000 - $149,999
6.4%
5.6%
11.3%

$150,000 or more
1.7%
1.8%
2.8%

Figure 11. Salary ranges, by race, 2020.

"White" as one of their options for the race or ethnicity question. The most common salary range for the sample was $55,000 to $75,000, as about 35 percent of participants selected that option, regardless of race or ethnicity.

Figure 12 shows response rates for salary ranges by age. Of 2020 survey participants, 34.5 percent earned at least $55,000 and less than $75,000 per year. Persons in their thirties slightly exceeded this at 37.4 percent, and 40.8 percent of persons in their forties reported this as their pay range. Only 14.5 percent of persons younger than

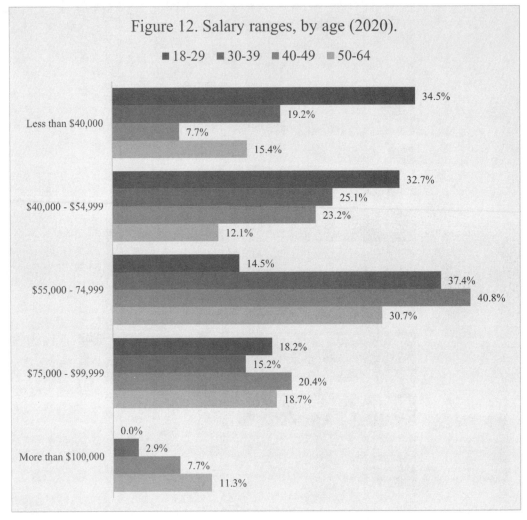

Figure 12. Salary ranges, by age (2020).

■ 18-29 ■ 30-39 ■ 40-49 ■ 50-64

Less than $40,000
- 34.5%
- 19.2%
- 7.7%
- 15.4%

$40,000 - $54,999
- 32.7%
- 25.1%
- 23.2%
- 12.1%

$55,000 - 74,999
- 14.5%
- 37.4%
- 40.8%
- 30.7%

$75,000 - $99,999
- 18.2%
- 15.2%
- 20.4%
- 18.7%

More than $100,000
- 0.0%
- 2.9%
- 7.7%
- 11.3%

Figure 12. Salary ranges, by age, 2020.

thirty earn a salary in this range, and that is a result of these persons earning less pay, as 67.2 percent of these respondents earned less than $55,000, versus just 39.8 percent for survey respondents of all ages. Conversely, 30.7 percent of persons in the fifty to sixty-four age group have salaries in the $55,000–$74,999 range, making this group 4.5 percent less likely to earn in this range than the total population. However, 30.0 percent of these persons earn more than $75,000 annually, versus 25.2 percent of the survey population as a whole.

As detailed in Figure 13, most respondents receive some core employment benefits. Of participants, 77.8 percent reported that their workplaces offer health insurance, 79.7 percent provide sick-day compensation, and 81.3 percent allow employees to

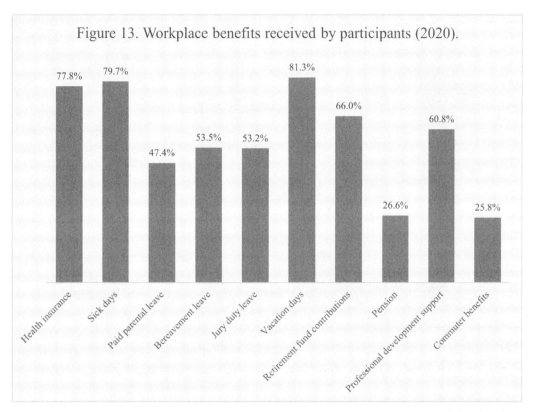

Figure 13. Workplace benefits received by participants (2020).

Figure 13. Workplace benefits received by participants, 2020.

take paid vacation time. However, a notable concern is that less than half of workplaces (47.4 percent) provide employees with paid parental leave. Likewise, pensions are somewhat rare, as just 26.6 percent of respondents receive this benefit, while only two-thirds (66.0 percent) of participants receive retirement fund contributions, showing that a significant number of persons in the audiovisual archives field may face challenges when they are ready to transition out of the workforce.

Figure 14 shows responses to a question about mentorship programs offered by participants' workplaces. Internships were the most common selection, at 41.1 percent. Only one-fifth (19.9 percent) of audiovisual archivists' workplaces offer planned mentorship programs for new employees, while 14.0 percent offer mentorship for people who express interest in advancing to leadership and management positions. Cultural affinity groups are organizations that allow persons of certain racial or ethnic backgrounds, gender identities, sexual orientations, or other cultural factors to meet with each other regularly to discuss their experiences and provide support for each other. Of participants, 13.2 percent reported that such groups exist in their workplaces.

As Figure 15 shows, the survey also asked participants about what types

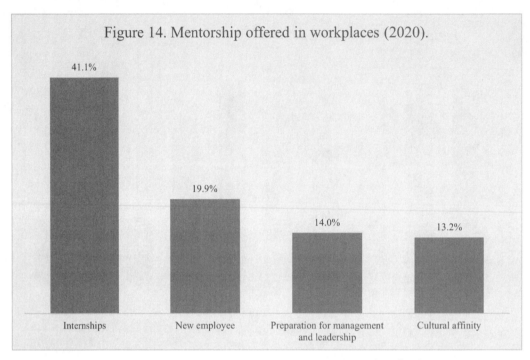

Figure 14. Mentorship offered in workplaces (2020).

41.1%

19.9%

14.0%

13.2%

Internships   New employee   Preparation for management   Cultural affinity
                                and leadership

Figure 14. Mentorship offered in workplaces, 2020.

of training and continuing education programs they would find useful. Just over one-fifth (21.2 percent) of respondents selected basic audiovisual history and theory, making it the least popular category. Considering that many people who enter the field came in with some sort of interest or educational or professional background in film and media production or studies, the majority of participants may feel that they have already been adequately trained in this area. Meanwhile, the most common area of interest for further training was digital technology, as 60.3 percent of participants selected this option. Part of this is undoubtedly due to the constantly changing nature of digital tools and the need to stay up to date, but more research is needed as to whether students feel adequately prepared for their careers coming out of degree and other training programs. However, archival standards was the second most popular requested training area, at 45.7 percent, followed by hands-on skills at 43.4 percent. Even if digital technology training is the most popular area, more traditional archival skills and the ability to handle physical artifacts are still relevant for professionals in the field.

Impacts of Covid-19

The authors discuss some possible indirect impacts of the Covid-19 pandemic in the discussion section. However, the survey did include some direct questions about how

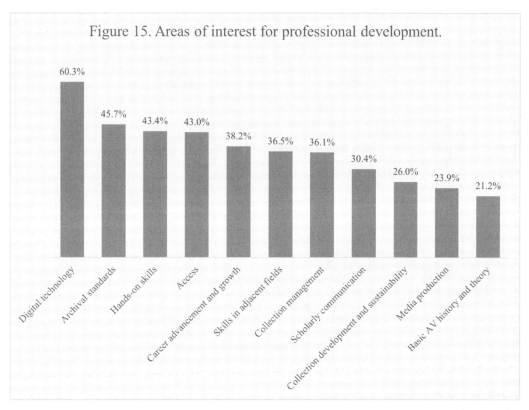

Figure 15. Areas of interest for professional development.

Figure 15. Areas of interest for professional development.

Covid-19 affected participants' lives and livelihoods, because data collection occurred in November and December 2020, when no clear end to the crisis was in sight. As Figure 16 shows, 22.9 percent of participants noted that they were the primary income earner for their family before the pandemic, but this increased to 26.0 percent afterward. Of respondents, 10.9 percent were the primary caregiver for a child or children, 1.9 percent acted as the primary caregiver for an adult, and 2.7 percent provided elder care after the start of the pandemic. The frequency of this occurring increased by less than a percentage point for all three categories, suggesting that the pandemic had only a minor effect on these matters.

Meanwhile, Figure 17 shows the most widespread impact of the Covid-19 pandemic: 82.8 percent of respondents shifted to remote work at some point during the shutdowns. Of participants, 8.8 percent saw their hours increase, while 9.9 percent saw their working hours reduced. Pay cuts affected 7.0 percent of individuals, while 11.5 percent saw their benefits cut or frozen. However, perhaps the greatest impacts were felt by the 5.9 percent of respondents who were furloughed and the 2.9 percent who were laid off during the pandemic. The authors of this analysis will follow up on these

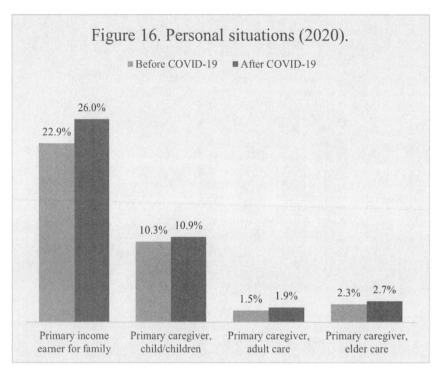

Figure 16. Personal situations (2020).

issues in future iterations of the AMIA Annual Salary and Demographics Survey of the Field to see if these impacts have remained past the end of the Covid-19 pandemic.

Figure 16. Personal situations, 2020.

DISCUSSION

It is impossible to make definite statements about the causes of some of the equity issues that the authors identified through the analysis of the AMIA Annual Salary and Demographics Survey of the Field. As such, the discussion that follows includes reasonable assumptions about why certain demographics are not adequately represented in the survey sample and the audiovisual archives profession as a whole, but these should still be read with some criticism. What is clear, however, is that AMIA is dedicated to acknowledging issues in the field and attempting to find meaningful solutions, such as the AMIA Pathways Fellowship Program (see the following section) and shifts to make AMIA spaces more welcoming, prioritizing inclusion and belonging for those who have been historically marginalized in the field.

Racial and Ethnic Diversity

One considerable limitation to the analysis is that issues of racial and ethnic diversity are often framed in terms of White versus non-White participants. This type of binary

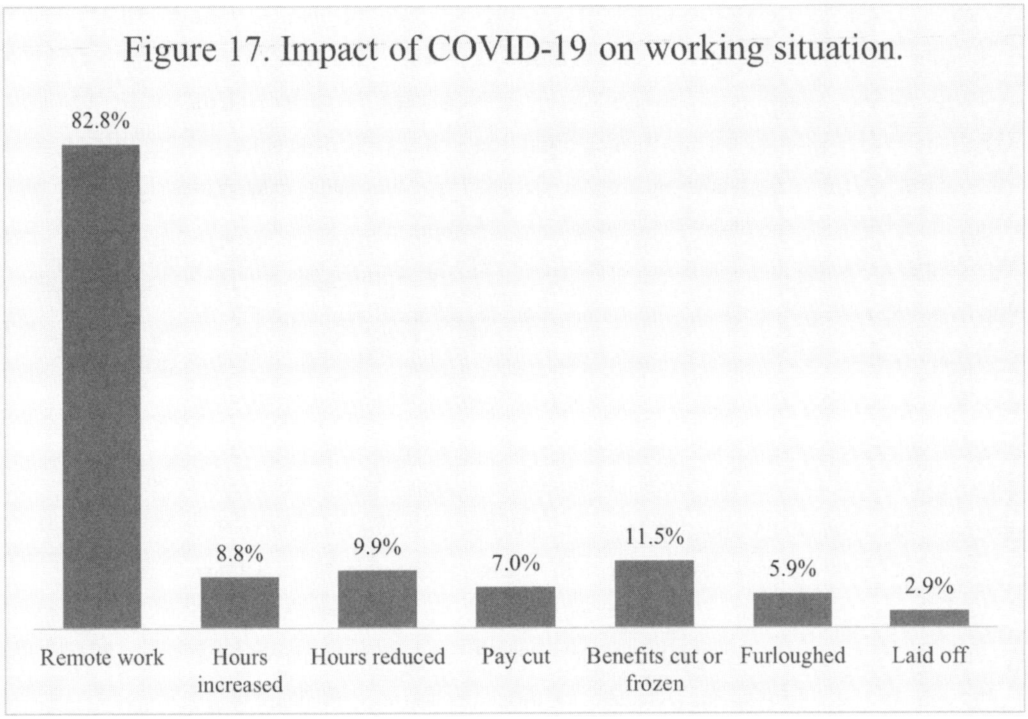

Figure 17. Impact of COVID-19 on working situation.

Figure 17. Impact of Covid-19 on working situation.

viewpoint is problematic, to say the least, because it agglomerates diverse groups of people and carries the risk of normalizing and centering Whiteness. This was not the intention of the authors; instead, they did this because breaking down data points by specific racial or ethnic groupings could create misleading arguments. As an example, only eleven participants, or 2.2 percent of the respondents, selected Black or African American as one of their options for race or ethnicity. While it would be possible to determine salary ranges or other data points for that specific group, this is a small enough portion of the sample that it would be irresponsible to describe this as the typical experience for such individuals at present or to suggest that these figures will remain stable as diversity increases in the audiovisual archives profession. Likewise, this also made it difficult to analyze trends according to people's always intersectional identities. However, the core message from all survey data related to race and ethnicity is that the field, and those within it who are in a position to advocate for change, must do better. The fact that no racial or ethnic group, other than White people, is represented at the same level or higher than they are in the U.S. population is unacceptable.

As stated, two target areas for improvement should be academic institutions and government, which respectively constitute 36.1 percent and 15.9 percent of survey respondents' workplaces. Despite these being areas where leadership should have more awareness of the need to create workplaces that reflect the general population, these subsamples are about as lacking in diversity as the field as a whole, at least in terms of employees working in audiovisual preservation and access. Encouraging these types of institutions to do targeted hiring and training could lead to direct improvement of the field's lack of DEI. The recent fellowship program launched by AMIA could also serve as a model for recruitment and retention for these types of institutions.

The AMIA Diversity and Inclusion Fellowship Program (ADIFP) was launched in summer 2020 as a pilot program, initiated as a direct continuation of the NFPB DTF report by Schneiter. AMIA wrote a follow-up grant proposal and received support from the Library of Congress's National Film Preservation Board and the Council on Library and Information Resources to support four emerging professionals of different races and ethnicities, gender identities, and sexual orientations in fellowship programs that would allow them to receive paid mentorship and training to help them enter and succeed in the audiovisual archives profession. Owing to the Covid-19 pandemic, the ADIFP Task Force had to retool its plans for each fellow to work in paid, in-person internships with a host. Instead, three fellows were able to complete hybrid (remote and in-person) internships safely. But the shift in focus to increasing online mentorship and curriculum-based training led to a reallocation of resources that allowed AMIA to expand the program to six fellows who hoped to pursue a career in the audiovisual archives profession. The lead author of this analysis is currently conducting an evaluation of the experiences of this first cohort, but AMIA plans to continue the program in future years under the new name AMIA Pathways.[10] In 2021, the project received a multiyear grant from the Institute of Museum and Library Services (IMLS) to continue the program for cohorts in summer 2022 and summer 2023. Beyond being a means to recruit and retain persons of different racial and ethnic backgrounds, persons of varying gender expressions, and those who have disabilities, the continuation of this program can serve as a way to address AMIA's challenges in encouraging and creating a pipeline for aspiring audiovisual archivists, especially the next generation, to be actively involved in the organization.

Younger Persons in the Audiovisual Archives Profession

Persons under the age of thirty composed 14.5 percent of the sample in 2019, but this declined to 10.3 percent in 2020. It is possible that this is due to differences in recruitment between the two years, but in both instances, the publicity mainly occurred through the email lists of AMIA and various other professional organizations related to the audiovisual archives profession. One notable difference is that the 2020 survey was also publicized during various panels at AMIA's annual conference. The authors will follow the data in upcoming survey cycles to determine if this was just a temporary drop-off for this age group and to see if reasons for relatively low participation from persons in this age group become more clear. One concern is that because younger persons are less likely to be at stable points in their careers and tend to have lower salaries; some of these individuals may have stepped away from their developing careers to pursue work in other fields that offered more short-term benefits or stopped participating in professional organizations during the Covid-19 pandemic due to cost or time.

On that note, several trends among persons under thirty defy expectations. According to the 2020 survey, these individuals were 14.9 percent less likely to have borrowed money for their higher education than persons in their thirties. Among those who did borrow money, persons who were under thirty were 2.9 percent more likely to have paid off their debt than respondents who are in their thirties. Meanwhile, while survey participants who are under thirty generally had lower salaries than older participants, 18.2 percent of these individuals reported in 2020 that they earned at least $75,000 and less than $100,000 per year, versus 17.1 percent for the survey population as a whole.

There appear to be a significant number of persons who come from privilege—the type of privilege that allows someone to complete their higher education without debt who are influencing trends in the data for younger persons. This is representative of only a portion of the younger participants, rather than the majority, but it is still a strong enough trend to skew the data. The authors will monitor the data from future surveys, and if the frequency of persons in their thirties having borrowed money for their education or still owing that debt declines, then this was clearly just a reflection of the state of the field. However, it seems more likely that individuals with personal economic advantage are able to enter the profession and become stable in their careers at an earlier point, which in turn makes them more likely to be involved in relevant professional organizations and thus more likely to have participated in the survey.

As such, it is a concern that aspiring professionals may not participate in AMIA due to cost, and this absence may have deepened during the time of economic uncertainty that came with the Covid-19 pandemic. If AMIA is going to continue to advocate for the needs of emerging professionals and work toward inclusion and belonging for a wide array of practitioners, it should want the people who would be best served by this to be involved. Although the organization already has a sliding scale for conference attendance based on salary, it is in the process of reviewing these existing rates and considering a sliding scale for membership fees. New conference and membership fees may be lower for new professionals in the field, and a "bridge rate" may be offered to persons who are unemployed or underemployed. Additionally, AMIA offers yearlong free memberships and event attendance, including all conferences and webinars, for ADIFP/ AMIA Pathways Fellows.

There are also AMIA student chapters at a dozen universities, and the organization takes other actions to promote itself to persons who are entering or considering entering the career. However, the data show that the field needs constantly to consider how it can do more to recruit and retain younger persons, especially those from less privileged backgrounds, and must find ways to ensure financial support for their professional pathways and career development.

Gender Bias and Disparities

It bears repeating that women making up about 60 percent of the audiovisual archives profession is not a problem in itself, but this does come with the risk of this labor being undervalued and salaries mirroring national trends of men being paid more for their work than women. As such, AMIA's decision to collect data on salaries, advocate for salary transparency through means like disallowing job postings on its job board without salary range information, and related actions will continue to be prudent and necessary. Any effort to make the labor of audiovisual archives more visible and understood by broader audiences, including constituencies like academics in film studies, will be useful for this purpose.

The authors' initial analysis of the survey data did not show clear evidence of widespread gender-based bias, which is not to say that the field is devoid of problems but instead that such issues did not become apparent through the type of quantitative data the survey was designed to collect. However, a notable exception is that 15.6 percent of women who participated in the survey are part of organizational leadership in their workplaces, versus 24.5 percent of men. There are numerous ways to approach this problem, and one of these is to ensure that women have access to the training needed for leadership. Only approximately one-fifth of workplaces offer mentorship for new employees, and just 14.0 percent offer mentorship for employees who are interested in advancing to management and leadership. AMIA has already started to take some action to remedy this and step into the role that most employers are not filling, with its launch of a manager training webinar series in June 2021 being one example. AMIA could also work with employers to help them develop their own programs. This could be an area for collaboration with related organizations, such as SAA, ALA, and the Association of Recorded Sound Collections.

Meanwhile, it is unclear if the increase in the number of nonbinary and transgender participants between the 2019 and 2020 surveys is representative of the state of the field or if this is the result of some form of sampling difference. Considering that there are no clear baseline data for the percentage of the population that falls into these categories, there is also no way to know at present if 2.9 percent of survey participants being nonbinary persons and 1.0 percent being transgender persons matches societal trends. The authors will continue to monitor responses to future iterations of the survey and other data sources to determine how AMIA can ensure that it is a welcoming environment and community for people to be their whole selves.

Disability

Unfortunately, the survey included only one question that asked about disability issues, and this contained rather broad categories. The authors are working to revise this for the next cycle of the survey, allowing them to capture more nuanced and granular data in this area. These revisions will be especially useful for understanding the experiences of persons with visible and invisible disabilities of all kinds in the audiovisual archives field, and the authors also plan to add questions to determine how many persons in the field have some form of chronic illness. However, the responses for both the 2019 and 2020 cycles indicate that there are considerably fewer persons with physical disabilities in the audiovisual archives field than there are in the U.S. population. Some of this may be related to the nature of the profession, because vision or hearing impairment may prevent individuals from performing certain essential tasks with audiovisual materials. The field needs to ensure that there are opportunities for those with mobility disabilities, but the fact that 13.7 percent of Americans have these forms of disabilities, while just 3.1 percent of survey respondents are persons with any form of physical disability, is alarming.

Revisions to the survey will help AMIA to understand these issues, but only so much can be done through quantitative means. It appears that persons with visible and invisible disabilities face barriers to entry to the profession, and the best way to understand these matters may be through qualitative interviews and other forms of discussions with individuals who are already in the audiovisual archives field and allied professions, such as libraries and archives.

Salaries, Education, and Debt

It is difficult to make definitive statements about certain trends with participant salaries, but this will become more clear as additional survey cycles allow for longitudinal data analysis. One immediately troubling issue is BIPOC survey respondents were four times more likely to earn less than $25,000 per year than White respondents. Future analysis should address structural racism, bias, and other issues that may be causing this gross inequity. The fact that approximately 35 percent of all participants, regardless of race or ethnicity, earn between $55,000 and $75,000 annually suggests that this might be the case. However, a situation in which BIPOC individuals are more likely to earn less in the early stages of their careers is certainly an equity problem on its own, and if this is in fact a systemic problem, it may act as a barrier to entry and work counter to retention in ways that have contributed to the audiovisual heritage field's lack of racial and ethnic diversity.

Educational trends in the audiovisual heritage field also present some areas for concern. The fact that 78.9 percent of 2020 survey participants have a graduate-level education is useful for advocacy purposes, because it supports arguments that audiovisual preservation and access require skilled, intellectual labor. However, more research is needed to determine if the need for a graduate degree for many positions acts as a barrier to entry for the field as a whole. Although the organization already hosts regular continuing education programs, AMIA is also considering the support and development of alternative training programs for new professionals outside of the structures of higher education, such as the AMIA Pathways Fellowship Program. If the organization takes further steps in this direction, though, it will be necessary to determine if biases in the field in favor of persons with graduate degrees would limit the prospects of persons with alternative training, and it would be important also to consider the potential impacts of this variance on long-term salaries.

The student debt for many participants was particularly concerning, as 40 percent of respondents have student loan debt and just below 10 percent of survey respondents currently owe more than $100,000. Further analysis needs to be conducted to determine why debt is so widespread in the field and whether this effectively negates the strength of typical salaries that many people receive once their careers are fully established. Two of the most popular American graduate programs for audiovisual preservation and access are located in Los Angeles and New York, respectively, which have high costs of living, and this is also the case for the graduate program Preservation and Presentation of the Moving Image at the University of Amsterdam. Students often have to complete internships as part of these and other programs, and considering that a combined 39.2 percent of U.S.-based survey participants work in or near Los Angeles, New York, or Washington, D.C., it would follow that many training and early career positions are in areas with high costs of living as well.

AMIA has already implemented certain actions to promote salary fairness and prevent the exploitation of labor in the audiovisual heritage field. The organization will not publicize any job postings for the field without a salary or salary range attached. This transparency ensures that employers cannot offer candidates less than they deserve, especially if due to conscious or unconscious biases. AMIA has also decided that it is unwilling to post advertisements for internships that are unpaid; the fact that student debt can increase as a result of unpaid internships was a factor in this decision. More research and analysis will be needed to determine what strategic, systemic, and ongoing steps need to be taken, however.

CONCLUSION

AMIA initiated efforts to understand representation, equity, belonging, and salary issues in the audiovisual heritage field as a core part of its strategic mission of DEI and its growth and sustainability as an organization. Some of the findings—especially in regard to fieldwide underrepresentation of people from different backgrounds and experiences, student loan debt, and the frequency of women being in leadership roles—may not be encouraging. However, because the first fieldwide survey of these conditions was conducted only in 2019, we do not have earlier data to show how the field has improved over past years and decades. More importantly, though, AMIA is committed to this data collection, as it intends to use this information as the basis for open and honest conversations about how audiovisual heritage professionals, organizations, and companies, and the association itself, can grow into a community that is of, by, and for all peoples. AMIA is committed to growing strategic equity initiatives, such as the recently IMLS-funded Pathways Fellowship, and doing the hard work ahead to ensure that a diverse workforce can learn about the field, are able to enter it, and are supported to thrive within it.

Brian Real (he/him) is an assistant professor in the School of Information Science at the University of Kentucky. He holds a PhD in information studies and a master of library science from the University of Maryland. His primary research areas are the historical impact of federal policy on film preservation and the modern social impact of public libraries on their communities. He is an active member of the Association of Moving Image Archivists (AMIA), serving on its Advocacy Committee of the Board and acting as the reviews editor for *The Moving Image*. Real has previously published research articles in *The Moving Image,* the *Journal of Archival Organization, Public Library Quarterly, Library Quarterly, Information Technology and Libraries,* and the *Historical Journal of Film, Radio, and Television.*

Teague Schneiter (she/her) is the founder and director of the Academy of Motion Picture Arts and Sciences' Oral History Projects Department, where she is responsible for new video productions and the acquisition and preservation of a collection of more than two thousand legacy interviews with filmmakers (1948 to present). Teague is a graduate of the University of Amsterdam's Preservation and Presentation of the Moving Image program and worked in the early part of her career with oral history, human rights, and other cultural heritage materials in Australia, the Netherlands, Canada, and the United States and with organizations like WITNESS and IsumaTV. From 2016 to 2020, Teague served as vice president of the AMIA Board of Directors, and she cofounded AMIA's CEA Task Force, Pathways Fellowship, Advocacy Committee of the Board, and Oral History Committee. Teague is currently serving as the inaugural project director for the AMIA Pathways Fellowship, funded by the Institute of Museum and Library Services.

NOTES

The National Film Preservation Board Diversity Task Force (NFPB DTF) funded the 2019 fieldwide assessment of key indicators on cultural equity and inclusion within the audiovisual archives profession. We are grateful for NFPB's support and especially for current NFPB chair and former AMIA board member Dr. Jacqueline Stewart's leadership in promoting a more diverse field. The 2020 AMIA Annual Salary and Demographics Survey of the Field built off of the momentum of this prior support, as well as feedback and encouragement from the AMIA Board of Directors and the AMIA Advocacy Committee of the Board (ACOB). ACOB Chair Brenda Flora was particularly generous with her time in supporting this project and publicizing the 2020 survey. The authors thank all members of the audiovisual archives community who participated in this research. Finally, none of these projects could have been completed without the invaluable support and feedback of AMIA managing director Laura Rooney.

1. American Library Association, "Diversity Counts," https://www.ala.org/aboutala/offices/diversity/diversitycounts/divcounts.
2. American Library Association, "Diversity Counts: 2009–10 Updated Tables," https://www.ala.org/aboutala/offices/diversity/diversitycounts/divcounts.
3. U.S. Census Bureau, "Quick Facts," https://www.census.gov/quickfacts/fact/table/US/PST045219.
4. Robin H. Israel and Jodi Reeves Eyre, "The 2017 WArS/SAA Salary Survey: Initial Results and Analysis," 1–74, https://www2.archivists.org/sites/all/files/WArS-SAA-Salary-Survey-Report.pdf.
5. Israel and Eyre, 1.
6. Israel and Eyre, 8.
7. Jeffrey M. Jones, "LGBT Identification Rises to 5.6% in Latest U.S. Estimate," Gallup, February 24, 2021, https://news.gallup.com/poll/329708/lgbt-identification-rises-latest-estimate.aspx.

8. Centers for Disease Control and Prevention, "Disability Impacts All of Us," https://www.cdc.gov/ncbddd/disabilityandhealth/infographic-disability-impacts-all.html.

9. This includes anyone who selected any of the three categories that began with "college or university." If a respondent selected more than one of these categories, that individual was only counted once.

10. Association of Moving Image Archivists, "AMIA Pathways Fellowship," https://amianet.org/about/amia-pathways-fellowship/.

PHOTO BLOCKS, SEX DOLLAR BILLS, AND "USELESS" PACKING CUSHIONS

ANTHONY L. SILVESTRI

Kenneth Anger and the Kinsey Institute, 1947–2015

In 2007, Kenneth Anger procured a photo block made by New Zealand

artist Eden Ripley depicting a close-up of a natural scene and sent it

to the Kinsey Institute for Research in Sex, Gender, and Reproduction

in Bloomington, Indiana (Figure 1). In the archives, it would be preserved in a box titled

after Anger, alongside such contributions as a handmade sign featuring a crude drawing

of a stick figure man with oversized genitalia crying "It Burns While I Pee!!!"; a satirical tin

of breath mints, titled "National Embarrass-mints," depicting former president George

W. Bush holding a sack of money and a Bible; the April 1997 Bettie Scouts of America

newsletter; and a copy of the June 1925 edition of Edwin Bower Hesser's *Arts Monthly*

Pictorial from Hollywood, among other items. Within this particular Ephemera Box are

some biographical items, such as two notes, one of which provides Special Collections director Liana Zhou with an update on a home robbery and another that supplies the organization with a brief review of *The Kite Runner* (2007) adaptation. This mix of materials is indicative of a pattern that exists throughout the rest of the Anger collections in the Kinsey archives. Though Anger has donated his own films, pamphlets for exhibitions of his work, and other materials about himself, most of the items held within the various subcollections in his archives were neither created by the filmmaker nor explicitly focus on him. Indeed, some of these donations contain such an abstract connection to both Anger's film production and human sexuality that the filmmaker's lack of explanations produces a deceptive problem for how to understand the objects' usefulness as historical records: after all, how could this photo block fit into a collection named after an experimental filmmaker that is maintained at an institution focused on sexological research? To approach this question, and Anger's collecting habits more broadly, this article considers the ways in which the reciprocal relationship that developed between the institute and the filmmaker has created an archive that provides new possibilities and alternative materials for researching and understanding histories of the avant-garde.

As stated on its website, the Kinsey Institute's mission is "to foster and promote a greater understanding of human sexuality and relationships through research, outreach, education, and historical preservation."[1] These contemporary aims are built on the foundations of an organization and staff that have always valued the mixture of scientific, statistical, and humanistic inquiry. Alongside his pioneering scientific publications, founder Alfred Kinsey built a Sex Library that, as Liana Zhou has argued, was reflective of his "view that sexual materials provide valuable insights into a culture's interests and that a sex research library should contain materials from a wide range of fields, including biology, medicine, psychology, sociology, anthropology, counseling, religion, history, law, literature, the arts and erotica."[2] Over the course of its history, the institute's relationship with Anger afforded it several distinct benefits in connection to this wide institutional focus. First, when the filmmaker was living in Europe in the 1950s, he had access to materials not readily available to institute staff. Kinsey noted at the time that the Sex Library was predominantly composed of American materials, so Anger was able to assist in expanding and internationalizing the holdings by filling in for the collections' relative lack of Italian and French materials.[3] Second, working with the experimental filmmaker functioned both as an extension of the institute's interests in gay culture and its efforts to collect both pornographic and nonpornographic erotic materials, as Anger provided the archives with his own work, the productions of filmmakers and artists with whom he was friends, and other materials he encountered in his day-to-day life. Third, as Anger's stature as a filmmaker continued to develop and the

Figure 1. A photo block designed by New Zealand artist Eden Ripley. Box "2007 Kenneth Anger." From the Collections of the Kinsey Institute, Indiana University.

impact of his legacy became more important to histories of avant-garde and queer media, the institute was able to receive unique materials and amass a series of collections related, even if sometimes tangentially so, to both his life and moving image productions.

Initiating and maintaining an active collaboration on these collections means that resultant archives rest at the intersection of the Kinsey's institutional goals and

Anger's personal aims. As I will suggest, Anger's connection with the Kinsey is a compelling demonstration of how an artist can use institutional connections to build and
sustain their legacy as well as how the unique materials they may choose to preserve
when given the freedom to do so can challenge and expand extant histories. At the same
time that Anger provided the aforementioned services for the organization (as well as
a range of others), he was given the ability to shape the contours of his collections,
and thus the boundaries of sexological research and biographical preservation, to suit
his own interests and creative ambitions. In many ways, the access to gay culture and
experimental film that Anger has provided to the Kinsey has given him access to a venue
that serves as an extension of his own mythos-building project, a part of his pursuits
made most apparent in the importance he has placed on his own start in film in Max
Reinhardt's *A Midsummer's Night Dream* (1935). As the donations suggest, the institute
has received an often idiosyncratic assemblage of materials that verges upon being both
an archive and an artwork in its own right. The Kinsey Institute's approach to curating
the Anger collections, a collaboration that reflects a shared, expansive view of what
types of objects can be relevant both to sex research and to research about Anger, has
ultimately resulted in a rich set of materials through which it is possible to re-view and
reanalyze Anger's oeuvre, opening onto new historical opportunities and connections
outside of those into which his work has traditionally been placed.

As Juan Carlos Kase has argued, the historical resources that are now available
to research a number of avant-garde filmmakers "provide new and exciting opportunities for a renewed understanding of experimental film history that is informed more and
more by archival research and materialist historiography."[4] Similarly, Ken Eisenstein has
demonstrated that histories that pay attention to the collecting habits of Ernie Gehr can
inform our understanding of the moving image productions of avant-garde filmmakers.[5]
The lack of scholarly research attempting to reconcile Anger's legacy as a filmmaker with
the materials he has sent not only to the Kinsey Institute but also to other institutions,
such as the Museum of Death and the ONE Archives, is especially striking given the
number of publications that have circulated based on the visual analysis of his moving
image productions.[6] Building on these accounts, new research on Anger's collections
in particular, as well as avant-garde filmmakers' archives and the displacement of collecting habits into institutional contexts in general, requires a framework that takes its
cue from Terry Cook's assertion that researchers from outside archival studies must
begin to incorporate the voices of those who are responsible for "defining, choosing,
and constructing the archive *that remains*" in their work.[7] Examining the Anger archives
is instructive in this regard, given the ways in which the shifts in archivists' decisions

for organizing the materials have all had tangible and apparent impacts on the ways in which objects are framed for researchers. Put simply, any account of Anger's archives must consider the collections as the combined product of both the filmmaker's collecting tactics and the contexts into which staff members have placed his donations.

Because of this, although the content of this article focuses on Anger's specific donations, its subsections are devoted to a chronological consideration of the Anger archives' subcollections. Though this is by no means a comprehensive analysis of the institutional labor that has gone into the Anger archives, ordering the information as such reflects the ways in which archival staff have mediated Anger's collecting habits and fit them into the institute's archives, thereby producing additional historical, sexological, and Anger-specific knowledge out of his contributions.[8] To make his donations legible for researchers, the Kinsey's staff members have split the Anger archives into several subcollections with titles designed to hold the wide range of materials the filmmaker sends. Some of the early donations that Anger made are scattered across thematic boxes with materials sent by other donors or are held in the general collections of the Kinsey Institute. The more recent materials that Anger has sent to Bloomington are held in five different subcollections under the filmmaker's name: one Kenneth Anger Art Box, the two boxes of the Kenneth Anger Film Collections, the twenty boxes that compose the Kenneth Anger Clippings Collections, and the three Kenneth Anger Ephemera Boxes. The donations I survey have been chosen as exemplary of the eclectic scope of the materials that the experimental filmmaker has collected and the genres of objects that tend to appear in each of these series of boxes.

That Anger has so fastidiously collected and produced archives with a variety of organizations also requires a reevaluation of his legacy and films as just one part of a dynamic set of pursuits he has undertaken that includes, but is by no means limited to, his moving image productions. A more thorough analysis of Anger's career necessitates attention to his pursuits as an amateur researcher, collector, and historian, arguably a field of activity in which he has been more prolific than in his more well-known pursuits as a filmmaker. This article provides a detailed history of the collections that Anger has amassed at the Kinsey Institute, examining such objects as the photo block within a history of his collaboration with the organization, a relationship that began in 1947 and culminated in the mid-2010s. Of course, Anger's attention to the potentialities of the archive is not only proven by the existence of these collections but also apparent in his use of archival footage and objects in such films as *Don't Smoke That Cigarette* (1999), *Ich Will!* (2000), *Mouse Heaven* (2004), and *Airships!* (2010). Without essentializing the two mediums, Anger's penchant toward creating a collage of

materials at once consonant with and deviating from sexuality as it is traditionally envis-
aged finds resonance in the ways in which films like *Scorpio Rising* (1963), *Invocation of My Demon Brother* (1968), and *Mouse Heaven* include inserts and cutaways toward appropriated footage and pop cultural references that erupt out of the films and create a sense of the omnipresence of, but lack of linearity or coherence to, the historical in the contemporary.

Anger's relationship with the Kinsey Institute has always exceeded the bounds of merely preserving personal items or objects related to his work. Participating in the institute's research activities, I will argue, not only provided a venue that he could be certain would safeguard his own legacy but also a space in which he could insert himself into the flow of sexological research alongside objects and articles that he had not authored, thus ensuring his own place in a curated history. This means that, although the donated objects do not always overtly tell us much about the workings behind his films, the contributions can still provide a sense of the histories that Anger believed his work to be a part of. Because of this, the collections allow us to re-view what types of filmic and, importantly, nonfilmic texts his creative output should be perceived alongside. Crucially, these collections decenter the importance of understand-ing solely his film production in favor of an assertion of his expertise as a historian on a range of subjects.[9] Yet, the absence of Anger from many of the clippings and items often necessitates speculation. Though certain correspondences and notes establish the logic behind select donations, the contribution of other items without notes about what their value is provides open-ended possibilities for interpreting the personal and general histories to which these objects might contribute. Allyson Nadia Field has recently argued for the importance of combining "meticulous historical research with informed speculation in the face of archival absence," which is necessary in dealing with the often opaque donations in the Anger archives.[10] At the same time, the institute's decision to store many of the items under Anger's name—a practice that began later in organizational history—means that the archive signifies personal history insofar as its contents are evidence of daily routine, reflecting Anger's existence outside of the labor of film production, even if the contributions do not always provide a specific diary of encounters in his day-to-day life other than the ritual of donation. The multivalent ways in which the objects produce meaning, contingent on both the larger institutional mission and the context of the ways in which they have been stored as items related to Anger in general, open up a fluid set of possible meanings for each donation that rebuts definitive analyses.

EARLY DONATIONS: THE KINSEY AND GEBHARD ERAS (1947–1983)

In 1947, Alfred C. Kinsey was completing what would become his best-selling monograph *Sexual Behavior in the Human Male* (1948). Gathering statistics by interviewing a variety of subjects was just one part of the collecting activities that were occurring as part of his research: in tandem with the creation of the Institute for Sex Research in Bloomington, Kinsey established the organization's Sex Library to preserve a variety of photographic, moving image, and ephemeral objects related to the history of sexuality, including diverse materials like stag pornography, sex toys, pictures of bathroom wall graffiti, and pubic hair.[11] Crucial to assembling these collections was Kinsey's relationship with a number of gay men. As Thomas Waugh has recounted, however, it was not just Kinsey's sympathy to gay culture that shaped the holdings at the institute. Rather, "also shaping the collection, most importantly, were the passion and commitment that the Institute's gay collaborators devoted to the task of preserving for science and posterity a record of their lives and loves."[12] While in Los Angeles, Kinsey would encounter yet another young gay collaborator eager to participate in the institute's mission. The sexologist had heard that Kenneth Anger's *Fireworks* (1947) was a film he should see. As a result, Kinsey and Anger met for the first time after a screening of the film at the Coronet Film Society. When the show was over, Anger would partake in the "famous Kinsey interview," meaning that, according to the filmmaker, his responses would eventually become part of the *Kinsey Reports*.[13] Not only would Kinsey purchase a copy of *Fireworks* for the institute's collections but Anger would also begin a seven-decade-long collaboration with the Institute for Sex Research.

The earliest detailed log of Anger contributions dates to the mid-1950s (Figure 2). At the time, Anger was living in Europe and, given his access to resources, such as booksellers and newspaper publications, that the staff in Bloomington could not easily or regularly meet or find, the institute advanced the filmmaker the sum of 52,000 francs. Of this, Anger had spent at least 23,900 francs on various items by April 1956.[14] The extant inventories suggest that Anger was, at once, producing an archive to safeguard information about himself and to participate in the general research of the institution, making his own life and legacy synonymous with the sexological mission of the organization. A few clippings that he sent to the organization are columns about his own films. Other items, such as a copy of Pauline Réage's sadomasochistic novel *Histoire d'O* (1954), foreshadow future attempts at film production. However, most of the contributions were created by and about others: these include a book by Oscar Wilde, thirteen photographs taken by the homoerotic photographer Baron Wilhelm von Gloeden, and special issues of magazines like *Le Crapouillot,* among other items. The correspondences also indicate that original film production was a minor part of the collaboration between Anger and Kinsey at the time, though by no means the central focus. In May 1956, Kinsey wrote to Anger, "Your film record from Rome is of extraordinary value. We have only a few comparable series from this country, and there are obvious reasons why the southern Italian material is even more important."[15] However, it is unclear what exactly Anger filmed for the organization beyond the setting that the sexologist referenced in his letter.[16]

When Paul Gebhard took over as director of the Institute for Sex Research after Kinsey's untimely passing, Anger's collecting practices remained largely intact. However, none of the correspondences mentions Anger receiving money from the organization at this point, which means that the transition from his status as an acquisitor to a donor providing the institute with gifts was likely under way, if not complete. Though it is not always clear when Anger sent the films he donated to the organization, he did contribute several 16mm reels to the institute's collection. This included *Scorpio Rising,* complete copies of Takahiko Iimura's *Onan* (1963), Jack Smith's *Flaming Creatures* (1963), at least one Brakhage film, and William Wyler's *The Collector* (1965), as well as a small extract of the "Vision of Dante" sequence from Harry Lachman's *Dante's Inferno* (1935). Such donations not only suggest the potential usefulness that the eroticism of avant-garde films held for sexological research but also the films that Anger thought were interrelated to the content of his own moving image productions through sexology. As expressed through the history of sexual representation he was building in the archives, the breadth of these film types suggests that Anger envisioned his own experimental films as participating in the Kinsey's studies alongside other corporeal avant-garde films, but also mainstream studio fare.[17] Rather than a recuperative gesture or a sardonic nod to popular culture, these donations encourage an understanding of films like *Dante's Inferno, The Collector,* and *Fireworks* alongside each other. Indeed, the sadomasochism that Anger indicated was important in the "Vision of Dante" reel becomes tied to both the representations of his own desire in *Fireworks* and the (criminal heterosexual) binding that occurs throughout *The Collector.* Though these films are not traditionally considered together in accounts of Anger's films, viewed together in the collections, they point toward a new genealogy of potential sadomasochistic influence and interplay.

Anger's collecting habits always exceeded the bounds of his productions and his expertise on film, as he assembled a collection of nonfilmic items that was much larger than the moving image magazines or 16mm reels that he gifted the organization. Similar to his contributions during the Kinsey directorship, these included the

```
INVENTORY OF BOOK SHIPMENTS                          (Anger)
FROM PARIS- March, April, 1956

Package # 1:    4 books;  "Histoire d'O" - "Passion dans le Desert"
                "The Hill of Dreams" - "Against the Law"

Package # 2:    4 magazines:  3 special issues "Crapouillot"
                1 special issue "Cahiers du Cinéma"

Package # 3:    2 books:  "Apollinaire" - "Considerations Objectives
                sur la Pédérastie"
                4 articles:  "Helmut Kolle" - "Du Nouveau chez les
                Flics" - "Franco Rossi-Amici per la Pelle"
                "Fireworks"
                13 photos:  von Gloeden, etc.

Package # 4:    4 books:  "Bijou de Ceinture" - "Les Amours Singul-
                ières" "Dernieres Nuits de Taormina" - "Enfant
                Hystérique"

Package # 5:    8 books:  "Der Tod in Venedig" - "Oskar Wilde"
                "Heliogabale" - "A Rebours" - "Madame Edwarda"
                "De Profundus-The complete Text" - "Catalogue
                Musee Gustave Moreau" - "De L'Androgyne"

Package # 6:    5 books:  "Les Cles de Proust" - "Les Mauvaises Anges"
                "Le Prince Eric" - "Le Bracelet de Vermeil"
                "Jeunes Proies"

                TOTAL 23 BOOKS
```

Figure 2. Inventory of packages sent by Kenneth Anger to the Institute for Sex Research in March and April 1956. Dr. Alfred C. Kinsey Era Correspondences. Copyright 2017, The Trustees of Indiana University on behalf of the Kinsey Institute. All rights reserved.

works of professional writers like Henry James as well as amateur typescripts, such as a copy of *Hyacinthe et Les Milles Plaisirs,* a short pornographic novella by an anonymous author that incorporates mythic themes as it tells the story of a gay French soldier. Anger also contributed sexual ephemera, including an item that he described in the correspondences as an "exotic pipe"; a large enough stream of newspaper excerpts to provoke Gebhard to call him "a fountain of clippings";[18] and musical items, such as a copy of Serge Gainsbourg's record "Je t'aime . . . moi non plus" (1967).[19] Well into the 1980s, Anger continued to donate other items, such as a monthly newsletter from the Church of Satan that included an Anton LaVey article about censorship and a copy of the WBAI-FM broadcast of Marquis de Sade's *Justine; or, The Misfortunes of Virtue.*[20] As this roster of contributions suggests, the sexological archives provided a venue through which Anger could preserve his own work, while inserting it into a larger history that included a range of historical records outside of film. Such archives afford, then, a window into the types of histories into which Anger saw his work fitting, and these established its proximity to elements ranging from pornography and sexual ephemera to mainstream representations of sexuality. At the same time, it is also undeniable that assets like the WBAI-FM broadcast are connected to the personal experiences that Anger was having with potential sexological records, imbuing them with a sort of biographical resonance with his day-to-day life, even if that was not his original purpose for sending them. After all, just as the copy of *Dante's Inferno* is as much a representation of sexuality in classical Hollywood cinema as it is material evidence of his relationship with Bob Chatterson, the collector from whom he procured it, the recording of *Justine* is indicative of the time he likely spent listening to the broadcast.[21] Though these histories are implicit in any donated object, the organization of the collections has framed certain items' value as including this component. The transition to organizing and maintaining items in the archives under his name has only further emphasized the ways in which the inherent, multilayered meaning of objects can be foregrounded for film historical research in archival description, suggesting, in this case, a framework that emphasizes both the sexological content of the films and the traces of everyday life they potentially provide.

THE ART BOX

During the Kinsey and Gebhard directorships, many of Anger's donations were stored in the archives thematically, meaning that it is necessary to cross-check the correspondences to confirm what materials the filmmaker was sending to Bloomington.[22] Others—such as the 16mm donations—are logged as being gifted by him on the digital Indiana University Library Catalog (IUCAT) system.[23] The organization of the Anger collections, however, has shifted toward preserving the filmmaker's contributions under a system of provenance (i.e., arranging and describing records under Anger's name both in the digital catalogs and in physical boxes).[24] Doing so suggests new institutional aims, wherein the connection of any donation to Anger has supplanted the gifts' content as crucial to their valuation as part of the Kinsey's archives and mission. The history and compilation of the materials in the Kenneth Anger Art Box, in particular, are distinct from those of the other subcollections maintained under Anger's name, in that the Art Box collection represents a reevaluation of older items in this manner. According to Shawn Wilson, associate director of the library and Special Collections at the Kinsey, the contents of this subcollection were donated throughout the course of Anger's collaboration with the organization, only to be pulled together later to create the Art Box.[25] Several items within the box relate to Anger's life and filmography, including ten small photographs used as police evidence against *Scorpio Rising* and a photograph of Anger, Dennis Hopper, and Alejandro Jodorowsky taken in 1975. The lengthy period captured by the box is made apparent by the fact that these items can be viewed by researchers in the same space as a frame enlargement from *Invocation of My Demon Brother* that was circulated to publicize an exhibition of film stills curated by Walter John Casidy III. This event featured a reception with Anger, and the markings on the object indicate that it was received in 2004. Anger has also sent other items that establish the continuing imprint his moving image output has on contemporary artistic production. A 2003 Tom of Finland Award–winning print by Hector Silver, for instance, was inspired by *Scorpio Rising*'s traffic cone scene.

It is those donations in the box that were not created by or about him, however, that gesture toward the types of histories that Anger was interested in using the Kinsey's archives to insert himself into. By far the most sizable group of items in this particular subcollection is a series of vintage lobby cards. Though these include advertising materials for studio works like the Metro-Goldwyn-Mayer production of *Freaks* (1932), most of these publicity materials were originally released in support of works of classical exploitation cinema produced by independent studios.[26] Exemplary of these donations are the lobby cards for motion pictures including *Stolen Paradise: A Story of Adolescence* (1940), *Girls in Chains* (1943), *Secrets of a Sorority Girl* (1945), and *The Flaming Teen-Age* (1956). Preserved alongside the *Scorpio Rising* frame enlargements, the archives suggest the resonance that might exist not only thematically between Anger's work and these particular exploitation films but also the censorship troubles that avant-garde filmmaking and exploitation cinema shared.[27] Anger also donated five photographs that might be understood as contextualizing these donations, insofar as they show the exhibition sites where exploitation films would have been screened and portray theaters, many of which are screening *The Story of Bob and Sally* (1948). Unlike for most of the contributions in the Art Box, Anger included a note on the logic behind this donation, using it as a venue in which to demonstrate his expertise on the subject:

> Enclosed are some photographs of movie theaters showing exploitation films, the so-called "Main Street Movies" dating from about 1948. Note that on the marquee of the theater showing "Bob and Sally" the showings were segregated according to sex, with separate shows for "Women and Hi-School Girls." These movies dealt with sexual content on the level of titillation wrapped in moralizing and the guise of "sex education." They were mostly Hollywood "poverty row" productions of a type that existed from the '20's to the 60's,

> when permissiveness made them redundant. It would be useful to preserve
> some samples of these films, but most have been destroyed as having no fur-
> ther validity on a commercial basis. "Reefer Madness" is one of the few that
> has survived and been revived from midnight showings, its sermonizing now
> the subject of hilarity.[28]

Anger flaunts his film historical knowledge, pointing out the relevant practices of exhibition to which the pictures testify, providing historical background on their production
style and tropes, and suggesting the photographic details that are most important to
draw out of the materials. At the same time, he uses this imagery as a way to suggest
that the staff at the Kinsey Institute furnish their collections with these films. While this
intent is not expressed with similar advertising materials elsewhere in the collection—
such as a poster of Lois Weber's *The Blot* (1921) donated without mention of the film's
content—it does seem to suggest that Anger might have considered sending paratextual
materials not only for their relevant artistic content but also as a means to advertise,
so to speak, the films that he believed the collections should acquire that he could not
provide himself.

Although Anger did once refer to these exploitation posters as "folk-art," there
is no indication in the correspondences that he envisioned the specific subassemblage
of materials that exists and has become the Art Box.[29] Taken together, however, the
donations stored in this box suggest that Anger did envision sexological research as a
crucial discipline that could serve as a point of intersection including, but not limited to,
histories of experimental media, carnivals, exploitation films, studio features, gay pulp
literature, and other pieces of pop cultural ephemera. For instance, the filmmaker sent
a photo placard of the Ringling Bros. troupe that was originally taken for the group's
Golden Jubilee in 1933. Although there is no explanation behind this donation, it is quite
likely that it is intended to function as a contextual item for the *Freaks* lobby cards, given
that the Ringling Bros. employed several of the actors in the film, including Johnny Eck.
This photograph is not necessarily a representation of human sexuality in the way that
the lobby cards for sex education films were, yet this item no doubt alludes to Anger's
expansive ideas of what might constitute sexological research, while also enabling
further connections to arise between Browning's work and his own. At the same time,
preserved in the Art Box by the institute staff, it is also linked through Anger to other,
ephemerally circulated items, such as a series of postcards originating from the Gay and
Lesbian Historical Society that replicate the book covers of *Behind These Walls* (1962),
Gay Whore (1967), *Gay Safari* (1968), and *Boy Meets Boy* (1968). Like the photograph of

the exploitation theaters, it is quite possible that these serve both as testaments to the circulation and repurposing of queer imagery in contemporary contexts and as references to texts that would be valuable in the Kinsey's collections, while also providing additional queer literature alongside which his own production should be understood. Similarly, parodic currency satirizing the Clinton sex scandal—one of which is titled a "sex dollar bill"—gestures toward both the breadth of materials that were under consideration by Anger and the lack of cultural hierarchy located in the definition of "art" under which they are kept.

That the archives present a lively site of discourse between the contents of these modes gestures toward new historical possibilities for analyzing the ways in which Anger's work is in dialogue with forms of cultural production that are not often included in experimental film histories. At the same time, the staff has no doubt structured these specific connections under the notions of the items' shared status as art as well as their links to Anger's daily life. For instance, Anger also donated an "Exotica Calendar" for 1987 produced by pinup artist Olivia De Berardinis. Not only is this item exemplary of the range of sexual products beyond queer representation in which Anger was interested but it is indicative of how we must reframe and rethink each item in the collection as both a record of Anger's life and a possible testament to changing sexual mores. Included with the donation is a note saying that the calendar is "drawn by a beautiful young lady friend" of his, and an inscription on the cover wishing Anger a happy new year confirms the intimacy of their relationship. Although it would be a mistake to assume that every donation has this type of potential, affective charge, the inscription also emphasizes the fact that every donation in the subcollections implicitly serves as an insertion of both Anger's personal life and the contents of the material into the Kinsey's archives.

THE CLIPPINGS COLLECTION (1994–2015)

Donated over the span of two decades, the contemporary clippings collection is stored across twenty boxes, with the items that Anger sent held in the original envelopes in which they were received. An issue with researching this subcollection is the sheer mass of letters that Anger has sent to the institute: one envelope may consist of more than fifteen clippings culled from an array of newspapers with a focus on both national and international current events, while the box holding it may contain well over fifty envelopes.[30] Some of the clippings record the spaces in which Anger has shown up in print publications: though over four decades old at the time of its receipt, one such extract is of the lengthy interview with Anger titled "Aleister Crowley and Merlin Magick" that was printed in *Friends* in 1970. Much like the Silver print, other clippings demonstrate Anger's enduring imprint on popular culture and a new legion of writers and artists. An interview with the late American journalist Marc Spitz about his dedication to twee, for example, contains a photograph in which the author holds a copy of *Hollywood Babylon*. A note below points out that this is the relevant visual information to be garnered from the donation, as Anger writes, "Note that in the photograph Marc Spitz is shown reading 'Hollywood Babylon.'" Of course, the filmmaker does not make any remarks as to his thoughts on his book being appropriated as part of a twee aesthetic. Given the size of the collections, however, the clippings are rarely about Anger. Notes written by or columns written about Anger are also not the norm for this collection; these instances are mostly interspersed throughout a wide range of donations.

Many of the clippings are columns that concern human sexuality, with a broad focus ranging from issues within the LGBTQIA+ community, such as articles about laws in Brunei that have called for death by stoning as a punishment for gay sex or updates from and about AIDS activist groups like ACT UP, to records of high-profile events like the Clinton–Lewinsky scandal in the 1990s. Other articles focus on topics like sexual medication, such as Viagra; abortion laws; interviews with straight porn stars; sexual assault; and child pornography arrests. Thus, although recording information about queer histories is certainly a part of this project, Anger's own interests are in clipping a diversity of sexualities as they appear in print publications. Though clipped articles are the primary objects in this subcollection, Anger has also included other types of ephemeral objects, such as an exhibitor's press sheet for *Nightmare Alley* (1947). While the reasons for these donations may seem self-evident, like every part of the Anger archives, there are deviations from an explicit focus on the filmmaker and sexuality, for instance, a Human Rights publication titled *Harming Artists: Psychiatry Manipulating Creativity*. Because of the lack of information, one might suggest that this magazine links to the representations of creative personnel and artists throughout the envelopes or, alternatively, that it might be linked to a broader suspicion of mental health professionals arising out of the ways in which the field has had its roots in pathologizing nonstraight individuals.[31]

As an example of how the newspaper clippings might be received in the context of the envelopes, on August 25, 2014, Kenneth Anger sent a letter stuffed with clippings to the Kinsey Institute. An extension of his own fascination with the star, Anger included a variety of articles from a 1953 issue of *LIFE* about Marlon Brando. Other clippings compiled alongside these range in thematic focus: one provides information on the Museum of Modern Art's plans to digitize the films that fellow underground filmmaker Andy Warhol produced between 1963 and 1971, while another is an advertisement for the

Figure 3. The contents of one set of clippings sent by Kenneth Anger to the Kinsey Institute, emptied from its folder. Kenneth Anger Clippings Collection. From the Collections of the Kinsey Institute, Indiana University. All rights reserved.

Matthew McConaughey AIDS drama *Dallas Buyers Club* (2013). Many clippings expand the focus of the envelope beyond film historical matters, such as a *New York Post* opinion editorial penned in defense of the catcall, an article about the ban on gay men donating blood, the death of Westboro Baptist preacher Fred Phelps, and an article about curing Ebola. Despite being maintained as part of the Kinsey's Kenneth Anger Clippings Collection, Anger is mostly absent from the contents of this envelope:

none of the stories directly references his life and work. As with many of his donations, almost all of the clippings from this particular letter do not contain any notes to indicate why Anger sent them to the Kinsey Institute, let alone what Anger's thoughts on the content might be. In fact, the only markings that Anger has left are highlights on the article on Phelps, with one drawing attention to the preacher's lectures about the lusts of the flesh and another pointing out that four of his thirteen children had broken from the church. Otherwise, Anger's connections to, investment in, and relationship with the subjects surveyed within the envelope form an absence in the envelope.

Researching the clippings collections, thus, presents a vexing problem: the articles are ingrained into Anger's day-to-day life, reading preferences, and particular interests such that they cannot provide a symptomatic history of human sexuality or current events, even within the framework of a donation pattern that includes, sometimes, sending multiple letters a day. At the same time, while some articles do either speak about the filmmaker or contain notes, the largest part of the content that Anger provides is so detached from the concrete details of Anger's life that they cannot function as evidence that might contribute to a biographical account of his life. At once, the materials contain enough personal information about Anger to distinguish them from traditions of queer opacity and the refusal of meaning or knowledge, yet not enough to create a transparent history of his life insofar as they do not provide conventional biographical evidence.[32] For example, should we read the clipping opining about the demise of "catcalling" as indicative of Anger's agreement with the article? An op-ed the filmmaker shared about noise pollution and leaf blowing, in which he agrees with the writer, suggests that this is a possibility. Though it is preserved in the Ephemera Boxes, an IQ card circulated by the Church of Scientology that Anger donated with the written inscription "FRAUD" suggests that just because Anger sent something does not mean he agrees with the information it provides (Figure 3). Though it is usually not the focus of the materials, the clippings might serve as much as a reminder of the history into which Anger seeks to insert himself as they do, in a circuitous fashion, a record of how and when Anger encountered certain pieces of information, the places he has been, and a profile of his own tastes.

THE FILM COLLECTIONS (2003–2009)

As an extension of Anger's earlier practice of donating moving image works on 16mm, the Kenneth Anger Film Collections comprise DVDs and VHS tapes the filmmaker donated between 2003 and 2009. The size of these collections, in comparison with the relative paucity of donations on celluloid from the Kinsey and Gebhard era, suggests that both the loosening restrictions on obscenity and the advent of home video were likely crucial for Anger's ability to afford to buy and gift films to the organization. This subcollection contains several late Anger films that are neither circulated as widely as the films of *The Magick Lantern Cycle* nor available on home video, making the Kinsey Institute a crucial repository through which to access and view them. This includes *Green Hell* (2007), a satirical film in which Anger appropriates a pornographic video of a man fucking a watermelon; *I'll Be Watching You* (2007), a short film set to the Police's "Every Breath You Take" that presents a security guard's voyeuristic viewing of gay sex in a parking lot; and *Uniform Attraction* (2008), Anger's film about homoeroticism in the military, the conditioning of young men to become soldiers, and nationalist propaganda in America. However, not all of the films that Anger has made and subsequently donated to the organization fall as clearly under the framework of the Kinsey Institute's mission to collect and preserve materials related to the study of human sexuality and reproduction. The presence of these items suggests the self-perpetuating nature of the collection—Anger's life has become a subject of sexological inquiry in its own right, and that, in turn, enables even his nonerotic work to be framed and preserved within the contexts of the sexological archives. This is the case for *Airships!,* a film in which Anger hand-tinted footage of Graf Zeppelins and converted the imagery to 3-D. The film builds the eerie beauty of these vessels flying over New York to a revelation that the airships are adorned with swastikas, a reminder of fascism's encroachment on America.

Much like the Art Box, the Film Collections provide new directions and contexts in which those works of his own that Anger has donated can be analyzed and historically situated. His moving image productions are less the central focus of the subcollection than materials he is inserting into a historical collection intended for sexological research. The largest group of items in the Film Collections are gay pornography. These include productions such as *Uniform Britain, His First Huge Cock, Circus of Torture,* and *Military Ass Initiation.* However, hard-core meets avant-garde in the collections box, with DVDs like a compilation of Amy Greenfield's cine-dance films and a sampler of *Unseen Cinema* included alongside *Assablanca* and *Straight Abuse.* Some of the films, however, break from extant understandings of Anger's work as being understood in historical inquiries that revolve around queer media and experimental film, including a DVD that contains both the murder-melodrama *The Sin of Nora Moran* (1933) and the crime movie *Prison Train* (1938), a copy of the Criterion Collection edition of *Pandora's Box* (1929), and the underground prank film *Uncle Goddamn* (1987). The lack of notes accompanying many of these films leaves the precise history that Anger is attempting to curate open to a

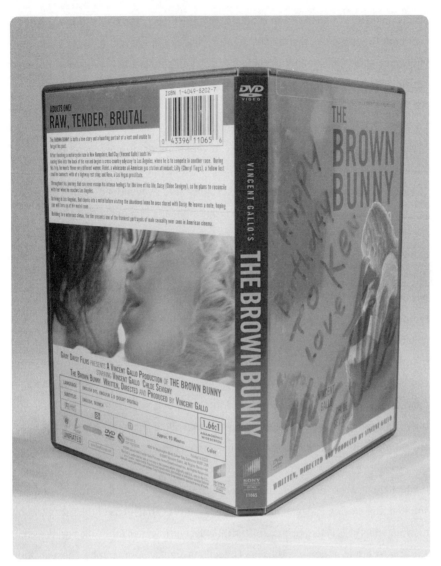

multitude of interpretations. Exemplary of this is *Uncle Goddamn*, a film that boasts a unique editing style and cuts from its prank numbers to odd, nonnarrative moments, such as a puppet singing for the camera in a manner that distinguishes it from commercial, narrative cinema, even if it is not experimental in the way that Anger's work is traditionally understood. At the same time, it is possible that the connections between the sadistic aspects of the family of hillbillies torturing each other and the sadomasochism present across the collections were the impetus for this contribution, even if the film does not present itself as necessarily pornographic. Moreover, we must question whether Anger has donated this item because he enjoys the film or if it is a detached, scientific interest in the content. Each interpretation, and many more, exists as a possibility for explaining how this item might inform our understanding of Anger and how Anger might inform our understanding of this item.

Though the origins of most of these films cannot be concretely traced—with the exception of a pamphlet for Peter's Outrageous Videos, there exists very little indication of where Anger found the materials—a few films in the subcollection are exemplary of how these films often exceed just the content that appears on-screen. A copy of *The Brown Bunny,* Vincent Gallo's experimental road film that tracks a motorcycle racer's cross-country trip and subsequent confrontation with traumas from the past, might be seen as relevant to the Kinsey Institute's mission insofar as it is notable for holding a textual record of a real blow job in an art film. An inscription on the cover, however, shifts focus toward how it was received and the types of alternative knowledge for which the film might serve as a record; here Gallo has written "Happy Birthday, To Ken, Love Vincent" (Figure 4). Similarly, a copy of Jason Wade's experimental water sports film *Golden Afternoon* comes with a letter that details how and when Anger received the gift and provides information on how he viewed it (claiming, in this instance, that he took notes on the film before sending it to the institute). Such materials remind us of Jacqueline Stewart's argument that certain traces in the archive emphasize the singularity of each film and allow us to learn about the circulation, exhibition, and content of the movies while encouraging us to reconsider what we think of as a film's "content."[33] Yet, that the donations so often do not include overt indications of the specific histories that lay behind each project means that the evidence that many of Anger's film donations provide about his day-to-day life and viewing patterns, as well as the precise connections he might draw between the contents of the films, remains speculative.

THE EPHEMERA BOXES (2007–2010)

The final, and newest, subcollections in the Anger archives are the three Ephemera Boxes, composed of materials received by the institute after 2007. While it is beyond the scope of this article to capture just how eclectic the compilation of materials stored in these subcollections can be, the contents do present an enticing mixture of items, including DVDs, magazines, CDs, and detritus capable of sustaining a variety of studies. Not only does this give us a sense of Anger's expansive view of what sexological and personal histories may contain but the institute's preservation of these materials under the framework of ephemera presents future opportunities to re-view the types of materials that are included in, and understood alongside, avant-garde film histories. Several biographical items are present in the Ephemera Boxes; in just the 2010 box, for instance, one can find two professionally drawn portraits of Anger; the program for the forty-eighth Ann Arbor Film Festival, which featured screenings and an interview with him; and a booklet and poster for a series of Anger screenings in Brazil between May 4 and 15, 2011. Other donations foreground the ways in which Anger has used his relationship with the Kinsey Institute as a way in which to cultivate his mythos, ensuring his placement in a variety of mainstream histories that cannot be forgotten. Exemplary are two magazines that touch upon the filmmaker's friends and former associates. In the July 2009 issue of *Los Angeles* magazine, for instance, Anger has underlined in pink pen every mention of his ex-roommate and musical associate Bobby Beausoleil in a lengthy article on Charles Manson. Similarly, within the winter 2011 issue of *Monsters from the Vault,* Anger inserted a notecard on an article about *Bride of Frankenstein* (1935), saying, "Note caption of still on page 6—the director James Whale was a friend." This caption references the potential reading of Praetorious's relationship with Dr. Frankenstein as an allusion to homosexual blackmail. The contribution of *Monsters from the Vault,* arguably, encapsulates how Anger uses the institute's mission to produce a multifaceted article that serves his own legacy: the magazine becomes both a record of queer representation and readings as it relates to classical Hollywood cinema and a record of Anger's personal relationships, as he uses the card to insert himself into a story about Whale in which he was not, originally, mentioned.

It is worth noting that Anger not only sent these objects that reference his life alongside additional DVD donations, such as the solo masturbation film *Aim to Please* (2006), a recordable disc including both *White Zombie* (1932) and *Perversion for Profit* (1965), and a copy of *Suburbia Confidential* (1966) and *Office Love-In* (1968) that references the *Kinsey Reports* on its cover, but also clothing, music, sexual aids, shopping bags, and detritus. In addition to such materials as the photo block or the drawn sign, these boxes mix and match a diverse set of contributions, including publications that range from several copies of the gay fetish magazine *Instigator* to the summer 2011 *Athleta* catalog for women's athletic wear and even copies of catalogs for *Taschen*. Exemplary of the nature of these holdings is a donation of an issue of the magazine *Frontiers 4 Men*. The issue itself, which includes photographs of male models, reviews of pornography websites, interviews, and classifieds, is a relatively routine queer publication within the context of the Kinsey's archives. However, nestled between its pages, as if part of the issue, is an additional set of contributions: a trio of deflated, biodegradable air cushions that Anger has marked "packing deflated—useless" (Figure 5). Not only does the issue

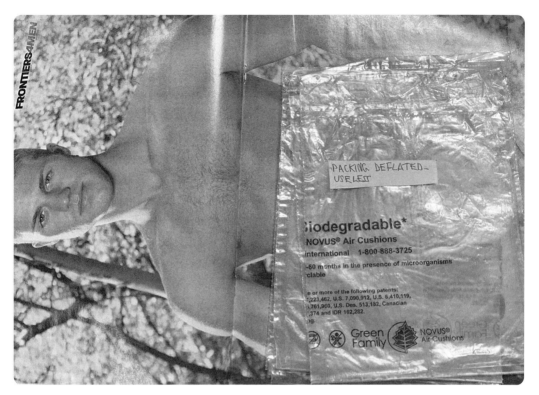

Figure 5. A set of three "useless," deflated biodegradable packing cushions, as found between the pages of an issue of *Frontiers 4 Men* magazine during research. Box "Anger 2010." From the Collections of the Kinsey Institute, Indiana University. All rights reserved.

of *Frontiers 4 Men*, then, have content that is explicitly useful for sexological research but it functions as something of a moment in which Anger has been, quite literally, inserted into the materials that he is sending to the institute. A reminder of the process of collecting and mailing that has gone into his collaboration with the Kinsey, the air cushions reassert the presence of Anger's day-to-day life in the collections inside a mass-produced magazine that may elide it. Yet the packing cushions can also be understood as a reference to the longer history of collaboration between Anger and the institute: this is not the first time that Anger has given the institute advice on how he mails materials safely. The cushions cannot be divorced entirely from a history of Anger, the institute, and the post office and the precautions the filmmaker has had to take to protect the objects that the institute is receiving from potentially careless handling by the postal service.

At the opening of this article, I posed a question about how one might understand the inclusion of Eden Ripley's photo block as a part of the archival project that Kenneth Anger has undertaken at the Kinsey Institute. At the intersection of the institutional context and personal collection practices that it represents, the photo block held in these Ephemera Boxes can be viewed as the dual function of many of the preserved objects in the collection that arises out of the reciprocal relationship between the personal and the institutional, as well as the multitude of interpretations that a lack of explanation opens on to. It can be argued that the visual content of this photo block has its own links to the history of the Institute for Sex Research: after all, Alfred Kinsey began his career as a zoologist who studied and collected gall wasps, a practice that, as Donna Drucker has demonstrated, fostered his ability to discern order in mass quantities of data in a way that would reveal new patterns and connections between cataloged and previously uncataloged data.[34] Thus, though the particular piece of art does not depict a gall wasp, it can still function so as to reassert the connections between the study of nature and sexology. In fact, the inclusion of a magazine on ecological conservation titled *Bats Conservation International* featuring a cover asking "Can Bats Save Bananas?" in the same subcollection could be interpreted as yet another instance in which Anger has donated materials to allude to the relationship between these fields.

At the same time, Anger's inclusion of materials about himself beside objects like this photo block means that he, likely, believes his own films and life to be as valuable to creating a sexological history as these items. While it is, by no means, the only understanding of this donation, received as a part of Anger's legacy in an archive under his name, an additional interpretation might be to understand this particular photo block alongside the other objects across the collections that reference wildlife and nature. Even though the archival placement of some of the objects varies, Vincent Gallo's *The Brown Bunny,* titled after a rabbit that the main character's ex-girlfriend had once owned, is a crucial symbol in the film as it builds toward its sexual climax. Perhaps, then, these objects might be relevant when considering a film like *Rabbit's Moon* (1950), whose titular white rabbit Anger has suggested "is my soul."[35] This reading of the objects does not preclude the range of other ways in which the photo block (and the other donations) might be read within the archives. Of course, the content is only one fraction of the information that these contributions provide: the photo block itself stands as a record of Anger's day-to-day consumption, a specific object that he encountered and thought to be of use to the Kinsey Institute.

CONCLUSION

Between 1947 and 2015, Kenneth Anger amassed a series of collections at the Kinsey Institute including, but not limited to, his own films, erotic photography, commercial cinema, gay pornography, monthly calendars, newspaper clippings, and detritus. For the staff at the Kinsey Institute, Anger was providing a service insofar as he was giving the organization records of sexual mores and gay culture for sexological inquiry. In return, Anger was given the opportunity to build collections in which he could construct and safeguard his own legacy. The result of this collaboration is an idiosyncratic collection that establishes the many disciplines, objects, and histories to which Anger's work can be related while establishing the filmmaker's life and productions as particularly valuable for sex research. Anger's use of the Kinsey archives to build and sustain his mythology and their mythology was, of course, mediated by institutional practice, as expressed through the valuation, interpretation, and organization of the objects by staff members. At the intersection of Anger's collecting tactics and the Kinsey's decisions regarding preservation, many of the items within the Anger archives can function as (but are not limited to) markers of the histories in which Anger believed his work was participating, traces of the filmmaker's day-to-day life, and artifacts related to a general history of sexuality.

It may be apparent, given the sheer size and longevity of this collaboration, that the Anger archives cannot possibly be summarized, let alone sufficiently analyzed, within the confines of a single publication. While I have endeavored to survey exemplary materials across the archives, many more donations merit discussion. The Kinsey's maintenance of these materials and their support of Anger's collecting practices provide a rich source for future studies that consider not only the correlation between Anger's interests and practices as a collector and his moving image productions but also the intersection between sexology and the postwar avant-garde and the ways in which experimental filmmakers may have extended their transgressive on-screen practices to historical preservation. The long-term nature of this relationship also provides generative grounds on which to pay attention to several other facets of the impact of archival process on the Anger archives, including a potential focus on shifts in practices like accessioning, storage, and classification, all of which are made especially pertinent given the often transparent ways in which a series of archivists have interpreted and framed Anger's donations. The inclusion of materials in the collection that expand historical focus beyond moving image productions (and their usual related paratexts)—including parodic currency, ecological magazines, and the like—gestures toward the circumscribed nature of evidence that avant-garde historical research generally uses. Ultimately, the collections allude to the potential expansions of avant-garde film histories, envisioning a scholarly discourse and research that can receive photo blocks, sex dollar bills, useless packing cushions, and *Scorpio Rising* as interrelated materials.

Anthony L. Silvestri is an independent scholar who currently works as journals manager for the University of Minnesota Press. His research, which focuses on the Kinsey Institute's relationship with film culture, film, and moving image ephemera's role in sexological research, sexual archiving, and avant-garde film, has appeared in *Porn Studies*, the *Journal of Film and Video*, and the *Historical Journal of Film, Radio, and Television*. Anthony earned his PhD in media arts and sciences at Indiana University.

NOTES

I convey my gratitude to the archivists at the Kinsey Institute for their continued support of this project, including the immeasurable assistance of both Shawn C. Wilson and Liana Zhou. My research on the Ephemera Boxes was supported by the institute's John Money Fellowship for Scholars of Sexology. Similarly, research on the film holdings would not have been possible without the technical support and expertise of the staff at the Indiana University Libraries Moving Image Archive. Thanks are due as well to Joan Hawkins and Andre Seewood, each of whom provided suggestions on various versions of this article. Finally, I thank Devin Orgeron and the anonymous peer reviewers at *The Moving Image* for their generous feedback.

1. Explore Kinsey: https://kinseyinstitute.org/about/.

2. Liana Zhou, "Characteristics of Material Organization and Classification in the Kinsey Institute Library," *Cataloging and Classification Quarterly* 35, no. 3–4 (2002–3): 338.

3. Alfred C. Kinsey to Kenneth Anger, May 14, 1956.

4. Juan Carlos Kase, "Encounters with the Real: Historicizing Stan Brakhage's *The Art of Seeing with One's Own Eyes*," *The Moving Image* 12, no. 1 (2012): 2.

5. See Ken Eisenstein, "Ernie Gehr's *The Collector* (2003) and Ernie Gehr the Collector," in *Provenance and Early Cinema*, ed. Joanne Bernardi, Paolo Cherchi Usai, Tami Williams, and Joshua Yumibe, 275–86 (Bloomington: Indiana University Press, 2020).

6. A complete overview of the monographs, scholarly articles, chapters, and references to Anger's work that have been produced would be untenable to cover in a single note. However, I point to the following resources as good examples of the ways in which researchers have foregrounded Anger's film productions: P. Adams Sitney, *Visionary Film: The American Avant-Garde, 1943–2000* (Oxford: Oxford University Press, 2002); Juan A. Suarez, *Bike Boys, Drag Queens, and Superstars: Avant-Garde, Mass Culture and Gay Identities in the 1960s Underground* (Bloomington: Indiana University Press, 1996); David James, *The Most Typical Avant-Garde: History and Geography of Minor Cinemas in Los Angeles* (Berkeley: University of California Press, 2005); Anne L. Hutchison, *Kenneth Anger: A Demonic Visionary* (London: Black Dog, 2011); and Jack Hunter, *Black Leather Lucifer: The Films of Kenneth Anger* (London: Glitter Books, 2012).

7. Terry Cook, "The Archive(s) Is a Foreign Country: Historians, Archivists, and the Changing Archival Landscape," *American Archivist* 74, no. 2 (2011): 615.

8. The Kinsey and Gebhard eras, however, are referred to under the time in which the objects were received, as many of the items were not stored by provenance. Although the collections have received passing comments, no detailed research has been released on these archives. However, for more on one specific subset of donations and the logic behind these items— those pertaining to sadomasochism—see Anthony L. Silvestri, "'A Conflict between the Token Guardians of Society and a Man's Private Life': Kenneth Anger, Palo Alto Kodak, the Kinsey Institute, and the Circulation of Marvin Samuel's Amateur S/M Pornography," *Porn Studies* 9, no. 4 (2022): 413–29.

9. This aligns with the research that Amelie Hastie has done on actresses and the construction of women's film histories. Particularly, in the final chapter of *Cupboards of Curiosity,* she explores how women actors used such venues as cooking books to insert texts that proved their expertise in a variety of fields. See Hastie, "The Expert: Celebrity Knowledge and the How-Tos of Film Studies," in *Cupboards of Curiosity: Women, Recollection, and Film History,* 155–93 (Durham, N.C.: Duke University Press, 2007).

10. Allyson Nadia Field, "Archival Rediscovery and the Production of History: Solving the Mystery of *Something Good—Negro Kiss* (1898)," *Film History* 33, no. 2 (2021): 1.

11. On the last donation from Samuel Steward, see Barry Reay, "Autoarchivism: Alfred Kinsey's Informants," in *Sex in the Archives: Writing American Sexual Histories,* 66–97 (Manchester, U.K.: Manchester University Press, 2018). Similarly, James Crump provides an analysis of how Kinsey established a projection in relation to his quantification of American sexual behavior by assembling a massive archive of erotic photography in "The Kinsey Institute: A Taxonomy of Erotic Photography," *History of Photography* 18, no. 1 (1994): 1–12.

12. Thomas Waugh, *Hard to Imagine: Gay Male Eroticism in Photography and Film from Their Beginnings to Stonewall* (New York: Columbia University Press, 1996), 392.

13. Scott MacDonald, *A Critical Cinema 5: Interviews with Independent Filmmakers* (Berkeley: University of California Press, 2006), 22–23.

14. Invoice: Paris shipments, March–April 1956.

15. Alfred Kinsey to Kenneth Anger, May 14, 1956.

16. As the authors of *The Kinsey Institute: The First Seventy Years* describe it, this would eventually become such an issue that by the end of the Gebhard directorship, the state of the library and archives would be deemed an emergency, with materials and acquisitions unopened, stacked in closets, and on windowsills; art stuffed into drawers; and leaks causing damage. Gebhard suggested that this was due to the lapsing of grants and the cutting of staff positions. Judith A. Allen, Hallimeda E. Allinson, Andrew Clark-Huckstep, Brandon J. Hill, and Stephanie A. Sanders, *The Kinsey Institute: The First Seventy Years* (Bloomington, Ind.: Well House Books, 2017), 129–30.

17. The links between sexological research and avant-garde film are made apparent in other donations outside of the Anger collections, including items such as a copy of Barbara Rubin's *Christmas on Earth* (1963) and frame enlargements from such films as the surrealist work *Un Chien Andalou* (1929) and the experimental documentary *À propos de Nice* (1930) in the organization's Cinema Stills Collections.

18. Kenneth Anger to Paul Gebhard, May 16, 1983, and Kenneth Anger to Paul Gebhard, December 1, 1982.

19. Kenneth Anger to Paul Gebhard, April 2, 1969.

20. Kenneth Anger to Paul Gebhard, April 14, 1982.

21. Kenneth Anger to Paul Gebhard, September 16, 1965.

22. For example, a portion of the frame enlargements that Anger sent from the *Scorpio Rising* trial and imagery from *Fireworks* are stored in the Cinema Stills Collections, alongside stills sent by other donors, such as J. M. Lo Duca and Gideon Bachmann.

23. For example, as of August 30, 2021, *Onan* is listed on IUCAT as part of the "Kenneth Anger collection," despite the fact that the notes say the film is located in the organization's Assorted Erotic Film Collection, no. 52.

24. For more on shifting approaches to provenance, see Jennifer Douglas, "Origins and Beyond: The Ongoing Evolution of Archival Ideas about Provenance," in *Currents of Archival Thinking*, 2nd ed., ed. Heather MacNeil and Terry Eastwood, 25–52 (Santa Barbara, Calif.: Libraries Unlimited, 2017).

25. Shawn C. Wilson, email correspondence with the author, March 30, 2021.

26. Of course, as Joan Hawkins has noted, *Freaks* has a history in which its own classification was difficult: it was produced by MGM, purchased by Dwain Esper, and circulated on the exploitation circuit before undergoing an art house revival starting with a 1962 screening at the Venice Film Festival. For more, see Hawkins, "From Horror to Avant-Garde: Tod Browning's *Freaks*," in *Cutting Edge: Art Horror and the Horrific Avant-Garde*, 141–68 (Minneapolis: University of Minnesota Press, 2000).

27. Similarly, the link between experimental filmmakers and sexploitation has been documented in the case of Peggy Ahwesh and Doris Wishman in Elena Gorfinkel, "The Meeting of Two Queens: Doris Wishman and Peggy Ahwesh," *Cinema Scope* 79 (Summer 2019): 27–29.

28. Kenneth Anger, note to staff, August 2, 1983.

29. Kenneth Anger to June Reinisch, February 22, 1988.

30. Unfortunately, I do not have a precise count of the letters in each of the boxes. But, as anecdotal evidence, I can say that after a summer of twice weekly appointments at the Kinsey Institute, I had just hit above the fifty-envelope mark, and there were more to go in this particular box.

31. For a detailed analysis of how this phenomenon intersected with racial ideologies at the turn of the twentieth century, see Siobhan B. Somerville, "Scientific Racism and the Invention of the Homosexual Body," in *Queering the Color Line: Race and the Invention of Homosexuality in American Culture*, 15–38 (Durham, N.C.: Duke University Press, 2000).

32. Nicolas de Villiers argues for the possibility of nonmeaning and non-knowledge as queer strategies through the works of Roland Barthes, Michel Foucault, and Andy Warhol. He defines the tactic as such: "Against the hermeneutics of sex as a field of meaning to be deciphered and interpreted, the oeuvre is not decrypted for the secret truth of sexuality or seen as simply a result of sexuality. Rather, the strategies in each of the following texts should be understood as indicating a style of living, what homophobic political reactionaries call 'chosen lifestyle.'" De Villiers, *Opacity and the Closet* (Minneapolis: University of Minnesota Press, 2012), 15–16.

33. Jacqueline Stewart, "Discovering Black Film History: Tracing the Tyler, Texas Black Film Collection," *Film History* 23, no. 2 (2011): 163.

34. Donna Drucker, *The Classification of Sex: Alfred Kinsey and the Organization of Knowledge* (Pittsburgh, Pa.: University of Pittsburgh Press, 2014), 8.

35. Quoted in Hutchison, *Kenneth Anger*, 53.

Hard Drive Failures and Learning Curves

Results from Ingesting Twelve Years of Born-Digital Film at Eye Filmmuseum

MARTINE BOUW AND ANNE GANT

Eye Filmmuseum started receiving born-digital films (films whose master material is digital) in 2008, just a few titles as digital cinema packages (DCPs) on 250 GB hard drives. By 2011, digital films with much larger and more complex file structures were entering the archive on a monthly basis. In the intervening years, like many archives, Eye had to scramble to develop workflows and protocols to safeguard the material without having a sustainable digital storage plan in place. Following the simple LOCKSS[1] principle, which can be applied to most archives with no media asset management (MAM) or digital asset management (DAM), Eye held these on duplicate and triplicate consumer-grade hard drives in multiple locations. Naturally, this was not an ideal situation, as it meant that each drive had to be turned on yearly to avoid stiction. It felt like a fragile system of organization—hard drives on shelves with labels and accompanying Excel lists and information sheets of manually generated metadata.

The staff members who were caretakers of this digital material were concerned about the long-term stability of these titles. In late 2016, we finally were able to install a DAM on premises and start the ingest workflow for our growing backlog of films. The collection of material that needed to be ingested had grown to 974 drives of a wide variety of types and sizes, with approximately three thousand titles on them.[2] In March 2020, Eye Filmmuseum finally completed the ingest of our back catalog of digital material. The team continues to ingest new material at a rate of about 60 TB a month.

This article offers the team a chance to share the unpredicted results of a real-life, three-and-a-half-year ingest project, which included old and new drives, and to document some of the mistakes and successes in managing drives.

PRIORITIZATION OF THE WORKFLOW

Once the DAM was installed, one of the first questions was how to start with such a big backlog, when it seemed like everything was due for migration. We didn't have the staff or throughput to ingest everything at once, so we identified three "tracks":

1. newly arrived material, which was generally larger but well organized, with digital cinema distribution masters and supporting material
2. middle-aged material (2012–16), which was due for migration but was not so irregular in file types or organization of material
3. oldest material (2008–12), which tended to be smaller but not uniform in its delivery and the most unstable, owing to the physical age of the drives (although many had been copied in the intervening years), and requiring the most cataloging attention because of its unusual formats and organization

In the first months of ingest, we made the difficult choice to work on the new incoming material and the middle-aged material, instead of the potentially more problematic and risky old material. We did this because we were also busy with testing and optimizing the DAM itself, and we needed a consistent data supply that could result in clear throughput numbers. We needed to see some quick wins, as well as test the tape robot's limits. For management reasons, we needed to test that the robot functioned well and, as soon as possible, get estimates for the number of people and worktime it would take to ingest the material.

This meant that in addition to requiring a yearly spin-up, the older drives had to remain on the shelves until we got the workflows optimized. From previous projects, we knew that it usually takes significant time to get a workflow running at capacity and that at the beginning of establishing a process, there is a lot to test and evaluate, so we created weekly meetings for an "ingest group"[3] and closely monitored the progress. It took about a year to get the process up to speed, but we were able to accurately estimate the amount of time the project would take. After we got through the first year, and we had a good estimate of throughput, we switched from working on the newest materials and progressed through the backlog from oldest to newest.

DRIVE ANALYSIS, FIRST STEPS

Material was delivered, especially in the early years of 2008–12, on work drives, containing all sorts of material related to the movie creation, that could be of any size or drive format. Before being allowed into our digital environment, drives were virus scanned on an air-gapped machine using FSecure and Kaspersky. To see the content, they would be connected to a Mac computer preferably but also, later on, to a Windows computer. To allow for these machines to read drives formatted with different file systems, they were equipped with Paragon software to allow the Mac to access NTFS volumes and the PCs to access Linux ext2 and ext3 and Apple HFS volumes. The PCs ran a custom file-scanning application, which was developed for

us by Nils van der Meer, called Digiscanner. This application scanned the drive using MediaInfo[4] and also assisted later on in the process with harmonizing, checking, and renaming files.

An additional risk turned out to be the Paragon software, which on rare occasions would cause drives to appear blank. We had some problems in the beginning with the Paragon software on Mac, as it would wipe the partition table. This happened five or six times, so we would not recommend this software for NTFS on Mac; instead, we switched to using a PC.

Initially, copies of hard drives would be created simply by copying all the files of one hard drive connected to a computer to an empty hard drive, but this was vulnerable to human error (copy/paste mistakes) or a potential problem with a computer getting infected from a virus on the incoming drive.

To avoid this, a hardware solution to copy hard drives to a hard drive without a computer connection was implemented, using double docking stations, but this also introduced a human error problem, where the operator could copy a blank drive to the source drive, meaning that both the source drive and copy would be blank.

It's worth mentioning here that we considered using checksums during this phase, but it is very time consuming. Films from makers are not delivered with checksums, so there was no "original value" to compare with. Making two copies of original drives was procedurally simpler than running a checksum or parity program, though obviously not as thorough. At the moment that films were verified and evaluated for ingest, and material was written into our sustainable storage, checksums were generated as part of the ingest. Further on, the entire chain is controlled with checksums on restore/ingest. (Now that our DAM is running, and films are immediately ingested into the sustainable storage, we are no longer making

Figure 1. Celebrating our 1 PB ingest mark in 2019. *Left to right*: Andréa Seligmann Silva, Jim Wraith, Kirsten de Hoog, Martine Bouw, Annike Kross, and Anne Gant. Not pictured: Rob van Houten, Ernst van Velsen, and Nils van der Meer.

multiple copies on hard drives, and they receive a checksum upon ingest.)

RESULTS ANALYSIS

Although we tried to protect the drives, we were always concerned that some percentage of the drives would be unreadable. For the most part, the drives were able to sit on shelves in a storage closet with office temperatures and humidity. But, in 2015, we moved the entire collection to a new building; this involved transporting all the drives in trucks across town, so the material also had to endure some jostling and relocation.

We were pleasantly surprised to find, at the end of this ingest project, that a very low percentage of drives failed, and even fewer files were lost or corrupted. What follows is a report of those results, including the types of damage we encountered and the steps we took to repair the material:

Total number of drives: 974
Number of drives with some failure
    issue: 19
Failure rate: 1.95 percent

After processing hundreds of drives from more than a decade of manufacturing, we can observe in our experience that no single brand or type of drive is more unreliable and no size of drive is more problematic than others. Most of the drives we received from filmmakers were standard consumer-grade drives, from the major brands. Large drives contain a slightly

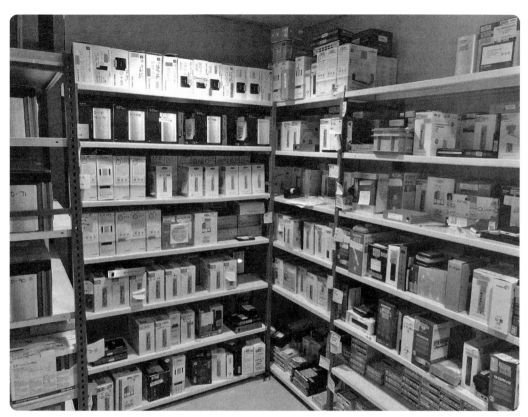

Figure 2. The original incoming drives from filmmakers are stored passively after the contents have been ingested.

higher risk, just because there is more data on them to lose, but not seemingly because they are more unstable. In some rare cases, we saw that fewer than 1 in 150 drives had manufacturing faults, which are discovered when we start to use them. In those cases, we returned them to the manufacturer for replacement before they were used.[5]

Types of Problems Encountered during Our Ingest

Physically broken hard drives. Most of these broke down while spinning up and were the older drives. It's possible that they had been bumped or dropped by someone and not copied. We have a rule that if a drive is dropped, the data should be copied off it immediately, but it's possible that it sometimes didn't happen. Martine remembers that about ten drives were not readable, but in those cases, we had backups already. In one case, we lost 190 frames from a DPX sequence from a large film and didn't yet have a backup, but we were able to go to the lab and get a new copy, which is a good argument for the necessity to check material as soon as it arrives, so that if something is missing, it can be retrieved from the depositor.

Corrupt renditions. For undiagnosed reasons, sixteen renditions from twelve titles were corrupt. This may have occurred in the creation of the rendition, before it arrived at Eye. In most cases, we simply rerendered the rendition from the master material. In other cases, the rendition that was corrupt was an "extra," and so we didn't bother to remake it.

Lack of/faulty documentation. One of the most time-consuming "errors" of our workflow involved not the data but the metadata. Sometimes films arrived without enough registration information or with incorrect information, and we made a policy that we would not ingest material with insufficient metadata. Of course, it is possible to store data sustainably but, without good cataloging, it is unfindable and as good as lost. In these cases, we would have to contact the makers to get more information about their films, which costs time. We learned that it is necessary to have a metadata form associated with each film that is filled in by the depositor, but also to check the material ourselves, as sometimes depositors would provide incorrect information. We also made a packing list of the drives, which was a text file that showed the entire contents of the drive. It was important to keep these forms (metadata list from the maker and packing list of the drive) somewhere digital and accessible.

Sequence types that couldn't be ingested, transcoding. Eye's current ingest workflow only supports DPX, TIFF, and CIN sequences. We received TGA files from animated films and PNG files in newer films. To be able to ingest them as sequences, so they will be migrated as sequences in the future, we transcoded everything to TIFF and also ingested the originals as "work material," which is a separate category in our system for additional files of a film. From a metadata standpoint, there was a documented link to indicate the original files and the resulting TIFF sequence and a different acquisition number for the TIFF, which indicated that it was made in-house.

Identification of file content. Sometimes we received unlabeled content. This could occur for many reasons, like the time we received pornographic material on an artist's hard drive or an extra film that was accidentally added to a delivery. In most cases, the curator who coordinated the delivery would know the correct assets to be ingested, or we could contact the depositor. If we had no idea what the material was, this of course delayed the ingest. This is not a new problem; it can happen with any archival deposit and requires stricter screening of material during delivery. In the earliest deposits, we didn't know exactly what to require, or what was useful, and we didn't screen the incoming drives as carefully. Unfortunately, once they were contractually registered in the collection, we had the obligation to preserve the material. We solved this problem by registering a lot of project files, outtakes, drafts, and extra material as generic work material, alongside the master material. This is a good cautionary tale about being critical and selective at the point of accessioning material.

Lack of policy for some new creative works. In new media cases like virtual reality files, 3-D films, multiscreen installations, films with apps, and other rare projects, we didn't have a policy developed before the material arrived. For our organization, this usually requires a few meetings with various stakeholders—curators, cataloging team, ingest team—to come up with solutions and, of course, this is an ongoing dialogue as new media formats emerge.

Practical issues. In the beginning, we just needed a variety of cables, plugs, virus-scanning stations, extra hard drives (for backups), and networks. We needed tables and spaces to work, where drives could safely run overnight and not be disturbed. This is relevant for most archives setting up a digital workflow.

Solution for Problem Drives

Of the small percentage of drives with data problems, about half were human inflicted. Human error, based on the statistics of this project, is the biggest threat at this point to our data. The biggest type of human error was to accidentally delete data and, in some cases, overwrite. This was easily detected because there were files on the drive from a more recent date. In these cases, restoring from the backup was the solution. The other human mishap was physically damaging a drive, usually by dropping it or knocking it off a table or stack. Our policy is to copy drives immediately if they have fallen or seem damaged but, in some cases, it's likely that the handlers just didn't have a chance to do this.

Physical Drive Repair

Although it is possible to recover data by physically transferring the platter(s) of a hard drive to a surrogate drive, or even by scanning the sectors manually, this is something we would need to outsource because we don't have the in-house equipment or expertise to do it. Rob van Houten, the IT specialist working on this project with us, would first check a drive simply by listening if the head might be bumping on the surface of the drive and would switch it off immediately to avoid further damage. Note that this trick will not work for solid state drives, as they don't make any noise.

If the hard drive was in an enclosure, Rob would remove it and connect it directly through a USB hard drive connection set. In a majority of cases of mechanical failure, the problem was the existing enclosure or its power supply. Once a drive was hooked up, the first check was whether any drive was recognized, which is simply a matter of looking in Windows to see if a drive appears. If it wasn't recognized at all, Rob would send the drive to a specialist repair shop, saying it might be the drive's internal controller or power supply. If it was recognized, Rob would check if Windows could see the partition table and at least recognize the drive, even if it couldn't read the specific drive format. If Rob could see that it was FAT32 or NTFS, he would make a file listing and simply copy all the files without having to run any recovery software.

Data Recovery

The other half of the problems (again, a small percentage of overall drives) could be attributed to either the physical age of the drives or the problems we had with the Paragon reader. In some cases where a file had unreadable sections, it was possible to export the readable parts to a new drive and ingest from there. In some of those cases, there was damage to the drive at the block level, and then our IT specialist, Rob, used four different pieces of recovery software to see if any files could be found: EaseUS Data Recovery, Active File Recovery Ultimate, GetDataBack Simple, and Active@ File Recovery. Each of these is free or inexpensive software, less than one hundred dollars.

Rob would then send a list of recoverable files to the curators and run the recovery software to copy the files to a new drive. This is a slow process of block-level copying and can take, in some cases, more than a week.

We didn't have to employ either physical or data recovery very often in this project, but it was great to have the expertise (Rob) and tools to do it.

IN CONCLUSION, OUR OBSERVATIONS AND ADVICE FOR OTHER ARCHIVES

After all our time worrying and fretting about the stability of hard drives in the collection, the drives performed surprisingly better than we had expected, and we had less loss of files. Because we had backups, could recover some files, and could retrieve a few more, we lost no files.

1. Make copies if you can't ingest into a storage environment. Store them separately. Lots of backups, with good documentation, will help and put less stress on the operation.
2. It is best to have as much information about the files up front before ingesting; documentation is important for finding the material later.
3. Clearly named files will save time in the long run and are worth the upfront effort.

4. Check drives as soon as possible once they are received: if something is missing or corrupted, it might be possible to get a copy from the donor.

5. Avoid accepting extraneous material, formats, or programs. If some material came by mistake, contact the producer and ask if it can be deleted or returned. This will save the future archivists time if they can't identify it or don't know whether they need to keep it.

6. Develop file-naming structures that make sense within your institution. This is especially useful for renditions or sound files, for example, to register from which copies the sound was scanned.

7. Be extra careful with the older material that hasn't been touched for a while. Carry out an extra virus scan. On most of the older drives, we found viruses that could be found with updated virus-scanning software.

8. Humans seemed to cause our biggest mistakes: we forget things, we drop drives, we forget the details of the metadata or leave fields blank, and we make mistakes in estimating the time something will take or the level of importance it has. One of the greatest leaps forward in this project was the development of workflows[6] and automated scripts that could extract technical metadata from files using MediaInfo and import that metadata into our catalog as asset records, with accompanying filmographic metadata. This helped us enormously in terms of accuracy and time savings. Although it doesn't solve the problem of dropped drives or miscopied data, it deserves a mention here, because it helped us eliminate some human error.

THE END OF THE STORY

Since 2017, we have moved to a system of immediate ingest for incoming born-digital material. Drives come in from producers; they are virus checked and organized; and the files are harmonized, registered, and moved directly to tape robot. The original drives are still stored with us, as a sort of third backup (two LTOs are made for each asset). To date, we have approximately 4.5 PB of original data ingested and more than 330 million discrete files.

Martine Bouw is an access employee at Cinémathèque Royale de Belgique–Cinematek, Brussels. She is also a programmer and researcher at the Nederlands Silent Film Festival (NSFF), Eindhoven. Previously, she worked at Eye Filmmuseum, Amsterdam, as a film collection trainee, digital film registrar, booker, documentalist, and digital ingest specialist.

Anne Gant is head of film conservation and digital access at Eye Filmmuseum, Amsterdam. She is currently head of the FIAF Technical Commission and participates on the AMIA Preservation Committee.

ACKNOWLEDGMENTS

A special thanks to the team that worked on ingest and also contributed to this article: Andréa Seligmann Silva, Jim Wraith, Rob van Houten, and Kirsten de Hoog.

NOTES

1. LOCKSS (lots of copies keeps stuff safe), https://www.lockss.org/about/what-lockss.
2. Some titles were not full films but soundtracks or single items related to a title. This included all drives, including backup copies. In the beginning, we didn't mirror drives but offset the contents, so drive A would be on C/D and drive B would be on D/C, and a third copy would also be made, perhaps with another offset. We thought this was clever, to split the risk that exact copies would both fail, but it was complicated to maintain.
3. For other organizations, it might be interesting to note the size of the group working on this project. No one was working on this full-time, but it had the attention of the following people: Jim Wraith, digital film technician; Kirsten de Hoog, informatiespecialist; Martine Bouw, digital ingest specialist; Andréa Seligmann Silva, digital registrar; Anne Gant, head of department; Annike Kross, film restorer; Rob van Houten, IT department; and Nils van

der Meer, external consultant and designer of the program for ingest workflow. The person responsible for system design and oversight of the DAM, and who was closely involved in the performance issues, was Ernst van Velzen, CIO.

4. MediaInfo (https://mediaarea.net/en/Media Info) is software that detects the technical data of video and audio files.

5. An extensive and seemingly transparent study of hard drive failure rates is published each year by Backblaze, using the test base of its own cloud center; see https://www.back blaze.com/b2/hard-drive-test-data.html.

6. It's worth mentioning that it took quite a lot of people to achieve this: this work was not done in-house but by developer Nils van der Meer, working closely with the in-house catalog managers and the developers of our DAM.

Are We There Yet?

*North American Road Maps
to Recovery*

VICTORIA DUCKETT

The conversations that I conduct with film archivists about the Covid-19 pandemic and its impact on their collections and working practices allow me to talk to people working globally to protect and promote film heritage in a period of tremendous change. I initiated this dialogue in early 2020 with Matteo Pavesi, director of the Cineteca Italiana, in Milan. At the time, Lombardy was the epicenter of the Covid-19 pandemic. I wanted to learn how a film archive was responding to the crisis at hand and learned that materials were being made increasingly accessible online. Looking locally (and teaching film history on Zoom from my home in Melbourne), I also wanted to explore the issue of online access and film heritage advocacy in Australia. When I spoke with Meg Labrum, the former general manager, Collections Branch, at the National Film and Sound Archive in Canberra, we had just experienced a disastrous summer of fires. Covid-19 appeared as yet another challenge to which a weary population had to adapt. However, it was not yet one driving significant change in terms of enabling web-led spectatorship for individuals and families experiencing, for the first time, home schooling, curfew, and lockdown.

In my next pair of conversations, conducted at the end of 2020, I turned my attention to archives in Asia. I wanted to learn about the archive experience of institutions that were geographically close but whose realities were very different. I talked with Shivendra Singh, founder and director of the Film Heritage Foundation in Mumbai, and Sungji Oh, head of the Korean Film Archive's Cinematheque team.

At this point, in October 2020, my questions were reflective. What had we learned from the last six months? How had archives adapted and changed? With almost a full year of online teaching under my belt, I thought I understood the challenges we were still facing. As Shivendra made clear, however, conditions in India were extremely difficult—perilous, I would say. After Prime Minister Narenda Modi mandated a strict and fast national lockdown on March 24, 2020, Shivendra's job of preserving film was put on hold while he cooked and cared for fellow citizens who were rendered homeless and unemployed. A season of early and unusually heavy monsoon rains, combined with this forced absence from the archive, took a material toll on the Film Foundation's collection. In contrast, Sungji explained that South Korea's early investment in digital culture (as well as the then comparatively negligible impact of Covid-19 in Seoul, coupled with remarkably supportive copyright laws) promoted and enabled public access to film online. Rather than highlighting materials that had been ruined and lost, or projects that had been interrupted because of the pandemic, Sungji explained that international partner institutions continued to collaborate with them through YouTube channels and online exhibitions.

Today, almost twelve months after these conversations with Matteo, Meg, Shivendra, and Sungji, I am reflecting on the very different dialogue I enjoyed in March and April with archivists in North America this year. At this point, and on the heels of Joe Biden becoming president of the United States in January, I spoke (respectively) with Mike Mashon, head of the Moving Image Section of the Library of Congress (LOC), and Haden Guest, director of the Harvard Film Archive (HFA). My aim was to hear testimony about how American collections are weathering Covid-19, a major health pandemic, as well as political change. I was also interested in learning about the experience of two quite different film archives within a single country. As a scholar who draws on the online holdings of LOC in her teaching and research, I was interested to learn how one of the largest collections of film heritage in the world is responding to Covid-19. What archival work was undertaken from home? How was this determined, organized, and actioned? I was also curious to know how a smaller (and what I consider a more bespoke, "artisanal") university archive like the HFA is responding to the pandemic. Are pedagogy, curating, and collecting differently negotiated in this period of change? What initiatives, if any, have been adopted and introduced to support the archive when the curatorial programs that so shape and identify its Cinematheque are forced closed? My discussions help me appreciate the "can-do" attitude of Mike, heading a staff and collection that dwarf most others. They also bring me genuine cheer, reinforcing my belief in the capacity for individuals to shape institutional directions and, with this, film heritage and public education. Most significantly, I newly appreciate the back-end, invisible work that archivists selflessly undertake.

PRESERVATION FOR ACCESS: PROBLEM-SOLVING THE PANDEMIC AT THE LIBRARY OF CONGRESS

When I talk to Mike, he is cheerfully ordering a pizza from a local restaurant. It is morning for me in Melbourne and evening for him in Culpeper, Virginia. I am reminded of the willingness archivists have to explain their collections to others and the welcome they extend to all members of the film community. What also strikes me is the depth of Mike's institutional knowledge. Head of the Moving Image Section at LOC, he has worked for LOC for twenty-three years. Mike's knowledge of the Moving Image

Section's collection is therefore one that traces itself not only through the many films and materials that I might access but the changing history of the databases that host and support these. As he explains—with an inclusive nod to an Australian legacy—Mavis was the National Film and Sound Archive of Australia's (NSFA) inventory system implemented by LOC in 1997. In 2021, Mavis is being replaced by a new system implemented by Axiell. This shift from one system to another is part of his team's experience of 2020 and 2021.

In addition to moving data across platforms, Mike tells me that it is precisely because colleagues have had more time at home "to play around , , , and think things through" that they have developed new, time-efficient practices. As he explains, LOC acquires a lot of material for its collection through copyright registration. Colleagues working from home throughout the pandemic had time to develop a Python script using OpenRefine that scraped information from the copyright database. Information from IMDb was similarly used to populate LOC inventory records. It is because of initiatives like these that, in 2020, the Moving Image Section of LOC processed more materials than it ever had before. This is just one way that, as Mike explains, the pandemic was a platform for positive change.

Other projects and initiatives emerged or were developed by the Moving Image Section of LOC through the pandemic. Remote Wikipedia training was provided for staff to embed material into Wikipedia pages. A lot of work (including rescanning into HD and editing work) was also undertaken on the 625 paper print titles that constitute the American Memory project, to ready them for a 2022 publication. Moreover, workplace culture adapted. This saw not only an expected change in meeting format (from the workplace to Zoom) but a shift in thinking around access to archives and the availability of online resources. As Mike succinctly states, "the archive as a destination is dead." While the difficulty in physically accessing the archive might be seen as a casualty of the Covid-19 pandemic, it has led to more materials being made available online. LOC is also increasingly willing to frame content with introductions and/or Q&A materials. For those who research and teach using available archival materials, this is a boon for writing, just as it is a resource reference for students. As I explain to Mike, my undergraduate cohorts are increasingly unwilling (and, possibly, increasingly unable) to read monographs or even edited collections without related audiovisual content. A meaningful and historically accurate introduction to a film or collection of film heritage materials can make the difference between youthful enthusiasm and detachment from the histories I am trying to teach.

THE HARVARD FILM ARCHIVE: COLLECTION, CURATION, AND CARE

I know Haden from my graduate school days in the critical studies program in the School of Theater, Film, and Television at the University of California, Los Angeles (UCLA). Our meeting is therefore both professional and social. What interests me about Haden's work is that he is both a lecturer in film and a collection curator. With our own graduate experience shaped by scholars like Peter Wollen and Janet Bergstrom ensuring meaningful connections between the UCLA Film Archive and their pedagogy, we know what it means to study film while exploring archival prints. We are also a generation that has seen the emergence and expansion of digital and web-enabled media as both a scholarly resource and an area of study. How can we continue to promote film as both an academic discipline and public history, particularly at a moment when we don't have access to festivals and screenings? What pedagogic possibilities have been enabled or supported by the HFA during the pandemic? Have the HFA's collection priorities changed in 2020 or 2021?

Haden is, like Mike, articulate about the changes the archive has faced in recent months. Haden's experience of Covid-19 saw him return from a film festival jury in Pamplona, Spain, to the new landscape of a university shutdown.

This meant that the program "Traveling Light: The Films of Kelly Reichardt"—scheduled for March 1–13, 2020—was suspended. Indeed, and most immediately, Haden returned to the United States with the in-person screening of Reichardt's *Wendy and Lucy* (2009) on March 10 at the HFA in negotiation because of the pandemic. Eventually, a reduced capacity of fifty people were allowed to participate in the screening, Haden's introduction, and his post-screening discussion.[1] Just three days later, students exited campus, and the HFA had to rethink work priorities and archival capacities. In parallel with Mike's focus on remote productivity, Haden explains that the forced need to focus on digitized collections spurred important work to completion. The recorded conversations the HFA hosts with makers (and hence the Reichardt visit) were cleaned, and transcripts were created, attached to programs as online educative resources. In addition to this important work—which speaks to public history and enabling access to this—the HFA was able to move forward with digitizing artist films and orphan films. The range of areas, genres, projects, and people that these films engage is remarkable. As Haden states, these include educational films, industrial films, and science films, as well as the works (including the papers) of artists like Anne Charlotte Robertson, George Kuchar, and Hollis Frampton. New collections are also being added: the HFA is currently working on the films of Aldo Tambellini, Robert Fenz, and Nathaniel Dorsky, as well as the work of pioneering African American cinematographer, photographer, and filmmaker James E. Hinton.

What is encouraging about Haden's discussion is not just the range of materials that I learn are available but the regard he gives curation. I newly appreciate, therefore, why films might or might not be released by an archive online. As Haden explains (in relation to his decision to suspend the virtual Cinematheque), there is a glut of available online content; he was best served by directing resources into other projects. I also newly appreciate the work of curatorial practice. While I have long advocated for a recognition of the work of programmers as curators in festivals like Bologna's Cinema Ritrovato,[2] I have not thought of teaching as a mode of curating (Haden's phrase) nor reflected on the curatorial energies that go into an archive's content creation. Indeed, as an Australian who cannot access primary source material on the NFSA website, I associate issues of access with issues of copyright. Instead, Haden speaks of the need to provide enough content to ensure learning but not so much that it becomes a deterrent to engagement. Given these views, it is hardly surprising that Haden is enthusiastic about the fresh perspectives researchers bring to HFA collections. As he contends, research seeds new connections, which regenerate thinking around film once more.

It is this repeated advocacy for the pluralizing of pathways into film history that reinforces Haden's indefatigable belief in our film future. Yes, the pandemic has greatly impacted archival work and the priorities of the HFA's projects, but it has also brought to the fore the significance of the film print. As Haden argues, film must be projected and watched as a live experience. Sitting in a theater and watching a film is not just any lived experience but the moment of a film's realization; it is where audience attention is focused on the lived experience of the moving image (and sound) and not on the screen as a transmitter of web-led media. As Haden eloquently explains,

> many assume it's easy to watch films at home, now so much is available streaming, but in fact it can be very difficult. Objects speak to you and distract you: this coffee cup insists you want another cup of coffee, the cat comes in and demands attention, and so on. You are constantly being pulled away and reminded of everyday demands. It's very hard. That's one of the reasons why watching film in the theater can be so powerful, and can open up the revelatory dimensions of cinema. I think that for younger audiences, those who are learning to watch film, it's so important that they do that in the right space.

SAVORING SPACE

I am writing this conclusion during Le Giornate del Cinema Muto's fortieth anniversary. I miss the community that the festival promotes and am finding the experience of watching online holdings even more difficult this year than I did in 2020. This difficulty has possibly more to do with the fact that Melbourne has officially become the city with the world's longest lockdown than with the experience of watching festival film streaming per se. I join Mike, however, in affirming that it is the communal experience of watching early films, particularly in the convivial atmosphere of Pordenone, that is one of the things I currently miss the most. I also join Haden in affirming that it is the projected image that ties our field to the experience of live performance, rather than to the many web-led screens that digital media promote. And so, following a final strand of Haden's conversation with me, I would position the online curation that the HFA and LOC undertake as a Janus-faced creative practice. Online archival curation pulls us inward, into discussions of internal cataloging systems and procurement processes, as well as outward, toward the recognition of projection contexts and spaces. Interestingly, where it was once apparatus theory that joined a discussion of cinema's positional spectatorship to the medium specificity of film, it is now the archivist who articulates this. Uniquely positioned to bridge inside and outside, preservation and exhibition, process and projection, archivists are educators who speak of film's specific artisanal construction, as well as the breadth of its contemporary community. Haden and Mike ensure access to film heritage online. During a pandemic, and in the absence of live screenings, they also remind us that the darkened theater is never a passive space of proletariat submission. It is, instead, the experiential promise of a future we still long to share.

Victoria Duckett is associate professor in screen at Deakin University, Melbourne. Author of the award-winning book *Seeing Sarah Bernhardt: Performance and Silent Screen* (2016), she has published extensively on actresses, archives, and early film. Her forthcoming monograph is titled *Transnational Trailblazers of Early Cinema: Sarah Bernhardt, Gabrielle Réjane, Mistinguett.*

NOTES

1. See "Wendy and Lucy Introduction and Post-screening Discussion with Haden Guest and Kelly Reichardt," https://harvardfilmarchive. org/calendar/wendy-and-lucy-2020-03 (with the recorded conversation and transcript available).

2. See my series of interviews with film archivists and programmers, published in the "Archives and Archivists" special issue of *Feminist Media Histories* 2, no. 1 (2016): 93–197: "Interview with Bryony Dixon, British Film Institute National Archive," "Interview with Giovanna Fossati, EYE Film Institute, Amsterdam," "Interview with Karola Gramann, Kinothek Asta Nielsen, Frankfurt," "Interview in Melbourne with Meg Labrum, National Film and Sound Archive of Australia, Canberra," "Interview with Mariann Lewinsky, Il Cinema Ritrovato, Bologna," and "Interview with Elif Rongen-Kaynakçi, EYE Film Institute, Amsterdam."

Conversation with Mike Mashon, April 7, 2021

VICTORIA DUCKETT

VICTORIA DUCKETT (VD): Thank you very much for agreeing to this interview. It is really nice of you to make the time, so I do appreciate it. Could you briefly tell me what your role is? I do know that you are head of the Moving Image Section of the Library of Congress.

MIKE MASHON (MM): I came to the library in 1998, so I've been here for twenty-three years. My first job was as the moving image curator, and I served in that role until 2005, which is when I became the head of the Moving Image Section. I work in the National Audio-Visual Conservation Center, and my section is responsible for film, video, and, increasingly, digital. There is also a Recorded Sound Section, and we have three preservation laboratories for film, video, and audio, in addition to research centers for both moving image and recorded sound in Washington, D.C.

VD: As head of the Moving Image Section, what kind of team do you have?

MM: We're responsible for the acquisition, description, preservation, rehousing, storage of, establishing preservation priorities for, and providing access to the largest collection of moving images in the world. It has 1.8 million physical items, in addition to all the digital objects. We have processing units with catalogers and technicians. Some of the catalogers create MARC records, while the processing technicians typically create inventory-level records. Then we have a curator and preservation specialists who are responsible for ensuring the physical integrity of the collection, in addition to coordinating various access initiatives. We also have a digital conversion specialist who is responsible for born-digital ingest and a variety of other digital projects that we're working on. All of our activity is, of course,

Figure 1. Nitrate vault.

in the service of making the collections more available for access.

Our section also feeds the video and film preservation laboratories. The videotapes that we process ultimately make their way to the video lab for preservation. And, by the same token, the films that we're responsible for ultimately make their way to the film lab, usually for digitization but sometimes for photochemical preservation. We still operate a web lab.

VD: It's a massive undertaking. I was looking through your website and was gobsmacked in terms of the amount of materials and the facilities and resources you have. It's quite overwhelming, really. How many people are on your team?

MM: Right now, there are twenty-seven people in the Moving Image Section. At one point we had more than forty people in the section. Certainly we'd always love to have more people, but we're doing well with the folks that we have.

VD: It sounds like a very large and very functional operation.

MM: It is. There are about a hundred people altogether who work at the Packard Campus for Audio-Visual Conservation in Culpeper, Virginia, with another six reference staff in Washington, D.C. When we designed the building here in Culpeper, it was for max capacity of 180–190 people. It's half a million square feet. It's a really, really big building! Right now, we have around 40 percent of the staff on-site at any given time because of Covid-19 restrictions.

VD: It's a beautiful building. I hope to see it, when I can travel again.

MM: You can read about it online. It opened in 2007, and it's worked out really well for us. Sometimes you feel isolated from the mother ship in D.C., so there's been good and bad in that. But, overall, it's nice to have a building that was built specifically for all of this activity surrounding moving image and sound recordings. We have a lot of resources.

VD: It does look brilliant. You said that you've got about 40 percent of your staff on-site now. When did that transition happen, in relation to the Covid-19 crisis and where we are now?

MM: Maybe it is best if I talk a little bit about the trajectory of how we've adapted to Covid-19. Obviously, it wasn't necessarily a slow train that was coming, but we could see events unfolding in February [2020]. We started making some provisional plans then. But when everybody was sent home in March, we were scrambling a little. I have to tell you, in the past year—and I was reflecting on this, in advance of our conversation—I'm really, really proud of the work that we have done. So let me explore what our thinking was.

First, I will clarify that in the Moving Image Section, there are two supervisors who work with me. Broadly, Andrea Leigh supervises the catalogers and the techs who work on copyright and Kelly Chisholm the technicians who work on the analog arrearage. We were asking, what can people do when they're working at home? Now, one of the challenges we had was that the library was in the process of replacing everybody's desktop computer with a laptop. I had a telework laptop, so I could take it home. I'd been doing this for a while. I could take home work on the weekends and get into the library's VPN, and so get into the internal databases. I therefore had everything I needed; it was just like I was at work. But a lot of our staff didn't have telework laptops, so they could get into some resources they needed but not into all the databases that we had. So we created a chart of who had a telework laptop and who didn't and then what projects people could do based on their situation.

Kelly and Andrea and I were constantly talking to each other the first month or so. We have a project, for example, to make the paperwork [available online] that was submitted along with copyright submissions, dating back to 1912. We've long wanted to get scans of that paperwork online, so one of our manuscript archivists devised a way to create a finding aid to which we could link descriptions. But this required the creation of a spreadsheet containing all the pertinent information

Figure 2. Packard Campus entrance. Photograph by S. Miller.

that would eventually result in a finding aid—but each entry in the spreadsheet had to be entered by hand. So, we had staff throughout the facility and not just our section working on the project, and since it didn't require a telework laptop, anyone could participate. It kept a lot of people busy on a project of great value and, to be honest, we couldn't have put nearly as many resources on it if not for the pandemic.

I arranged for people to have remote Wikipedia training with the express intent of linking some of our online content and embedding it in a Wikipedia page. The library continues to have big crowdsourcing projects that weren't necessarily germane to the Moving Image Section but were, however, definitely germane to the library. So some staff helped transcribe the Clara Barton Papers or the Theodore Roosevelt Papers, while others wrote blog posts. We did a couple of blogs on staff pets since those were our new coworkers.

By the summer—and this had not taken too terribly long to emerge, because we have really clever people on our staff—everyone in our section had their telework laptops, and we started developing new processes for working on our collection. There were two [processes] in particular that I'll call out, without getting into the details.

Figure 3. Safety film vault.

There are two primary ways that we acquire material for our collections. One is registrations through copyright, and the other is through gift and purchase. The Copyright Office changed the way that they were documenting video, film, DVDs, whatever else that was coming in and being registered for copyright. A couple of my colleagues developed a Python script and, using OpenRefine, they figured out a way for us to scrape information from the copyright database. We also used information from IMDb to automatically populate inventory records.

We stood all this up fairly quickly be-

cause my colleagues had more time at home to play around with it and think things through. When I did the annual report for the calendar year 2020, Victoria, [I found that] we processed more material in 2020 than we ever had before. This is because of all of these processes that my colleagues developed. It was really remarkable. You always acknowledge the pain of the pandemic, but we [nevertheless] had a great year. Same with the arrearage. Working from home and using various inventories and spreadsheets, my colleagues created skeletal records in our Mavis inventory system. When folks finally did get back on-site, they could go get that unprocessed material for which they had already created records, complete the physical processing, and finish out the record. Much of the work was [therefore] done before you ever laid hands on the can of film.

By the end of the summer, we could bring 20 percent of the people back in the building for short amounts of time. Sometime in the fall, it was 40 percent occupancy full-time. As long as we didn't get over about forty, forty-five people in the building with proper social distancing, then we could bring more people back in the building. We're very fortunate that we work in a large building. For example, our audio engineers work in isolation rooms, so it was perfect for them. When we are thinking about who should be coming back on-site, we're going to prioritize the people who actually touch collections. The people who need to get back are the people who work in the preservation laboratories and the people processing those analog arrearage collections. And then there are other on-site workflows like born digital, where files on hard drives, data tapes, DCPs, and other physical media are prepped for ingest.

The other thing I should say is that the library has been sterling, absolutely magnificent in its communication. For a long time, there were daily phone-in meetings, with updates from all around the library. Then it went to three times a week, and then once a week. Now it's every other week [that we meet virtually]. For a long time, there were daily coronavirus updates. I got coronavirus update number 200 the other day. I will give the library a tremendous amount of credit for keeping those lines of communication open.

There are a couple of other things that we've focused on, including getting more of our material online. That was always going to be a very important thing for us, regardless of the pandemic. But, boy, is it really important now, because the archives as a destination is dead.

VD: Please don't say that!

MM: OK, "dead" may be a little strong. But we cannot always expect people to come to Washington, D.C. We need to make more of our material, at least our public domain material, available online.

We have the National Screening Room as our primary portal through which we're putting more material online. We don't have a lot now. It's a little over four hundred titles. The library's first go-around with putting digital moving images online was with a project called American Memory, in the 1990s. These were all very low-res[olution] versions of some of our paper print titles. Some years ago, we started a rescanning process, rescanning all the American Memory titles at a minimum of HD. We want to do a comprehensive upgrade on all titles—roughly 625—that are in the old American Memory presentation. The pandemic, honestly, Victoria, was the greatest thing that ever happened to that project. By the time we left in March [2020], of the 625 titles, I think we probably had 550 of them scanned. At that point, we needed to have a ProRes version of the JPEG 2000 (our master file) made, and then those ProRes files needed to be edited. That was a big thing, editing those files so we could get ready for publication. Because another clever colleague of mine had created a way for me to be able to transcode these JPEG 2000s remotely, I was able to make ProRes on all of these files from home. I had colleagues also at home—some worked in the film lab, a couple worked in my section—who had Final Cut Pro on their home computers, and so they could do all the editing. We hope to publish all these upgrades in early 2022.

The final big challenge I have to mention is Mavis. Are you familiar with an older database that originated with the [National Film and Sound Archive of Australia], Mavis? Mavis is our inventory system that we implemented back in 1997 and is more than end of life. We're moving away from Mavis, and we're implementing a new system made by a company called Axiell. That has occupied a tremendous amount of staff time, sometimes multiple meetings a day, but the team has been very dedicated, and we've done a good job adapting to having all these meetings online. I've actually come to prefer them to most in-person meetings.

I think the final thing that I wanted to say is that while I prefer an in-person conference (especially for the junior staff, because I think it's important to them to create those professional networks), I think we've also seen that those [online forums] can be enjoyable. It's a way to increase access or visibility of your collection. And it's something that I'd really like to see the library do more of. I can definitely see us putting more of our preserved content online with a taped introduction or Q&A or something similar.

VD: That's a great idea. You do have the essays, which I was quite interested to see. You have great two-page In Focus essays on given titles. But, absolutely, I thought it would be really good to have exactly what you're saying. I'm thinking about my own undergraduates: they would happily sit and watch a ten-minute, fifteen-minute chat more than read an article. What you're saying is therefore also possibly generational. Your point about your junior colleagues needing (and necessarily needing) to build networks is also generational. We've got our established networks, and you have obviously managed to move in an incredible way because of this. You know your staff well, you know how they work. And you were able as a team to make a really difficult situation an opportunity, in terms of reviewing your processes. So you have done so much work around preservation for access.

MM: That is the animating principle of the Packard Campus, preservation for access. We're not doing this for giggles; we are doing this because we want people to be able to access the material. And we have a lot of content that can be made freely available. Again, I work for a very large organization. My friends who work for LOC.gov are fantastic. We have some highly creative people who are engaging in a lot of interesting data experiments. The web team is responsible for putting up the photographs, the maps, presidential papers, and all the vast treasures of the library. They are responsible for a lot. I'm there patiently in line, they like the moving image collections, and I appreciate it. I'm not impatient, but we also have a tremendous amount of content that we want to make available.

One of the things I'm always interested in, Victoria, is hearing from researchers, academics, and students about the kind of material that they're looking for. Sometimes it's hard to sync up our priorities with those needs, so I rely a lot on the reference staff. They are the front line. They work with researchers all the time, so they're the ones to ask, of all of the things that we have in the collection, what should we focus on in terms of putting them online?

From that, we keep a priority list. We have some really interesting things in the pipeline that'll be coming up. One of our newer focuses—I shouldn't even call it a new focus—is the preservation of Black films, what used to be referred to as "race films." We have a lot in the collection, many are in the public domain, so we want to digitize them for online access. We have all the film shot by George Stevens when he was with the U.S. Army Signal Corps. We have all those films he shot from the D-Day landings through the liberation of the death camps. We want to get those online. People also ask us about Margaret Mead films all the time. Can we put the Margaret Mead films online? We can. Like I say, it's a lot!

VD: As a teacher and researcher, I am impressed with what you do have online. You seem to be able to curate good packages of material, even though there is an enormous amount of material to choose from. I like your vaudeville program, for example, because I'm thinking in terms of my performing arts colleagues, and I'm trying to teach classes on the related histories of stage and screen. Also the Black films, as well as one of the first queer demonstrations in 1968.[1] I flicked that through to my colleague running the gender and sexuality studies units at Deakin. And so your initiatives enrich our own research focuses within my own university. It's also really nice to see the access you give—your site is an open-facing initiative—but also the way you can draw people into collections. Your material is really on the ball in terms of critical debates and pedagogy.

MM: Thank you for those kind words. Pretty soon we're going to be upgrading the vaudeville presentation that you're referring to (it's one of the American Memory presentations, called American Variety Stage). That happens to be my favorite. I mean, who doesn't love monkeys riding bicycles? All of those are going to be upgraded. And, Victoria—this is important—if a film is available (and eligible) to be downloaded, we provide MPEG-4 and ProRes LT options. So it's not the highest-resolution flavor of ProRes, but it's really solid. It even looks good broadcast on TV. These are all available and freely downloadable now.

Not all of our films are available for download. Lilli Vincenz's movies—*The Second Largest Minority* [1968], *Gay and Proud* [1970]—are not available for download because of an agreement with her estate. But the vast majority of what we have is available in high-resolution formats. We want people to be able to have these films for themselves and to be able to repurpose them however they want. They can put them into a presentation. They can use them in their papers; they can remix and reuse.

VD: Yes, I think this is really great. So, going back to what you have been working through—did more materials become available in the library because of the pandemic?

MM: We were able to work on our backlog. We still have a long way to go on that. But we were able to get through a lot of copyright backlog. These things are picking up again. We would like to see more direct digital deposits.

People are getting back in the building in D.C., where the Copyright Office is located, and we have more people on-site in Culpeper. We are starting to get more

materials in from Copyright. During the pandemic, we did acquire some fairly large collections that had been started before the pandemic. We got twenty-eight pallets of 16mm film from the BBC. These were all film prints of movies that they used to show in the 1950s, and they don't need those 16mm prints anymore, so we took them. We didn't have a lot of those titles in our collection. But, by and large, we slowed the pace of acquisitions.

VD: I know you have your screening programs, and that also you have the film library (and from what I understand, there are 350–400 film titles lent during the year). What has happened to these?

MM: Our 205-seat theater is completely shut down. The library has said not to expect any live programs until 2022, so we're following their lead. I'm glad that you mentioned the film-lending program. That is starting to pick up a little now since more theaters are reopening. We're seeing more of that in the United States. We had that burst in Europe for a while, and then they retreated. I was on-site today, and a colleague of mine was in there inspecting film because we have a couple of loans coming up. We are also expanding our digital loans. We haven't really gone heavily into DCP production but are trending in that direction. However, we want to support 35mm exhibition for as long as we can.

We're motivated by providing maximum access to folks like you, your students, and live audiences. This is how culture is perpetuated and celebrated. We're a taxpayer-funded institution, and it is our imperative—our mission—to make this material available, not only to the American taxpayer, but to people around the world. It's a privilege to do this. Sometimes, when I really get bogged down in being a bureaucrat, I have to back up and say what I do is a privilege and I'm really lucky to do it.

VD: I've luckily been given access to archives, to films this year, that I couldn't physically go and visit. But we need to remember also—and it's a concern, I suppose, as a film historian—that I have missed

[Cinema Ritrovato in] Bologna, Pordenone, as well as other forums for live screenings. Specifically, when I'm trying to teach to students, I can stream the films online, but I'm trying really hard to explain to students what it's like in a cinema theater, when you're looking at films together. And that becomes the loss.

MM: I try to be really optimistic about it. I told my wife, I'm just letting you know, I'm going to every festival there is. So I'm going to the San Francisco Silent Film Festival. I'm going to Pordenone. I have to say, that is one of the things that I miss the most—that communal experience of watching a film. Already, from the beginning of 2020, I decided that I was going to devote myself to watching more films at home and in theaters. I was watching a lot of television series, and I felt like I'd lost touch with my film side. And that has continued right into 2021. Hardly a day goes by that I'm not watching a film or two.

VD: It's a lot.

MM: Yeah, it's a lot. But I am really looking forward to getting back to Pordenone. The point that I also keep making any time I talk to my friends who go to all these festivals is, think how great it's going to be when we are all there again. It will be the best, the most joyous thing.

VD: On another tack, but still pointing to questions of access, I have seen the library blog *Now See Hear!* I really enjoy it.

MM: I don't write for it as much as I'd like to but have wonderful colleagues who do, in addition to maintaining a Twitter feed. Please follow us, @LOC_AV.

VD: So that's an impact of Covid-19, the increased outreach we might achieve through online forums like this. What do you see going forward in terms of your theater? Will it take a more centralized and important role for your own facility?

MM: We're thinking ahead to when we reopen, focusing how to expand our audience. There's a not insignificant Spanish-speaking population here. We'd like to show films that they might be interested

in. I've been living here for fifteen years now, and it really shocks me how many people don't know that we show movies for free.

VD: For free! That's what I noticed. I wish I could bring my classes to this. I was also thinking about my father, who has Alzheimer's, and how much it would help him to access TV shows and films from his own youth. I think it's really great there's a massive community of people that the film archive can bring a lot of joy to.

MM: Yes. You know, Victoria, so much of that material in America is rights restricted, and so we'll always work with that reality. There are positive developments, however. For example, we have a lot of silent films released by Paramount in our collection. In 2019, we signed an agreement with the studio allowing us to put their public domain titles online and/or distribute them on DCP without fees or permissions. We're delighted Paramount agreed to this—they have such a fantastically entertaining catalog—and I hope we can work out similar arrangements with other studios.

VD: Thanks. What I am really interested in is access. What you're saying is that your task is to do that outreach, to somehow explain and ensure the significance of film. And you do a great job on your website in terms of this. You make visible a range of things.

MM: Yes, it is a good and responsible organization to work for. I'm proud to work for the library. It's an advantage, in many ways, to work for the Library of Congress. People know the name, it opens up doors.

Earlier today, I had a conversation with several friends to talk about what archives are going to look like in 2031. A colleague is going to be in a presentation at the Association of Moving Image Archivists conference next week, to talk about that. [As we discussed,] we're going to be looking at more distributive models, archives that are interconnected with each other in the future. The library's not going to be a silo in the way that it is. I think there are some good, interesting things that can happen out there. I'm excited about that.

VD: What I found remarkable was that, for example, if you're interested in scriptwriting, on your site, there are links to go and get access to those scripts. These are not necessarily your own materials. I have not seen that on other sites.

MM: Well, just wait until this copyright description project that I mentioned earlier gets online this summer. Starting in 1912, when people registered films for copyright, they had to submit paperwork along with them. We didn't keep the films because they were on nitrate. And a lot of those films disappeared. We did keep the paperwork. So we haven't scanned all of it, but we've scanned a lot of it. So if there's a film from 1923, and you want to see the paperwork submitted for copyright, you're going to be able to find it. Maybe it'll just be a synopsis, but it might be the whole script. It might be a press book. It's going to be fantastic. I am so excited about that. This copyright descriptive material is gold.[2]

VD: That's great. I'm going to stop this conversation here, on such a tremendously positive note. I look forward to looking at those materials. Thank you so much for making yourself available, Mike. It's been an incredibly interesting conversation.

Victoria Duckett is associate professor in screen at Deakin University, Melbourne. Author of the award-winning book *Seeing Sarah Bernhardt: Performance and Silent Screen* (2016), she has published extensively on actresses, archives, and early film. Her forthcoming monograph is titled *Transnational Trailblazers of Early Cinema: Sarah Bernhardt, Gabrielle Réjane, Mistinguett.*

NOTES

1. See *The Second Largest Minority* (Lilli Vincenz, 1968), https://www.loc.gov/item/mbrs 01991429/.
2. This collection is now online: https://www .loc.gov/collections/motion-picture-copyright -descriptions/about-this-collection/.

Conversation with Haden Guest, March 5, 2021

VICTORIA DUCKETT

VICTORIA DUCKETT (VD): Thank you for agreeing to talk with me, Haden. I haven't yet spoken with anyone in America about what it's been like to work professionally in your current circumstances. I know you're the director of the Harvard Film Archive. So before I ask about Covid-19 and its impact, I would like to know more about what you do in the archive.

HADEN GUEST (HG): As director of the Harvard Film Archive, I am chief curator of both the HFA's year-round cinematheque and its film and manuscript collections. I also work closely with our preservation and access team to define strategies and priorities for the care, access, and promotion of HFA collections. During regular times, a lion's share of my time is devoted to the Cinematheque, where we present originally curated programs in our 188-seat theater located in the historic Carpenter Center for the Visual Arts on the Harvard campus.

I oversee a total of seven full-time employees. We also have some part-time employees, who are a part of the Cinematheque. I also serve as a senior lecturer in the Department of Art Film Visual Studies [AFVS], where I teach on various topics of film history and curatorship. The HFA is a division of the Harvard College Library [HCL], and so I am also active within various library initiatives and committees. All of this keeps me rather busy!

VD: It sounds like you've got archival duties, plus the teaching and administrative duties. That's a big load. It's really interesting, as you are a bridging figure. You can probably therefore speak to both the archival and academic impacts of Covid-19. Maybe we can start, first, with the question of when you started noticing the impact of Covid-19. You're doing a lot of things—the collections, acquisitions, programming—so I am interested in when and where you were first impacted.

HG: The first week of March 2020, I was in Spain, as a member of the jury of the wonderful Punto de Vista festival in Pamplona. I remember that it was March 7, and I received a telephone call from then chair of the AFVS department, Robb Moss, alerting me that things were in motion in response to the emerging Covid-19 crisis.

We actually had a public program scheduled just a few days later, a screening with filmmaker Kelly Reichardt in person. Robb shared the updated university advisory that we could not have more than one hundred people in the theater. And then, when I returned home the next night, that number had been reduced to fifty people. The situation was very fluid, and we almost canceled, but our screenings of *First Cow* and *Wendy and Lucy* with Kelly wound up being our last in-person events. On March 10—I believe it was on that Tuesday—it was announced that the university would be closed, with students going home on Friday. I was teaching a seminar at the time, and that Wednesday would be our last in-person class. Students were crying, hugging each other, saying goodbye. Many in the class were seniors. The impact was immediate and felt on every level.

At the same time, at the HFA, we had to quickly try to understand what the move to remote work would mean for us as a team, as an organization, in terms of our day-to-day work and larger priorities. There was a lot to figure out, and it was a very stressful period. That said, the university did a really great job and really made the correct decisions. There was no hesitancy sending the students home and all of us into remote mode, and the wisdom of that decision has been proven. But it took longer to understand the next steps. Within the library and across the university, organizations were asked to identify those individuals whose work would be most profoundly challenged by working from home and to begin defining alternate work scenarios.

Very obviously, those who work with physical collections, such as conservators and our projectionists, were potentially most impacted. At the HFA, staff working with the Cinematheque programs were also impacted.

The Harvard Film Archive was quite lucky in a number of ways. We had just finished a full redesign of our website, after giving considerable time to reimagining the site as a place for increasingly enhanced and expanded access to HFA collections and other resources, such as online exhibitions. It took a long time to refine a design concept, but also to make it happen institutionally, because it was a major investment.

We were also fortunate because we had recently acquired major collections that were ready or nearly ready to be processed. Together we identified a series of priorities in terms of collections, driven partially by longer-term objectives and plans but also by technology and priorities. We identified those collections we could work on efficiently and effectively while remote. Digital collections were given a major priority. Whenever we have a Cinematheque event with visitors, we record the conversation. We have a growing collection of conversations with filmmakers that are really extraordinary, and we were at last able to work on those audio files to make them fully accessible. After cleaning up the audio files, and creating transcripts, we have been loading these conversations onto our website. The visiting filmmakers audio collection is just one example of a really rewarding pandemic project that we've been able to do.

We were able to identify a number of projects, a number of them ongoing projects, whose progress had been slow, simmering on the back burner. The pandemic and work-from-home scenario gave us the opportunity to focus upon these, now with a real sense of purpose. Some projects were very back-end; cataloging, database cleanup, and above all the processing of backlog collections. Some staff members who do not typically work on collections were able to do so, by doing data cleanup and entry. There was a general reorienta-

Figure 1. The HFA Theater. Photograph by John Quackenbush.

tion of HFA staff, in terms of priorities, during the pandemic. The HFA is a Janus-faced institution facing simultaneously toward the Cinematheque program and toward the collections. With the Cinematheque dark, we were able to focus almost exclusively on the collections. In order to maximize this orientation—which we understood from the beginning would be temporary, even without knowing how long it would last—I made the decision that we would not present a full-time program of virtual screenings, even though we have the virtual Cinematheque. This is also partially because there is such a glut right now of streaming programs available. There's so much to see online, many of it quite compelling. If we do not have to dive fully into these virtual waters, it seems a better investment of our time and resources to focus elsewhere.

Some months into the pandemic, we were given limited but flexible access to our space that proved really valuable. We were able to purchase a film scanner, something that we've been wanting to do for a long time, and set up a digitiza-tion studio in the Carpenter Center. We now have staff going into the office five days a week processing collections and digitizing select materials. It has been exciting to be busy on-site. We also have a number of film-to-film preservation projects under way with labs nearby in Boston, elsewhere in the United States, as well as in Europe and Japan. So, on a certain level, with the exception of the Cinematheque work, much of our work has continued.

VD: So this is all work that emerged after March 10, when you had immediate notice to stop events?

HG: Yes, right after our last event, with Kelly Reichardt.

VD: I love Kelly Reichardt! You said that event was reduced to fifty people. Who made that decision? As an archive, and even as an academic institution, who was directing the closures in that immediate moment?

**Figure 2. Agnès Varda et moi
(aka Haden Guest), 2009.
Photograph by Marcus Halavi.**

HG: All decisions about events came from the top, from the president's office and Harvard's Health Services. Harvard had formed a committee to focus on the pandemic early on in 2019, I believe, drawing experts from Health and Human Services and from various important administrative and medical departments. So they already had been putting a plan in place and thinking about this. In fact, their thinking was even further advanced than that of the U.S. government. We were just lucky. I should point out that the decision to go remote was made just right before spring break. So the instructions were quite simply that everybody will be leaving home for spring break early and will not be coming back.

In terms of the Harvard College Library, of which the HFA is a division, it was very soon after announced that HCL would not be coming back to campus either. We had to quickly decide what to take home: desktop computers, printers, chairs, etc. Other units and departments within Harvard took just a little bit longer, in terms of days, to figure this out. But it was pretty uniform.

VD: Was this an initial lockdown? Or have you been in lockdown since then [March 2020]? I don't expect you to remember every date, but what happened? When people went home, did you have to rethink how you were going to operate?

HG: Yes, exactly, we did have to rethink everything. The first question was, can we ensure that everybody has meaningful work to do? That was of paramount importance. The HFA is a small team, so we had a series of focused one-on-one and group conversations to determine what projects could move forward and how we could enable staff to work on projects that would normally be outside their regular work. We also asked ourselves, what kind of work would staff *like* to do? Because we did not want to suggest someone do something that they didn't particularly enjoy. Across the larger library organization, a significant number of people were identified as needing remote work projects. Divisions were invited to post projects that would be suitable for different skill sets, be they catalogers or conservators. We benefited tremendously from this opportunity. For instance, we were able to give new energy to a transcription project that we had never been able to fully focus on. It's exactly projects like this, as well as back-end projects, such as cataloging, that really benefited, in a certain sense paradoxically, from the pandemic. With all of this extra help on HFA projects, our productivity increased significantly during the pandemic.

VD: That's great.

HG: Yes, and we're seeing a kind of cascade effect too. As more collections are being digitized, we have been improving virtual access, and as a result, we are seeing a significant uptick over the last year in terms of visits by researchers.

VD: I was looking at your collections—and they are amazing—and you do have a lot of online content. Are you saying that you built new collections or that this period has allowed you to review the holdings you have?

HG: It allowed us to review holdings we already have. What's been really interesting is rethinking our collections. The HFA collection contains close to forty thousand audiovisual items that can be divided into two or three large categories. The first and the largest category is exhibition prints. These are prints of films whose original format is 35mm or 16mm, works meant to be seen, projected in the theater. These are usually commercial films, from around the world. Those are materials that we're not digitizing, for the most part. Instead, we're focusing on the other two categories, orphan films (academic, educational, industrial, and science films) and what we

call "artist films," films by experimental, avant-garde, and independent filmmakers. We have been digitizing a wide variety of orphan films, and certain artist films, to make them newly available.

VD: With the artist films, I was noticing when I was looking through your materials online that some of those people have come through Harvard, or are resident in your state, which I thought was really interesting. I was really impressed with that. So these collections are not new, but this period allows you to go through them again. Are you thinking about ways to give more access? Because I keep on trying to watch more [of your] films.

HG: Yes, we are focusing on access to certain artist films. I think one of the most important collections we have in this category is that of Anne Charlotte Robertson. The HFA has the entire opus of Anne Charlotte Robertson, and also all of her papers. Her *Five Year Diary* is an extraordinary milestone, an eighty-one-part (or chapter) work made over many, many years. The question is how to make that accessible. It's not enough to simply digitize things and then just put it out there. If you make too much available, in some ways, that becomes an obstacle and might even intimidate research. And then, if you don't give enough, that is also an obstacle. There has to be a balance.

In the case of *Five Year Diary,* there is still a lot of work that needs to be done. Anything that we make available online must also have closed captions available. Anne Charlotte Robertson's work is particularly complex in that way, because she used simultaneous voice tracks.

VD: Of course. Your collection is absolutely brilliant. It gave me the opportunity, knowing that I was going to talk to you, to look through the collection. I didn't realize how rich it was. It's really interesting to hear about your scanning of ephemera, diaries, or papers. You are now able to move forward more with that work? Is that what you are saying about your collections?

HG: Yes. We've been focusing on the digitization of film more than anything. The papers are a separate project. But the HFA has received a number of additional collections recently that include significant manuscript components. As a division of the library, we have negotiated a new understanding and arrangement with Houghton Library, the home of modern manuscripts at Harvard, so that HFA paper collections can be accessed there, in their fabulous and recently renovated reading room. The HFA has the papers of George Kuchar, Hollis Frampton, Warren Sonbert, and Godfrey Reggio, among other filmmakers. We're working on a number of projects right now. There will be a release of a big box set of George Kuchar films next year, and we are hopefully going to be able to include scans of papers as well. We also want to do some kind of release of Anne Robertson's work. I'd love to do a Blu-ray box featuring selections of her writings as well. So there are a lot of projects to do.

We've had a number of preservation projects. We're working on the films of James E. Hinton, who was a pioneering African American cinematographer, photographer, and filmmaker. We have the only collection of his film work. We're working now with his daughter to define access and preservation priorities for that collection. So there's a lot of work to be done. Working with donors, working with artists, oftentimes it's a longer conversation that leads to the final projects. Each collection and each artist has their own needs. This patient work has to be done first. I've been spending a lot of time talking in conversation with different artists. We're working on a project now with Nathaniel Dorsky's early films. We're also working on the films of two artists who recently passed away, Aldo Tambellini and Robert Fenz, as well. There are a number of collections that we're really engaged with right now. My time is usually divided between collections work and curating the HFA Cinematheque, which is driven by urgent deadlines—it's show business, after all. Being detached from public programs has allowed me to focus more steadily on important collection needs. This has been really rewarding for me, personally. But, more importantly, it has been great for the HFA, too, because we have been able to give new focus to existing collections as well as make new acquisitions, often of films or collections that have been waiting at the threshold of the archive but needed extra work to welcome them in.

I think the pandemic has caused everybody to rethink priorities. A number of artists who were saying they wanted to wait before archiving their films and papers are now discovering that that is actually a good time [to engage] with us on the preservation of their work and legacy.

VD: Has Covid-19 created, in a sense, a more reflective space for donors or for artists?

HG: Yes, I think this is the case. This time, and space, for reflective conversations has been really fruitful. But at the same time, this period has also seen some things moving at a more accelerated speed than would be normally possible. We were waiting to purchase a film scanner for some time. And suddenly this became a very high priority and one we were able to work through institutionally very efficiently, even though equipment purchases required special approval during the pandemic. But suddenly we could make the argument much more forcibly and directly: we can't do this work unless we have this scanner. And then—boom—thanks to the generosity and understanding of our colleagues within the library, we have new digitization capabilities.

VD: There's two questions around this. First, who works the scanner? Obviously, that's physical work. So that's a question about access and work. And secondly, there is the role of your work as director of the HFA. You are touching base with people, but you are not in the same physical space. This can be difficult.

HG: Absolutely. The HFA is in this really amazing building, the only Corbusier-designed building in North America. The main HFA office space is one of the most intimate in the entire building: a large room with five smaller offices branching off it. The main space serves almost like this little

Figure 3. Recent arrivals in the HFA vault, August 3, 2022.

piazza that inspires conversations with one another that are very important to our work and esprit de corps. We definitely missed spontaneous interaction. The idea of having to schedule everything took a while to adjust to, but we've been having more regular staff meetings as a result. We were so in touch with each other on a daily basis that we did not hold staff meetings as often as other organizations. But now Zoom meetings have become a really important space for different kinds of interaction, both agenda-driven meetings but also more open-ended explorations of different topics. Especially during the early days of the pandemic, they also provided important time just to be to-

gether, which was really appreciated.

But in terms of building access, this needed to be a little complicated because we share the building with the Department of Art Film Visual Studies and the staff of the Carpenter Center for the Visual Arts. There had to be certain protocols to determine how many people can be in the building, a number determined by airflow and the actual physical space itself. So at first we determined that we could have one member of the HFA in our space per day throughout the week, and gradually this number was able to increase. We soon had a schedule where three of us (not myself) were able to work in our space. Among these is our head technician and projectionist; he runs the scanner. It's a perfect fit, because he is threading film through the scanner and making sure it registers properly. He's also great at working with digital files. So he's in charge of that. The other two who are coming in are a collection manager and collection archivist. They are both working with physical collections, principally paper and films. These are new collections that have come in that need to be inspected and cataloged.

We are also able to bring certain materials from some special collections home. I contribute to some of the work on those collections. I have a few boxes of Anne Robertson's papers here now. This is important work that can be done safely from home. I only go into the office to retrieve books every now and then, when nobody else is there and with clearance.

VD: This has been since March? As you said earlier, you shut down at spring break, and there is no mixed-mode or "blended" teaching?

HG: Teaching in the spring semester was 100 percent virtual. There are exceptions— certain science classes in labs, and some studio courses, for example, where students and faculty require access to specialized spaces and equipment. In the spring, there was also a small group of international students who couldn't travel home, and there were also some students who didn't have an environment at home where they would be able to study. So there was a small population of students who were on campus, but that was a restricted place in terms of where they could go. In fall 2020, a larger population came back, including all the freshmen. In spring 2021 semester, seniors and juniors were allowed to return to campus, as well as some others. Those students here now have limited access to spaces, outside of their dorms, but there are very few faculty members coming back onto campus, just as there are staff working and within the

libraries, and within the science labs. In terms of teaching, it is all virtual and it's all on Zoom. You know what that is like. It has more pluses than I had realized, but at the same time, it's not the same for teaching. I'm teaching Harvard's introductory film class, and there's so much I would love to screen. I would have screened so much more experimental cinema, and I would have used film prints. It would have been amazing, immersive, and impactful. I'm doing my best, but there are things that I do miss.

VD: You can use your collection in your teaching?

HG: Oh, yes, that is a great reward and benefit of the HFA's incredible collection. The main AFVS classroom is in fact the HFA theater, and film prints are projected regularly for classes. These are distinct from our public screenings and are treated like research screening—they are not publicized. The HFA collection makes possible the teaching and study of film as film, allowing students to watch films in their original format, be it an original 35mm Technicolor release print or a hand-painted 16mm print. Or a silent film with live musical accompaniment. I was teaching a Hitchcock class last spring. When we started it, there was an HFA silent Hitchcock program running at the same time. It's planned so students could experience Hitchcock's silent films with live music.

VD: I saw that. I am so envious.

HG: It was great. All of the class screenings were on 35mm. I can't remember the last film we saw, maybe it was *Rebecca*. It was painful scheduling *The Birds* to watch online. But such is life. And I really can't complain too much.

VD: They are lucky students. I noticed that you have teaching showcases online. Is that internal to your teaching? There are artist films, student films, home movies, and documentaries, as well as shorts mentioned.

HG: We're trying to think of different ways to encourage scholars and teachers to use database collections. Home movies, for instance, are really interesting and important as teaching resources. But often these are overlooked. We're trying to do more outreach to individual faculty and to encourage them to use these different kinds of collections for their classes. That's what those teaching showcases are for. But we continue to think about better ways to do that. One interesting project that we have been doing is to work with a number of artists who have research-based practices and work with film. That has been really fascinating. In the case of one artist, Christopher Harris, he is working on a film that involves rephotographing film prints and manipulating them in various ways, a found footage film. Because we have been doing a big deaccessioning program, we were able to give him some prints that have deteriorated such that they cannot be projected but still have excellent imagery. It has been so great to give a second and last life to these materials.

We're trying to think of different ways to bring people into the collection and give them unfettered access.

VD: I wish I was teaching my courses through your institution! This development of on-line resources goes back to what you were saying initially, about how lucky you were to develop your online presence around the time of coronavirus emerging.

HG: The new HFA website went live earlier, we actually won a Webby Award for design.

VD: I saw that. I wanted to ask about this. You won the "cultural institution" category in 2020.

HG: Yes, and it was against the Rock and Roll Hall of Fame, MoMA, among others!

VD: It is a beautiful design.

HG: We're really lucky because my good colleague Brittany Gravely, who is our publicist, is also a hugely talented artist. She is both a filmmaker and also a self-taught designer who does all of our publicity material, including posters and our printed calendar. She led the design conversation, working with an interesting design team based in Warsaw called Huncwot.[1] I joined them at the beginning, and it was very exciting to watch it come into being. What is important about the HFA website is not just design but its functionality. The website is designed to showcase collections that are unique to Harvard, that are significant and worthy of further study. We want to synergize our collections, to help discovery of connections between them. We also want to encourage new research and scholarship, especially of certain collections—like the films of James E. Hinton—about which very little has been written. In that case, we have been doing outreach to our colleagues in the history department, and the African American studies department, to see if we can find a junior or senior scholar who would be interested in working with us on this. And that's just one example.

VD: That's great. That speaks to your unique position, in terms of bridging academic, scholarly work with archival work.

HG: Absolutely. The archive is this tremendous resource, and we want it to be fully appreciated and used as dynamically as possible. At the same time, we also want to learn what we can from the experts around us. You learn so much from researchers who approach collections with a new set of eyes, a new, unique perspective that often cuts a unique cross section across collections. You start making connections and discoveries that can be really important. I think that this is one of the great benefits of the university film archive. It's able to draw from different energies and synergies.

I should also say that I think the work of the curator is really important as a position and a profession that bridges academia as well as creative artistic practice. I think that it's also something that is underappreciated, as such. I'm part of an initiative now under way at Harvard to create a place for curatorial practice within the academy.

VD: That's a great idea.

HG: I think it is vitally important.

VD: You're right. It's a capacity to bring together disparate—or even similar—objects and to make the case for the significance and relevance of these in creative terms.

HG: Absolutely. In some ways, teaching is a mode of curating. You know, when you think of your syllabus, and you make arguments, that's a kind of programming, it is a kind of curating. That's one of the reasons I find this job endlessly stimulating. I feel like I'm constantly overstimulated, and it's just so great. I feel like sometimes, in academic studies, there's a kind of territoriality where there is pressure to publish and then to be an expert in a certain defined area, a delimited part of a field. There are of course many exceptions to this. But I feel like, in general, academia fosters microclimates of intense specialization, where people can't really talk to one another. I feel that cinema is so much more than that. It's more than a collection or a single topic.

I find that curatorial work can allow you to think more broadly, more openly, about cinema and film history, and I find that really exciting. I hope this excitement and insight of a generalist and collection can benefit the university as a whole.

VD: When I looked at the Harvard Film Archive online, you do get this sense of excitement. It is a bit of a candy store. For me, it was honestly thrilling to look at what you hold. I'm not just saying that because I know you and I like you. I'm saying that because your collection really opens my eyes and makes me aware of what's available as a film scholar, as a teacher, and as someone interested in archives. When I was looking through your collections, I thought that they did not all match. And that's what I liked. It was genuinely interesting. The other thing I realized, when I clicked on some of the showcases, is that you are unique and interesting because you obviously focus internally, within Harvard, to promote teaching and pedagogy, but also externally, to show the world what you have. You've got a fine balance there, which I found encouraging as someone who teaches film and also likes archives.

HG: Thank you for saying that. I would love us to be even more connected globally with a larger community. This kind of global public outreach is a larger mission for the Harvard libraries as well. I'd like to think that we're at the forefront of this. But there's a lot more to do. There really is.

We're learning a lot now, in terms of how to connect globally with this larger community that we're talking about, as well as how to think about digital collections and virtual access. We've been forced to rethink that. That said, it's also equally important that we maintain, when we can, our Cinematheque screenings, our classroom screenings, and that we don't just preserve film but the film experience. We don't want to dilute that or change that. Because the film experience is so vital for teaching and learning and fostering a deep, ongoing mode of engaged cinephilia.

That's a very important goal. On campus, we sit next to the Harvard Art Museums, which is a world-class collection of paintings, sculpture, and all kinds of art. That's where you can see the original [artwork]. When you study a painting, it is important you understand its texture and the touch and direction of the brushstrokes. There is something equivalent when you are studying film designed to be seen on the big screen, even digital cinema. The pandemic has only reinforced just how essential but also difficult it has become to attend a live screening. We had long taken it for granted, and now we are being reminded that watching film requires a certain discipline. Many assume it's easy to watch films at home, now so much is available streaming, but in fact it can be very difficult. Objects speak to you and distract you: this coffee cup insists you want another cup of coffee, the cat comes in and demands attention, and so on. You are constantly being pulled away and reminded of everyday demands. It's very hard. That's one of the reasons why watching film in the theater can be so powerful and can open up the revelatory dimensions of cinema. I think that for younger audiences, those who are learning to watch film, it's so important that they do that in the right space, and ideally with access to an archival collection.

VD: That's good to hear. I just was asked why I want my screenings physically on campus in my class next trimester. I was like, how do I teach film history if the students have no recollection, or no sense, of sitting in an audience? I'm teaching twentieth-century film, and I'm allowed two screenings on campus.

HG: What are you going to screen?

VD: That's what I've got to think about! What are the two films that I should screen? Next trimester is the first time that students will be allowed on campus for around a year. I understand that teaching designs have shifted and everything is online, but it's really reassuring and reaffirming to hear you talk about being in the vicinity of the art and sculpture [in the Harvard Art Museums] and also the importance of screening original film prints. It is important for the younger generation to understand that, and to see that, and to have that as a value.

HG: It's strange to be teaching now because there's a rich body of film that I just can't even draw from because nothing is available. Streaming from YouTube for a class can be such a disservice to a film on so many levels. It's like trying to read a book that's been xeroxed upside down, and trying to read it on a subway or in the rain. It's not the way to experience films intended for a theatrical setting, or even (and perhaps especially) experimental work meant to be seen projected in special situations (silent and/or at an alternate frame rate, for example). It is an argument you just have to continue to make. But you also have to teach whatever the circumstances, and you have to teach thoughtfully, which includes the importance of seeing film as an experience that has certain needs and requirements. Film is not something to be consumed however *you* want; you have to listen to it, understand what it needs. Anybody who studies architecture understands that if you haven't seen the building, been inside it, walked around it, understood how sound and light work in and upon the building's surfaces, then you don't yet understand that building. Looking at a photograph of it doesn't do justice to dimensionality, experiential qualities. And the same is true of so many films that are not experienced in the correct circumstances.

VD: Looking forward, do you think that there will still be a focus on the human-centric—or whatever you might call it—value of film? Do you worry about this?

HG: In terms of Harvard, I don't worry about this institutionally. Because the human-centric, as you call it, is true for so many things here. I don't mean to equate them, but, for instance, take athletics. It's really essential for many students, for their learning, and for college life and culture in general. And so athletics *will* return, because it is recognized as important. It hasn't been able to happen now, but it will. So, too, will theater, and all the different kinds of performing arts, including dance. And the Harvard Art Museums and other museums will open. And our Cinematheque program will begin again. My prediction is that the HFA public screenings will not begin again until the calendar year 2022, and then will begin gradually. I think there's going to be a period where there may be some hesitation or nervousness about being in a theater. We will need to rebuild our audience.

We also still have some work to do before we can welcome back a full house for our screenings. We have been reviewing and selectively renewing heating, ventilation, and air-conditioning systems to create better airflow, which is badly needed, I have to say. Our building is from the early sixties, so that's a really good change. But no, the human-centric, the live experience, the in-person screening with the filmmaker remains absolutely crucial to our mission. I predict that the pace of the Cinematheque in general will change. In recent years, we often welcomed up to forty different filmmakers a year in the HFA. It was extraordinary. But it's going to take a while for us to return to such a fast pace. In fact, I wonder whether we ever will. I feel like this whole experience has allowed us to rethink what our values are and what's important. We met last in Bologna, and I love film festivals, I really do. But part of me doesn't miss that hectic pace, rushing from film to film, gorging on cinema. It's not natural to watch eight films in a day, which I would push myself to do. I would watch five to eight films a day for, like, ten days. I feel the same way about art fairs which drive you to exhaustion, not the best state of mind to experience difficult art. Maybe there will be fewer festivals at the end of it all. And maybe that will be a good thing, a way to give a space for slightly more reasonably paced and sized events, human-centric events. I hope we as a community can reflect on this before returning to something proximate to the previous "normal."

VD: I agree. I think it's interesting that we began our conversation with you talking about flying back to Harvard from a film festival. Now we are ending our discussion with the question of returning to the film festival experience. We don't know when the film festival experience will again be available to us and what we mean by a return to this. Thank you, Haden, for your time and comments. It has been a pleasure to learn more about your work in the Harvard Film Archive.

Victoria Duckett is associate professor in screen at Deakin University, Melbourne. Author of the award-winning book *Seeing Sarah Bernhardt: Performance and Silent Screen* (2016), she has published extensively on actresses, archives, and early film. Her forthcoming monograph is titled *Transnational Trailblazers of Early Cinema: Sarah Bernhardt, Gabrielle Réjane, Mistinguett.*

NOTE

1. See https://www.awwwards.com/case-study -harvard-film-archive-by-huncwot.html.

REVIEWSREVIEWS

Book

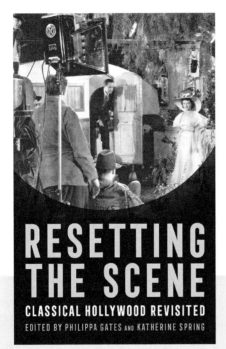

Resetting the Scene: Classical Hollywood Revisited
EDITED BY PHILIPPA GATES AND
KATHERINE SPRING
WAYNE STATE UNIVERSITY PRESS, 2021

Mandy Elliott

To a scholar of classical Hollywood cinema, the title *Resetting the Scene: Classical Hollywood Revisited* is at once exciting and nerve-racking. After all, the prospect of "revisiting" beloved, yet increasingly fragmented, subject matter has the potential to disappoint by rehashing previous scholarship or to elate with new and necessary approaches.

Thankfully, *Resetting the Scene* decidedly invigorates classical Hollywood studies.

Editors Philippa Gates and Katherine Spring have put together a remarkable collection of essays that not only present new ways of exploring and understanding the effects of classical cinema on audiences and scholars alike but argue for its ongoing relevance and the need for continued scholarship. The book reads as a survey of recent academic research and moves from close readings of style to elements of production to topics of race and gender to the poststudio era and new approaches. Moreover, essays by David Bordwell and Janet Staiger—the coauthors with Kristin Thompson of *The Classical Hollywood Cinema: Film Style and Mode of Production to 1960,* the urtext of classical Hollywood studies—demonstrate the book's through line of reverence for past scholarship and excitement to build on it. As a result, *Resetting the Scene* affirms not only the study of classical Hollywood but interest in its accessibility to a contemporary audience, ensuring that the field of classical Hollywood scholarship remains evergreen.

The result of a 2018 conference titled "Classical Hollywood Studies in the 21st Century," the book considers various innovative approaches to classical cinema organized into eight sections, each of which blends issues of aesthetics, labor, economics, history, and intellectual trends of contemporary cinema studies. The essays are short yet concise, which aids in the book's remarkable readability and inclusion of such a wide range of interests.

In a stand-alone essay composing section I, "Setting the Scene," David Bordwell reflects on *The Classical Hollywood Cinema* before addressing classical cinema studies after 1960, alternatives to the continuity style, and classical contributions to narrative tradition. Bordwell advocates the tracking of continuity and change in contemporary cinema, noting that while general narrative schemas seen in classical cinema have become more flexible, they have also remained surprisingly consistent.

Bordwell's essay ushers in several innovative reflections on classical films and practices found in the book's remaining sections. In section II, "Film Style and Practice," Scott Higgins discusses the "Minnelli swirl," a compositional technique in Vincente Minnelli's musicals that he connects to artistic virtuosity and narrative depth; Kathryn Kalinak discusses the common practice of Hollywood film composers appropriating their own work when warranted by the narrative; and Chris Cagle's essay, "Hollywood Mannerism," highlights classical Hollywood's stylistic tendencies, such as lighting, editing, and camera movement, and how they serve the narrative and exemplify the era.

In section III, "Classical Genres," Katherine Spring points out the genre history of 1950s integrated musicals and notes the terminological slippage in the early days of the genre to suss out categorization and promotion. Steven Cohan then tackles the back-studio picture as exemplified by A Star Is Born (1937) and Hollywood's self-reflexive efforts of rose-tinged transparency. Blair Davis rounds out the section in a study of the origins of science fiction films and the importance of B filmmaking to cementing sci-fi in the cinematic firmament.

Charlie Keil and Denise McKenna begin section IV, "Studio Labor and Operations," by discussing Hollywood as a physical place in which cinema could ground itself and the crucial collaboration between the establishment of Hollywood as an industry stronghold and classicism's inception. In "Disney, Dupont, and Faber Birren: Hollywood and the Color Revolution," Kirsten Moana Thompson links animated color and industrial modernity by noting the relationships between the rich, synthetic pigments for which Disney was known and Disney's business with DuPont. Kyle Edwards discusses B film production by examining 1930s Warner Bros. film series and the Warners' ability to use B movies to mitigate risk and increase production. Bradley Schauer rounds out the section by discussing the life span and missteps of Universal-International's Talent Development Program.

The essays of section V, which discuss classical Hollywood's experiences and depictions of race, are particularly noteworthy. Philippa Gates considers Chinese Americans, the Production Code Administration (PCA), and the reasons behind the racialized images of Chinese Americans on-screen. Gates's argument that the PCA was motivated by commercial protectionism rather than social progressivism to avoid racist representations emphasizes the importance of studying Hollywood's treatment of racialized bodies. Ryan Jay Friedman then offers an examination of the African American specialty number and the racial roots of "excess," seen specifically in Lena Horne's performance in Broadway Rhythm (1944) and its striking diversion from the film's narrative. Friedman compellingly claims that these aesthetic contributions connect classical Hollywood to Russian formalism. In "Dark Desires and White Obsessions: Sam McDaniel as a Marker of Blackness in Double Indemnity (1944) and Ice Palace (1960)," Charlene Regester argues for actor Sam McDaniel's Blackness as a control measure for White characters' perceived approximation to moral Blackness through their villainy. To Regester, McDaniel provides a common Black presence in both films that allows for the "darkening" of White protagonists through composition, lighting, and general othering. Barry Keith Grant follows with "Incursions in the Forbidden Zone: Genre and the Black Science Fiction Film." He argues that films like The World, the Flesh, and the Devil (1959) and The Meteor Man (1993) use the conventions of the classical Hollywood science fiction film to address Black experiences in place of the traditional exploration of outer space.

In section VI, the book features persuasive arguments about women's agency and contributions to classical cinema. In "Doing Her Bit: Women and Propaganda in World War I," Liz Clarke explains forms of gender representation during the early classical period and notes that stars like Mary Pickford, Mabel Normand, and Lillian Gish were able to increase their following by promoting American nationalism and demonstrating women's adeptness at playing war heroes. Helen Hanson writes about gender, genre, and MGM's Arthur Freed Unit and details the roles of those working "above and below the line" (referring to elite moviemakers and anonymous movie workers, respectively), noting that women occupied many of the below-the-line roles. Hanson focuses particularly on Lela Simone, "the girl for everything," who served as Freed's music coordinator during 1944–57. Finally, Will Scheibel looks at classical star Gene Tierney and the ways in which her professional life opened doors for women, while her poor mental health prompted the doubling down of expectations that women work through illness and blur boundaries between their personal and professional lives.

Section VII, "Classicism after the Studio Era," explores classical Hollywood's legacy. Tino Balio discusses landmarks in MGM's decline as a major studio, and Lisa Dombrowski argues that scholars should rethink the idea that director Robert Altman's work is uniquely anticlassical given his alleged resistance to classical conventions. Using *The Gingerbread Man* (1998) and *Gosford Park* (2001) as primary sources, Dombrowski highlights the importance of collaboration and the use of classical techniques to better structure and clarify their respective narratives. Janet Staiger ends the section in a piece on the difficulty of screenwriting in the package-unit era and reflects on what she sees as an industry paradox: that an aspiring screenwriter needs to rigidly adhere to the industry's rules to be considered professional and, at the same time, manipulate standard narrative style.

The book's final section, "New Approaches," underscores the rhizomatic areas of study regarding classical Hollywood. Eric Hoyt discusses the importance of trade papers and their participation in creating Hollywood as a cultural touchstone. Hoyt also examines Tamar Lane's vision of a more artistic film industry and argues that distributors like A24 and fan sites like Indiewire have taken up that mantle. Patrick Keating's "The Video Essay and Classical Hollywood Studies" explores the use of the video essay as a new and refreshing way to study classical cinema in more personal and creative ways. Paul Monticone then analyzes modes of production and classical Hollywood in contemporary media studies, noting Bordwell, Staiger, and Thompson's work and the ways in which it has influenced and reinvigorated recent classical scholarship; Charles Acland's and Haidee Wasson's contributions to historical analysis; and Richard Maltby's work on audiences and their consumption of movie culture. Monticone claims that, far from being passé, classical cinema studies is alive and well and rife with scholarly avenues to explore. Finally, Richard Maltby breaks down his understanding of "new cinema history" and reminds us that there is yet much unexplored ground to study regarding the American motion picture industry's legal and legislative history and that classical Hollywood scholars must lead this scholarship.

Resetting the Scene boasts impressive scholarly work on a variety of topics, and it does so clearly and concisely. What's more, although a few of the essays cater to seasoned scholars of classical Hollywood, many have the potential to engage classical Hollywood fans beyond the ivory tower and into the realm of public scholarship.

Mandy Elliott is an assistant professor of English and film studies at Booth University College in Winnipeg, Manitoba, Canada. Her scholarly interests include issues of gender performance, sexuality, and war in classical Hollywood cinema.

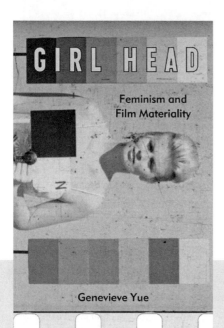

Girl Head: Feminism and Film Materiality

By Genevieve Yue

Fordham University Press, 2020

Patricia Ledesma Villon

Archivists, curators, projectionists, celluloid filmmakers, and their respective institutions contribute to each other's structures and functions as they interact within the field and rely on the presence of one another for the continued existence of their practices. Operating in tandem with the exhibition context, within this social economy of film exists three central sites of exchange: the film laboratory, the editing room, and the film archive. However, looking beyond them, one can find figures in the margins of their industrial conditions—the anonymous feminine figure at the start of the reel, otherwise known as the China Girl.

Genevieve Yue's *Girl Head: Feminism and Film Materiality* challenges our innocent reliance on these locales as cherished assets to cultural heritage and dives into what is otherwise invisible, gendered labor embedded within their practices. Yue, an associate professor of culture and media and director of the screen studies program at the New School, brings a new focus to film preservation by investigating and critiquing the three aforementioned sites and their contributions to film techniques and mechanisms. By retelling, highlighting, and conducting meticulous research across the field, Yue's insight is an invaluable contribution to contemporary film and media scholarship.

The concept of the China Girl unites the three sites and builds a rich foundation for Yue's investigations. China Girls, sometimes referred to as "leader ladies"—a name with less racial connotations, yet still gendered in focus—establish themselves as an omnipresent existence across all three of the aforementioned industries. Chapter 1 builds and expands on the core questions of Yue's research as she outlines a brief history of the China Girl and its role during the rise of various color motion picture processes, such as Technicolor and Eastmancolor. The China Girl's labor contributes the most within a film's core site of visuality: the correction of the image's hues as conducted by the film laboratory color timer. Here she poses as the color for timing reference and becomes a major figure in the development of a work. Yet, readers come to realize that her ubiquity within the industry is not to be wholly accepted. There is an ongoing need to question the presence of the China Girl and her silent communication with those who witness her.

However, while she is spliced alongside a feature film and lives with the film in a can, the China Girl is strictly utility. In the words of Yue, "the China Girl is a condition of industrial production, rather than a 'film' in its own right" (36). The China Girl is connected to the film leader and useful for processes of creativity and fabrication yet is intended to vanish from the final product and its display. She is dubbed merely an "accident" if the work of the projectionist reveals her frames—often flashing by on the screen for less than a second—to an audience. Introduced to the social economy as a visible object, she is soon rendered invisible by practice.

Yue does not limit herself to celluloid methods within her examinations. Chapter 2's "Gone Girl of Escamontage" juxtaposes Alfred Clark's *The Execution of Mary, Queen of Scots* (1895) with David Fincher's 2014 film *Gone Girl* to extend her investigation into the editing room and the digital realm. The splice in *Mary, Queen of Scots,* being the earliest known to film historians, plays a key point of discussion in the chapter and highlights Yue's definition of escamontage. By "creating meaning through the act of concealment" (75), escamontage transcends the notions of visual effects and continuity and is transformed by digital practice, notably in Fincher's *Gone Girl,* where "the vanishing woman's body is both thematized and integrated as part of a production process" (79). The transition into digital editing may estrange readers drawn to Yue's book with interests in celluloid film and its relation to materiality; however, it is the ideology applied to the digital medium not only serving as a platform for branching out but strengthening the applications of Yue's work.

The final chapter of *Girl Head* ends with a discussion on the film archive and Jacques Derrida's use of Sigmund Freud's understanding of Wilhelm Jensen's *Gradiva* in *Archive Fever.* The quest for *Gradiva* functions as an origin story for the archive per Yue's discussion as the need for knowing and seeking manifests into archival desire. She expands on Cheryl Dunye's film *The Watermelon Woman* (1996) and the main character's search for the fictional Fae Richards in the historical record as one of her many examples illustrating a Gradivan model. Connecting dreams with the material world, the film archive itself was born on the acknowledgment of loss, illustrating a motivation connecting desire to the field at large. Although Yue refers to archival scholars in her work, such as Terry Cook, Michelle Caswell, and many others theorizing about the archive throughout history, she argues that archival scholarship has lacked a self-reflexive approach and is instead more concerned with how archives have been conceived. She concludes that her aim is to focus on "a gendered logic of materiality" (105) and how it has sustained the archive—a discussion she finds many before her have lacked.

Girl Head provides a new approach to our understanding of film, its practices, and what it means to create and preserve by blending analysis on a range of film and media practitioners. Parts of the book also focus on artist-made films as shorter case studies, such as Barbara Hammer's *Sanctus* (1990) and Jennifer Montgomery's *Transitional Objects* (1999), and include a rich color section of "leader ladies"

and film frames to visually refer to while reading. With its multifaceted approach, Yue's work is able to bridge a range of audiences: film scholars, film archivists, filmmakers, and anyone else interested in the history and practice of film and celluloid. She notably thanks a wide range of recognizable industry names, cultural heritage organizations, and experimental/avant-garde filmmakers in the book credits for aiding her work, such as DuArt, Fotokem, Kodak, the Society of Motion Picture and Television Engineers, the Chicago Film Society, the Library of Congress, the George Eastman Museum, filmmaker Phil Solomon, and filmmaker and preservationist Mark Toscano, among a wealth of many other esteemed institutions operating with film in the past or to this day.

Yue's academic text connects fiction, non-fiction, gender and sexuality studies, and film theory, making it a unique and accessible angle for interested readers of various disciplines. Although the three chapters serve as the main pillars of the work, readers can approach these sections of *Girl Head* as distinct essays after reading Yue's introduction and still find plenty of value in the writing. When read together in chronological order, the chapters map three compelling avenues of film technicality and its relationship to notions of gender by following the life trajectory of a film from the laboratory to the archive. Industry practice and its choice of actions are not separate from film and media studies but can shape their greater intellectual trajectory and play stronger roles of influence. It is its focus on materiality and its intersections with film technicality from an outside yet still very adjacent perspective that makes Yue's writing a valuable insight on an overlooked topic of film and archival scholarship.

Before *Girl Head,* we wondered, what does it mean to represent on the screen, and what challenges do we face in achieving inclusion? Groundbreaking feminist film theory, such as the work of Laura Mulvey, taught us about the gaze, yet it is time to extend beyond meanings of diversity and observation within media discourse. Yue states in response to these feminist analyses that "the China Girl is a challenge to a scholarly emphasis on representation because it presents a different relationship between the film image and gender than the one such an emphasis presumes" (3). In doing so, her work forges a new feminist film scholarship transforming meaning beyond the frame. Perhaps it is those not formally trained in the social economy of film preservation who may have the most well-suited vantage points to generate refreshing reflections on the moving image archive and its related fields.

Patricia Ledesma Villon is the Bentson Archivist and assistant curator in the moving image department of the Walker Art Center. She is a graduate of the University of California, Los Angeles's master of library and information science program, specializing in media archival studies, and is a coprogrammer for *Light Field,* an international exhibition of recent and historical experimental moving image art on celluloid in the San Francisco Bay Area. She currently serves on the board of directors of Canyon Cinema and as a cochair of the Small Gauge and Amateur Film Committee of the Association of Moving Image Archivists.

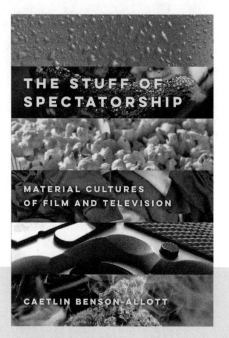

The Stuff of Spectatorship: Material Cultures of Film and Television
By Caetlin Benson-Allott
University of California Press, 2021

Suryansu Guha

In *The Stuff of Spectatorship,* Caetlin Benson-Allott analyzes the material means through which media are often experienced and consumed—literally the "stuff" or "the commodities and comestibles that surround viewers" (2). What this essentially means is that she looks at a diverse array of material objects and their ensembles, including television programming catalogs, the commercial packaging of DVDs and Blu-rays, branded merchandise, and even the consumption of alcohol and marijuana in movie theaters. One can question how these diverse material objects of consumption relate to each other or what they have in common so as to have their histories written in the same book. I would argue that the material objects (like DVD covers) or the ensemble of objects (like movie theaters and alcohol) are united by their understated importance to consumer rituals. This is part of what makes this research project so complex and yet so compelling. Though this "heterogenous mix of case studies" (249) is sometimes part of a greater continuity (like popcorn, alcohol, or even weed as constitutive of inhibited viewing experience), sometimes they have their own histories separate from the other case studies. For instance, the fifth chapter centers around case studies of violence in cinemas, which does not share a lot in common with material objects and consumption. But the organizing rationale has something to do with their centrality of significance to how audiences want to watch or consume media content or the ideological lenses that inform what they watch.

Benson-Allott herself addresses this seeming discontinuity between the foci of her analysis, stating that "the book's eclecticism is meant to demonstrate the breadth of material objects influencing film and television reception, which exceed the materials of its production and distribution" (14). She constructs the history of these material habits of consumption or the stuff of spectatorship, simultaneously bringing out the ontological significance of these nonhuman objects in conditioning viewers' responses to film and television. The thread that connects these individual chapters dealing with diverse sets of human and nonhuman objects is the idea that the culture of contemporary film and television spectatorship is inextricable from the material culture through which film and television are experienced. Benson-Allott further argues that these material objects, which are often taken for granted by consumers and invisible to critical enquiry, are an extension of the cinematic apparatus (something that has, in fact, been a subject of critical scrutiny in earlier decades). Expanding on the existing work of apparatus theory, her work simultaneously draws from four critical traditions—media industry studies, reception studies, new cinema history, and materiality/material culture. In the same way that her work is informed by a diverse range of subfields within media studies, her methodology consists of close textual, archival, and oral historical methods.

In her first chapter, for instance, Benson-Allott looks at how the packaging of physical media, such as DVDs and Blu-rays, influences our relationships with shows, films, and genres. Her case study of *Battlestar Galactica—The Video* illustrates the way DVD or VHS packaging can act as a form of remediation. *Battlestar Galactica—The Video* was released in 1985 by MCA Home Video as a stand-alone product and was not marketed as part of a serial narrative. Benson-Allott goes on to effectively demonstrate how the VHS box art disavows and "actively conceals its televisuality" (39). A close textual reading of the VHS packaging design reveals attributes like the Universal logo or the placement of the name of Academy Award winner John Dykstra to show us how the creators wanted to promote it in a specific way. According to her, the distributors did not want to sell *Battlestar Galactica—The Video* to fans of *Battlestar Galactica* the television series, nor were they interested in having it be understood as part of a larger continuum of the Battlestar Galactica universe. Rather, they wanted it to be promoted as an autonomous product in the same vein of blockbuster sci-fi action film franchises like Star Wars. This is one of the ways in which the design and packaging of box sets and VHS covers "encourage reparative reading of the televisual season as an object discrete from outside histories" (49) and how prerecorded video can often reinterpret television history to serve the commercial interests of the distributors.

If the material conditions of a film and television show's emergence and continued presence are the key ideas in the first chapter, Benson-Allott devotes her second chapter to the idea of the obsolescence (planned and otherwise) of filmic media. She takes up the case study of Richard Brooks's 1977 film *Looking for Mr. Goodbar* and tries to reevaluate her own position as a film historian with respect to the film and its "disappearance," meaning its lack of availability on disc or through streaming services. This chapter is not so much a commentary on general spectatorship as much as it is a reflexive commentary on humanities scholars' motivations to historicize some objects over others. She invokes Eve Kosofsky Sedgwick to address the fact that often humanities scholars have a predisposition toward affirming their own pessimistic suspicions. However, like an adept reparative reader, she shows how the circulation of the film has stopped because of purely commercial reasons, arguing that "all possible scenarios suggest that the film is not being deliberately suppressed" (73). But it is this state of disappearing and its entry into what Benson-Allott calls the "abject archive" that now condition its reception. "The power of *Looking for Mr. Goodbar* now emerges in part from its abjection, from the very economy of scarcity that limits viewers' access to it" (93).

Benson-Allott's third chapter looks at how Turner Classic Movies (TCM) transformed classical Hollywood movie watching on television into a lifestyle in the 1990s. Through a curatorial emphasis on taste making, cinema tourism, branded cinephilia, and merchandising, Benson-Allott shows how "TCM organized a new psychic relationship of viewer to screen, a new mode of cinematic interpellation" (132). Chapters 4 and 5, meanwhile, look at the idea of inebriated spectatorship and attend to its concomitant class and ethnic anxieties. The history of adult concessions chronicled in chapter 4 shows how James and John Duffy, who opened the Cinema 'N' Drafthouse, a second-run theater outside Orlando, Florida, in September 1975, got the idea from the illicit practice of cinematic drinking and the culture of "sneaking in" six-packs at drive-ins. Although this was a second-run theater pub, Benson-Allott talks about how it helped "demystify the ordinary pleasures of moviegoing and reintegrate alcohol into US cinema culture" (149). The "big three" theater chains—AMC, Regal, and Cinemark—were still slower to adopt alcohol services. AMC lobbied for and introduced alcohol to target Latinx moviegoers, whom it believed "spend more money on food and drink than other ethnic groups" (167). Chapter 5 similarly looks at inebriated spectatorship in the context of television and cannabis. Both chapters, drawing on racial and ethnic complexities, show how sobriety and intoxication "are not universal categories but social constructs that help enforce other ideologies" (213).

Benson-Allott's final chapter is an exploration of how actual incidents of violence in movie theaters condition the reception of certain films, specifically films about Black men. She takes up the case study of "cinema violence" during the exhibition of John Singleton's 1992 film *Boyz n the Hood,* along with numerous other case studies, and shows how it "shapes viewers' perceptions of movies, their makers, and their audiences, not because of the material violence itself but because of how the press represents that violence" (247). Benson-Allot shows how the overall audience perception of *Boyz n the Hood* was dramatically transformed because of the incidents of violence that took place during its screening in theaters. The book opens up several avenues of investigation and shows how taking the material culture route in film historiography and textual analysis can answer several questions and provide a platform for new ones.

There are several directions in which further research could build on the foundation that Benson-Allott crafted in this volume. Each of the material histories that she maps out in her five chapters could lead to expanded research projects on its own, in the direction of both reception studies and production studies. For instance, building on her work on the history of adult concessions and alcohol in movie theaters, one could ask how the history of adult concessions impacted studios' assessment of viewers? Could it have in any way impacted how some films were made or even what films were made, like how she documents Netflix's launch of the series *Disjointed* (2017–18) in her fifth chapter? Perhaps most importantly, what makes this work significant is the fact that such a lens of studying film history and production through material conditions is inevitable after the Covid-19 pandemic, which is something she duly acknowledges in her coda. Besides opening up newer avenues of investigation and critical inquiry, Benson-Allott's *The Stuff of Spectatorship* is a rich sourcebook of historical information about material histories that are so easily brushed aside, taken for granted, forgotten, and made invisible. Its importance lies in its making visible the several conduits of reception that structure our responses, critical and otherwise, to a filmic text.

Suryansu Guha is a PhD student from India in the Department of Film, Television, and Digital Media at UCLA. His areas of interest are media industries studies; precarious labor; media, science, and technology; and the philosophy of humor. He holds a master's degree in English literature and critical theory from Jawaharlal Nehru University in India.

GLOBAL
PERSPECTIVES
on AMATEUR FILM
HISTORIES and
CULTURES

Edited by **Masha Salazkina**
and **Enrique Fibla-Gutiérrez**

Global Perspectives on Amateur Film Histories and Cultures

Edited by Masha Salazkina and Enrique Fibla-Gutiérrez

Indiana University Press, 2020

Gaurav Pai

Masha Salazkina and Enrique Fibla-Gutiérrez's ambitious new edited volume, *Global Perspectives on Amateur Film Histories and Cultures,* builds on the stellar work by their colleagues at Concordia University, Haidee Wasson and Charles Acland, in the service of advancing the cause of nontheatrical and amateur film. The philosophy of the Concordia school of film studies is clear: gently displace popular, commercial film, which has traditionally been at the center of film studies for more than sixty years. We could summarize the objectives of the book as answering questions in three broad directions: (1) What is the relation between amateur film practices and commercial film, avant-garde aesthetics, and "useful cinema"? (2) How should historical amateur production, traditionally associated with democratization

of media and a tool toward mobilization of the population, be contextualized in the backdrop of the state? and (3) How can we conceptualize film and media history away from the European and North American scenarios as the central axes of reference? The answers to these questions seem to be the following:

1. The "spaces, networks, and institutions" of amateur cinema absorbed and reflected several other media practices, often constituting a "shared field with experimental productions, forms of political activism, and educational media" (6). This was different from its current entanglement in the dominant logic of digital media and neoliberalism.

2. The ideal of social mobilization through the democratization of media inherent in some conceptions of amateur film production is what gave rise to its rapid institutionalization and the involvement of the state in this process in many historical contexts (16). The state even co-opted the phenomenon on occasion.

3. We traditionally associate amateur film with wealthy dilettante filmmakers, but amateurism in older media was realized under multiple economic models of employment, circumstances, and wherewithal to create moving images. Furthermore, there existed circuits of sharing and viewing these films.

The collection of essays is divided into four sections: "Medium Specificity and Expanded Media Ecologies," "Institutions, Industry, and the State," "Politics of Legitimization and Subversion," and "Transnational Networks: Amateur Cinema Travels." This review, however, is organized under the three aforementioned questions to explore how the various contributors to the volume answer them individually. The message of the book is in line with the general manifesto of the Concordia school: the idea of great filmmakers making great films as the history of cinema needs some serious correction.

One could argue that the opposite of "useful cinema"—a Wasson and Acland concept—could be commercial cinema, where a viewer exchanges their monies in return for the undefinable experience of entertainment, the latter mostly translating as escapism or a moralistic "message." Then, the obvious question is whether we can also include modernist experimental and avant-garde film as contra useful cinema. We could argue that this category of film is more invested in the exploration of medium specificity and self-awareness. On the other hand, amateur film as a mode of production is plainly associated with pursuits other than that of profit, but that doesn't really explain its relationship to useful cinema. But as the Concordia school has often demonstrated, and this volume gives more corroborative evidence of, such taxonomy is fraught with foolhardy risk. For instance, James Rosenow's chapter on *The Lesson of Even—as You and I* (Roger Barlow, Harry Hay, and LeRoy Robbins, 1937) shows that the film highlighted its own amateurism (even as it is a film within a film) to veer toward what came subsequently to be known as modernism, even as it mimics a traditional Hollywood narrative structure, and where "(film) makers were comfortable enough to employ all cinematic modes of address" (60). Meanwhile, Yvonne Zimmermann analyzes filmic production of the Swiss company Sulzer, highlighting the blurred boundaries between amateur and professionally produced films as well as between "corporate home movies" and industrial films, alluding to the fact that amateur film also intersected with the universe of useful cinema. Mariano Mestman and Christopher Moore explore the amateur origins of Fernando Birri's Documentary School of Santa Fe founded in Argentina around 1956. The essay demonstrates how Birri relied on amateur *fotodocumentalista* methods that later became the model for Third Cinema and radical documentary in many parts of the world. In other words, amateur cinema should be seen as part of different modes of cinema, and the chapters in this edited volume combine to show that the sum is greater than the parts.

Global Perspectives presents nonprofessional film as a "creative practice that inhabits a liminal space between public and private spheres, state institutions and civic platforms, politics and leisure" (8). If this space was born out of negotiation between the various intermingling aesthetics and styles, then it was inevitable that amateur filmmakers would eventually run into the gaze of the state—or start off with an oppositional disposition to it. This could be subversion from the inside or explicit resistance, as examples from Vichy France and Francoist Spain reveal. Julie Guillaumot's essay documents the brave attempt to set up a state-controlled organization of amateur filmmaking in Vichy France that sought to reorganize the nascent amateur film movement in the country and document everyday life under Nazi occupation. Pablo La Parra-Pérez's chapter explores militant, radical, resistance filmmaking in the Francoist Long 1960s and highlights the need for further research and documentation of nonprofessional militant film practices in the post–World War II period. Resistance filmmaking could also take the form of circumventing restrictive state laws, as in the case of the *duli* (Chinese Independent Documentary) movement of the 1990s and 2000s, as demonstrated by Margherita Viviani's chapter. These films were not submitted to the Chinese state, famous for its censorship, and were therefore exhibited in noncommercial and unofficial venues, giving them a chance to record "changes in Chinese society, with a focus on marginalized groups or forgotten histories" (85). The most remarkable chapter, however—certainly written with the greatest flourish—is Laliv Melamed's, on Israeli military commemorative videos, where the home movie emerges as "a technique of self-formation and self-representation implemented by the state" (107). As she puts it, "while the state withholds its power through the rhetorical form of 'advice,' the freelance filmmaker emerges as a constellation of labor and creativity through which mourning is formed while acts of governance are privatized and rendered intimate" (106–7). Thus family video making becomes an extension of the apparatus of state power and regulation, turning upside down our conventional understandings.

The collection does a splendid job in charting the movement across geographies of amateur film in the twentieth century and the contexts that enabled (or forced) such a flow. For instance, Rachel Webb Jekanowski examines the contemporary collection of historical amateur Yiddish films held at the YIVO Institute for Jewish Research in New York City and underlines the "significance of amateur films as historical traces of vernacular Jewish life and Yiddish world-building, particularly at the cultural level . . . (of) Yiddishland, an ephemeral country held together by its shared *mamaloshen* (mother tongue) . . . (and the) negotiation of the vernacular within a postvernacular moment" (369). The examples of amateur film festivals in Tunisia (starting 1970) and Venezuela (1976–80) in chapters by Samhita Sunya and Isabel Arredondo, respectively, present fascinating histories of transnational networks of distribution and exhibition through which amateur film traveled. Finally, Maria Vinogradova showcases the international success of a Soviet amateur film, *A Gift to Mother* (Movshin, 1963), in the United Kingdom, Canada, and the United States at the height of the Cold War. As the last few essays recounted here illustrate, there existed substantial interactions between amateur film movements across borders, putting in sharp focus the internationalist spirit that pervaded amateur circles worldwide and their ability to connect with each other. It is impossible to fully represent all facets of a global phenomenon within the confines of a single edited volume, just as this reviewer only had space to address some of the book's eighteen chapters, but Salazkina and Fibla-Gutiérrez did an admirable job of bringing in varied cultural perspectives.

Amateur film studies is a relatively new field, although we already see the formation of a canon with the aforementioned work of Wasson and Acland; varied contributions from Charles Tepperman, Liz Czach, and Ryan Shand; an edited volume by Karen L. Ishizuka and Patricia Zimmermann; another by Laura Rascaroli, Gwenda Young, and Barry Monahan; and the seminal 2003 special issue of *Film History* on small-gauge and amateur cinema edited by Melinda Stone and Dan Streible, which is frequently cited in this volume. Having said that, one essay from the current volume that should enter the rapidly evolving canon is that by Benoît Turquety. This is the first essay in the collection, but indeed, it could serve as its conclusion. Turquety argues that amateur production decenters the spectator from traditional apparatus theory, which took shape in the 1970s. As he puts it, "if the cinematic apparatus is no longer centered on the spectator but on a user of machines, we will have to rethink the changes this movement brings about beyond the history of nonprofessional filmmaking devices" (39). Citing Tepperman and Michel de Certeau, Turquety argues that we should think of an amateur moviemaker as a craftsman and that "to be able to appreciate an amateur film, a scene, a gesture, a certain virtuosity in the highly coded art of selfies, food porn, or didactic films, one has to develop a sensitivity that may be closer to the assessment of technical objects or gestures than to classical high art" (42). This is probably true of new media, as well as old media, and functions as the long-standing message of the Concordia school of film studies.

Gaurav Pai is a PhD candidate in the Department of Cinema and Media Studies at the University of Washington in Seattle, where he studies and teaches media technologies and documentary, amateur, and nontheatrical film. He is writing his doctoral dissertation about small-gauge film technologies in Mexico prior to 1960.

Eugène Frey: Inventeur des célèbres décors lumineux à transformations du Théâtre de Monte-Carlo appliqués pour la première fois à l'Exposition universelle de Paris 1900
EDITED BY JOÃO MARIA GUSMÃO
NOUVEAU MUSÉE NATIONAL DE MONACO, 2020

Nico de Klerk

Eugène Frey is a lavishly illustrated, bilingual (French and English) exhibition catalog on the career of this Belgian painter, lanternist, and set designer (1846–1942). It was published on the occasion of a show of his innovative work at the Nouveau Musée National de Monaco, February 7–August 30, 2020. The many illustrations consist, on one hand, of a generous selection of his artwork and glass plates and, on the other, of a selective record of the imagery projected by the installations that Portuguese exhibition creators João Maria Gusmão and Pedro Paiva designed to both evoke and reflect on Frey's projections. The visuals are complemented by three essays and a story on

more or less relevant contexts of the exhibition and on Frey's work.

Work, of course, is a thorny term in this case. Obviously, the artistic legacy of Eugène Frey consists only partly of objects (brought together from a number of repositories) that can be seen directly, such as his studies in graphite, ink, gouache, photographs, and models as well as the paintings and painted glass plates used in shadow theater and sets in various other performing arts (variety, cabaret, dance, opera). But although he was a painter, and called himself such, Frey did more than design and paint these objects: he projected them too, either as stand-alone stories or as light sets *(décors lumineux),* notably at the 1900 Paris Exposition and at the operas of Paris and, most famously, Monte Carlo. There, for twenty years, he cooperated with chief set designer Alphonse Visconti. And although he was regarded by some as mere "chief electrician" (which he certainly was too), in realizing Visconti's designs, he combined his engineering skills and artistry to accomplish unprecedented visual screen spectacle.

However, apart even from the fact that some of these performing arts are extinct, reconstructions of these projections in situ, that is, in actual performances, would have been practically impossible and possibly disappointing after the lapse of a century. Still, today's set designers are indebted, wittingly or unwittingly, to Frey's accomplishments. His pioneering, electricity-based, changeable scenographies through light projection and superimposition predominantly define his legacy. In fact, Frey's legacy—his foresight ("un homme clairvoyant") and the significance of his light sets—was already noted at the time, the early twentieth century, for instance, in the cited reviews of French film and music critic Émile Vuillermoz. *Eugène Frey,* the exhibition and the book, mark the *re*-discovery of an artist and a theatrical projection practice.

At first sight, it may seem somewhat strange to read that a lanternist was called clairvoyant. After all, the emergence of film technology and the subsequent rise of a cinema industry all but eclipsed the popular lantern show in contemporary entertainment. These developments were nonetheless coincident with the high point of Frey's career at the Opéra de Monte-Carlo between 1904 and 1924, pointing up that a "progressive" or even a purposive perspective tends to overlook other, persistent manifestations of lantern culture—a tendency screen-based entertainment studies have not quite overcome yet. Besides Frey's career, one can point to the lantern's widespread educational use in the shape of the illustrated lecture, which continued well into the second half of the twentieth century. Conversely, whatever stuff the dreams and expectations of early twentieth-century entertainment practitioners were made of, a scenography by means of projection—what Loie Fuller had called the "theatre of light"—didn't necessarily need to be filmic. Indeed, stage design did not turn out to be a cinematographic growth industry.

As for Frey, Swiss film scholar Stéphane Tralongo argues in his essay that he "resisted" film. His approach, he writes, "was a way to reassert the artistic dimension of the elements of scenery." Or, in Frey's own words, taken from a lecture on February 20, 1925, in the Belgian town of Liège,

> light sets are paintings on glass, executed *by hand,* which are then projected through the transparent glass onto a white screen using powerful machines. The screen stands alone in a dark area, while the stage is lit by the usual devices, whose manner of use, or more precisely position, has been modified. (215, my emphasis)

The quote strengthens Tralongo's argument, partly based on this excerpt, that "the physical qualities of painting [were] reinforced by the co-presence on stage of pictures projected on a 'screen' and painted scenery mounted on 'frames.'" Citing Swiss film scholar Laurent Guido, he concludes that Frey's light set designs "still relied on a value of 'authenticity' guaranteed by the presence of performers on stage, and more generally, the presence of the human body" (110). This included, most importantly, the offstage crew, under Frey's direction, whose skills and meticulousness were critical to a show's success (as Frey said in the quoted lecture, "I think the crew members

would like me to go to hell, as my innovations disturb all their comfortable well-established habits" [224]).

The book's first illustration, a photograph of Frey and crew amid a bank of slide projectors, foretells Frey's position, literally and conceptually. It is a position, too, to heed when we think of the history of modern media, more specifically of screen practices. It is for this reason that the essay contributed by French media historian and archivist Laurent Mannoni rather grates with Tralongo's argument. Instead of a reasoned account of the use of the lantern in a specific artistic niche in the latter, one gets a sweeping statement or two in the former, such as "*féerie* became popular as a means of forgetting the catastrophic end of the second Empire" in 1870 (while on the same page, it was first described as being "hugely popular . . . *during* the Second Empire" [55, my emphasis]). But how, where, and for whom was this forgetting attained, one would ask. Surely the example of the performance of "certain scenes" of a stage production of *Le voyage dans la lune,* in 1875, is insufficient to account for *féerie*'s alleged power to consign an entire era to oblivion. Nor, incidentally, do we learn why, "during the 1890s *féerie* gradually went out of fashion" again (56). And instead of Tralongo's approach to Frey as a specific instance of projection practices, one gets teleology. In what seems like a précis of his 1994 book *Le grand art de la lumière et de l'ombre,* Mannoni's long run-up, from 1659 to be precise, spends itself at the moment, in the early twentieth century, when "plates whose large size and complexity indicate why the time was ripe for the cinematograph to appear" (61). Hence the exclusive focus on cinema in the last section of his essay, as if all theatrical lantern entertainment had been conjured away. Notwithstanding the announced topic of the piece—an exploration of "magic lanterns in theatre"—the quoted statement not merely narrows the emergence of film to "improvements" in theatrical technology (while it conveniently bypasses the many innovations in plates, light sources, and projectors that Frey—*inventeur*—made himself); it also obfuscates the fact that the development of a technology and its applications are two different, even quite contingent things.[1] Given Frey's major work in opera, one would have settled for a well-researched essay on the history of moving light sets in this performing art alone; recent studies demonstrate that up-to-date, expert knowledge is sufficiently available.[2]

The other two texts deal, in one way or another, with the exhibition. The first, a story by João Maria Gusmão, the exhibition's co-creator *and* editor of the book, is to my mind a case of self-indulgence. It is well known that artists consider a show without a catalog—functionally alike to a CV—as nonexistent, but this feels overdone. While the story is meant to illustrate the curators' intention to "bring together scientific and literary personalities from Frey's era" (287), its "what would happen if . . . ?" approach, by combining a Faustian story with Plato's allegory of the cave, is too far removed from the exhibition's subject. Closing this conceptual gap seems to have been left to Célia Bernasconi, then head curator of the Nouveau Musée National de Monaco, in the final essay. It may be the reason that her text reads like an extended audio guide, providing background to Gusmão and Paiva's curatorial work and their research for this exhibition and commenting on the installations they designed for their exhibition.

Much more instructive and exhilarating are the book's many illustrations, of both Frey's work and the two curators' response to it. In fact, the *raisonné* order of the visuals makes Gusmão's and Bernasconi's texts to a certain extent superfluous. The chronological presentation of the works by Frey, beginning with shadow theater (although not all his) through his light sets for the Palais de la Danse at the 1900 Paris Exposition, the simulated movement for the opera *La damnation de Faust* in Monte Carlo in 1905, and subsequent productions, is matched by the spatial order of the exhibition, the curators' installations especially. The latter reflect on a number of aspects and technologies of Frey's creations by allusion. The "denuded," either abstract or simplified projected images—sometimes next to Frey's original studies—simulate the processes and procedures Frey used in his own projections; although one can no longer see the original projected works, one is allowed to see their working. And although the illustrations are stills, some of these pages fold out to suggest

the phases of a movement (e.g., sunrise to sunset) or the additive color synthesis, the basis of Frey's manifold superimpositions.

All in all, *Eugène Frey* is a partly successful attempt to inform its readers about the origins of a way of creating set designs that we nowadays take for granted. Given that, as noted, the materials Frey made came from a number of archives and other repositories, the many illustrations may ease the disappointment of those who were not able to visit the exhibition—what with the Covid-19 pandemic. But one would have wished for a well-advised concept and more illuminating information that offer a fuller sense of a particularly dynamic period in the history of screen practices in a variety of performative settings.

Nico de Klerk has a BA in English (Leiden University, 1983) and an MA in discourse analysis (University of Amsterdam, 1986). In 2015, he completed his PhD at Utrecht University, published in 2017 as *Showing and Telling: Film Heritage Institutes and Their Performance of Public Accountability,* partly based on his experience as a film historical researcher and curator at the then Nederlands Filmmuseum. He is currently a postdoc researcher for the project "Projecting Knowledge: The Magic Lantern as a Tool for Mediated Science Communication in the Netherlands, 1880–1940" at Utrecht University. Recently, he coedited and contributed to *Films That Sell: Moving Pictures and Advertising* (2016) and coauthored the website *Mapping Colin Ross* (Ludwig Boltzmann Institute for Digital History, 2017). He is on the editorial board of *The Moving Image.*

NOTES

1. See, e.g., Wiebe E. Bijker, *Of Bicycles, Bakelites, and Bulbs: Towards a Theory of Sociotechnical Change* (Cambridge, Mass.: MIT Press, 1995).
2. See Gabriela Cruz, *Grand Illusion: Phantasmagoria in Nineteenth-Century Opera* (New York: Oxford University Press, 2020), and Gundula Kreuzer, *Curtain, Gong, Steam: Wagnerian Technologies of Nineteenth-Century Opera* (Oakland: University of California Press, 2018).

DVD/Blu-ray

The incredible 1915 Italian feminist, steampunk, jewel thief, cross-dressing, aviatrix thriller!

FILIBUS
The Mysterious Air Pirate

A film by Mario Roncoroni

"The spryest comic-book movie of the season
— J. Hoberman, *New York Times*

⬦ eye

Image courtesy of Milestone Films.

Filibus

DVD/BLU-RAY PRODUCED BY MILESTONE FILMS/EYE FILMMUSEUM, DISTRIBUTED BY KINO LORBER, 2021

Kate Saccone

If there were such a thing as the *ultimate* archival film, *Filibus*—the futuristic 1915 Italian crime caper produced by Corona Films—might just be a top contender. Not only is it beautiful, with gorgeous tinting and toning, but its central female character is a delight. A "master" of disguise, Filibus (aka Baroness Troixmond aka Count de la Brive) is a daring, technologically savvy, cross-dressing jewel thief who has her own dirigible and a group of henchmen at her bidding. *Filibus,* which was directed by Mario Roncoroni, is more than just an enjoyable film, however; the story of its recent rerelease, following a 2K restoration carried out by Eye

Filmmuseum in Amsterdam in 2017, is also a tale of film vault detective work, resulting in the correct attribution of Valeria Creti as the lead actress. You might say, then, that *Filibus,* which is now out on DVD and Blu-ray thanks to Milestone Films, is the total package: an engaging but heretofore underseen film that highlights how cinema history is always in process.

The full title of the Milestone release is *Filibus: The Mysterious Air Pirate.* It is an apt moniker, because Filibus relies heavily on her metal airship to carry out her schemes over the course of the film's five sections. (According to Milestone's press kit, *Filibus* was originally meant to be seen either as a feature or as a serial in five parts.[1]) Utilizing a small container to move between the airship in the sky and the striking Italian coastal area where the story takes place, Filibus attempts, via various means, to frame Detective Kutt-Hendy for the crimes she herself commits (sleeping drugs, the cast of his handprint, and a miniature camera all come into play). Along the way, she also gets her hands on some Egyptian diamonds, kidnaps the detective's friend, and, disguised as the Count de la Brive, woos the detective's sister. It's a game of cat and mouse that shows, as Monica Nolan rightly argues, that for Filibus—or whatever her real name is— "all of life is one big masquerade."[2]

As others have noted, Filibus the character resembles the indefatigable American serial queens of the 1910s, such as Grace Cunard, and *Filibus* the film shares similarities with more famous French crime serials like *Fantômas* (1913–14).[3] And like her literary contemporary, the popular "gentleman thief" Arsène Lupin, Filibus's disguises play into societal preconceptions. Just as nobody anticipates the dapper Lupin to be a burglar, nobody expects the well-dressed upper-class Baroness Troixmond to be a criminal mastermind or the urbane Count de la Brive to be a jewel thief, especially after "he" rescues the detective's sister from a kidnapping attempt (which "he," of course, arranged). Scripted by writer Giovanni Bertinetti—who himself used both male and female pseudonyms[4]—*Filibus* reflects his career-long literary interests in science fiction, technology, adventure stories, and flight. That *Filibus* and Filibus have various cinematic and literary cousins, as it were, is not to suggest that either is overly familiar; rather, this intertextual framing of both shows how the film is at once of its moment and an exciting (re)discovery for the present. In the final shot of the film, Filibus, now dressed as Baroness Troixmond, is aboard her dirigible, handling her stolen treasures and greedily dreaming up her next adventure. Although the film leaves room for further episodes, nothing else was made—World War I soon began, and Corona Films eventually closed its doors in 1919. So, we are left only to imagine what this scheming, industrious, and technophilic jewel thief would do next.

The visibility that this Milestone release brings to a lesser-known film from the mid-1910s made by a short-lived production company is important because it draws public attention to smaller titles and less prolific people and studios. In other words, it helps sustain a wider perspective on film history beyond canonical successes and major stars. Such an expansive approach, to paraphrase (and slightly take out of context) Milestone cofounder Amy Heller in her excellent essay "Canon Fodder," means "embrac[ing] and explor[ing] the concept of many worlds of culture, creativity, images, and imagination."[5] We do not know much about Valeria Creti, who seems to have acted in a dozen or so films for a few different Italian companies before her film career ended. (Her last known role was in 1922, in *Il fabbro del convento.*[6]) She clearly did not reach the same level of success as fellow Italian Francesca Bertini, for example, but, as releases like this one refreshingly remind us, (Italian) film history has room for both the Cretis and the Bertinis, and all those in between.

The release's special features constitute an intelligent curatorial intervention, although their presentation on the disc could have used a proofreader. Alongside *Filibus,* the DVD/Blu-ray also includes several short films that played at the feature's original Netherlands opening. Although the Blu-ray case announces "five short films," it lists only four (there are ultimately only four on the disc). The years of both the Netherlands opening and the newsreel also differ between case and disc menu. Regardless of these minor issues, the idea of including the film program from a Dutch screening of *Filibus* is wonderful (and likely only possible because

Image courtesy of Milestone Films.

of the meticulous records kept by Dutch distributor Jean Desmet, from whose collection at Eye *Filibus* is taken). Present are a Dutch newsreel titled *Laatste bioscoop wereldberichten* (1916), the French comedy *Onésime et la toilette de mademoiselle Badinois* (1912), the Italian travelogue *Rapallo* (1914), and the French drama *Amour et science* (1912). The last two are especially nice and share *Filibus*'s stunning Italian vistas and interest in technology and gadgets, respectively.

The special features also include three trailers for *Filibus* and a short behind-the-scenes video about Eye's Jean Desmet Collection, in addition to the Italian feature film *Signori giurati* (1916), which was also produced by the Torino-based Corona Films. A perfectly fine melodrama with a gorgeous colorful fireworks sequence, *Signori giurati* stars Fabienne Fabrèges as an immoral woman who, after coming into some money, opens up an opium den (the House of Forgetfulness) and ensnares many of the rich, hapless men around her in her web of deceit. Creti has a small role as the

daughter of one of the vamp's victims. As this was the film that Eye intern David Emery used to identify Creti as Filibus (as opposed to the previously long-credited Cristina Ruspoli, who actually played the detective's sister),[7] the inclusion of *Signori giurati* on the release feels appropriate. It is also a pleasure to see *Signori giurati* here because it gives us more access to the career of Fabrèges. A French stage and screen actress, Fabrèges worked in the Italian film industry from 1916 to 1923 before moving to England and retiring from cinema.[8] According to Elena Nepoti's profile on Fabrèges for the Women Film Pioneers Project, while in Italy, the actress wrote the scripts for a few films, including *Signori giurati,* and directed at least one.[9]

Like Milestone's previous silent film releases, *Filibus* contains excellent musical accompaniment performed by world-renowned artists in the field of contemporary silent cinema exhibition. Viewers can choose between Mont Alto Motion Picture Orchestra's score and two additional scores composed by Donald Sosin, with one featuring intermittent vocals by Joanna Seaton. Although all of the scores enhance the experience of watching this beautiful film restoration, the orchestral score turned out to be, surprisingly, a bit too muted for my taste. Sosin and Seaton's accompaniment, on the other hand, effectively captures *Filibus*'s bizarre and playful energy.

With a crisp seventy-one-minute runtime, *Filibus* would be a welcome addition to any gender or film studies course, although I hope it continues to have wider appeal as well. While one could argue that some of the promotional language around the release is a bit hyperbolic, it also seems to reflect Milestone's obvious and infectious excitement about this long-buried silent film and its plucky cross-dressing heroine. Like all of Milestone's releases, *Filibus* is a testament to the company's passion behind its catalog. It's one thing to distribute archival films to contemporary audiences; it's an entirely different thing to have done it with such enthusiasm.

Kate Saccone is a PhD candidate at the University of Amsterdam. She holds an MA in media studies (Preservation and Presentation of the Moving Image) from the University of Amsterdam (2022) and an MA in film and media studies from Columbia University (2013). She is also the project manager and an editor of Columbia's Women Film Pioneers Project (WFPP).

NOTES

1. Dennis Doros, Austin Renna, Marcello Seregni, David Emery, and Letizia Gatti, *Filibus* press kit (Milestone Films, 2019), 3, https://cdn.shopify.com/s/files/1/0150/7896/files/Filibus_Press_Kit_8888a58b-4bd7-4c55-b200-c5c1709a6944.pdf.

2. Monica Nolan, "Filibus," *San Francisco Silent Film Festival* [program essay] (2017), https://silentfilm.org/filibus/.

3. E.g., Daniel Lawrence Aufmann, "Filibus (Re) Introduces Us to the Wild Weird Women of the 1910s Cinema," *Persiphere,* January 23, 2022, https://www.perisphere.org/2022/01/23/filibus-reintroduces-us-to-the-wild-weird-women-of-1910s-cinema/.

4. Doros et al., *Filibus* press kit, 28.

5. Amy Heller, "Canon Fodder," *Caligari,* no. 1 (2021), https://caligaripress.com/Amy-Heller-Canon-Fodder.

6. Doros et al., *Filibus* press kit, 34–35.

7. Doros et al., 12–14.

8. Elena Nepoti, "Fabienne Fabrèges," in *The Women Film Pioneers Project,* eds. Jane Gaines, Monica Dall'Asta, and Radha Vatsal (New York: Columbia University Libraries, 2015), https://wfpp.columbia.edu/pioneer/fabienne-fabreges/.

9. Nepoti.

Conference

EYE INTERNATIONAL
CONFERENCE 2022
Global Audiovisual Archiving: Exchange of
Knowledge and Practices

29 - 31 May 2022

EYE INTERNATIONAL
⬦ eye ☀ AMIA

© Francis Alÿs, REEL-UNREEL (2011) BY-NC-ND

Global Audiovisual Archiving: Seventh Eye International Conference

MAY 29–31, 2022, AMSTERDAM, THE NETHERLANDS

Marek Jancovic

The opening and closing words of the first day of the seventh Eye International Conference (May 29–31, 2022, Amsterdam, the Netherlands) could stand in as a good outline not only of the whole event but also of the internal conflict with which the entire field of audiovisual preservation, as a global undertaking, is grappling. Following a welcome by Eye Filmmuseum's Chief Curator Giovanna Fossati, the title of the very first panel—"It's Almost Too Late!"—emphatically communicated the sense of dread, panic, and urgency that most of us concerned with audiovisual heritage experience in the face of rapidly deteriorating analog and digital carriers and multiplying environmental and political crises. And yet, Judith Opoku-Boateng concluded the last panel of the day with the words "but all is not lost." It's almost too late—but all is not lost. This ambiva-

lent but ultimately hopeful stance perfectly encapsulates the atmosphere at the conference.

Officially a three-day event subtitled "Global Audiovisual Archiving: Exchange of Knowledge and Practices," the conference was organized by the Eye Filmmuseum in collaboration with the Association of Moving Image Archivists (AMIA), the University of Amsterdam, and the Amsterdam School for Cultural Analysis. It took place in the cinema auditorium at Eye's gracious building on Amsterdam's northern waterfront and was flanked by additional days of screenings and poster presentations. The event brought together a truly diverse set of presentations and an audience from all corners of the world to discuss the challenges and global disparities in audiovisual preservation in all their complex political, technological, geographical, social, and historical facets. The audience was treated to fascinating photographic and videographic material, and the program was punctuated with emotionally impactful film screenings.

In many ways, this year's Eye conference was a model example of what a post-Covid-19 forum for practitioners, artists, and academics could look like. It was a delight to convene with colleagues and to finally catch up with old and new friends in person. It was equally gratifying to see the potential of online conferencing utilized so well, with a balanced presence of geographically remote presenters who seamlessly joined the discussions in real time as well as with prerecorded contributions.

And yet the hybrid format in itself subtly underscored the lopsided material realities of global technological infrastructure. While the conference was impeccably executed and streamed with an elaborate multicamera setup, some of the presentations occasionally got stuck because of slow hardware and network delays in places like Ghana and Tunisia. Another telling moment occurred during one of the discussions, when Rebecca Ohene-Asah from the National Film and Television Institute in Ghana, presenting on-site in Amsterdam, realized that she had never met Samuel Benagr (University of Ghana, joining virtually), despite both of them working in the same country on the same questions of national video culture and its preservation. Again, this accentuates the paradoxical position of venues like this: they carry a critical and necessary function in network building and enabling conversations, but in so doing, they also reinforce the status of established institutions in the "Global North" as ineluctable mediators of knowledge. Having said that, our field is clearly better off with this conference than it would be without. It may not be "best practice," but it is "good practice"—a refrain that echoed across many of the debates and presentations that took place.

Summaries of all the numerous, rich panels can be found in the conference program.[1] I shall try to inventory some of the subtending and overarching points raised in the presentations, roundtable discussions, and audience debates. I will first do so by means of a list that will initially appear very bleak. Some of the issues are well trodden and familiar but continue to worsen:

Much global audiovisual material has been irrevocably lost and continues decaying, sometimes due to intentional indifference or willed governmental forgetting.

Owing to political and/or financial neglect and infrastructural and/or staffing difficulties, many institutions lack even basic projection equipment, let alone appropriate tools for preserving or digitizing analog formats.

Old equipment is obsolete, and new equipment is expensive. This is exacerbated when rare tools, machines, or spare parts have to be imported across borders, especially from North to South.

National and international funding structures are set up antagonistically. Archives must compete for meager resources rather than collectively addressing shared concerns.

Under the guise of altruism, offers to digitize materials from Western/Northern companies are often paid for with loss of intellectual rights or the withdrawal of heritage from their local and regional contexts. (Commercial) archives in rich countries continue monetizing and profiting from the cultural memory of formerly colonized populations.

Despite public commitments and individual initiatives, restitution of looted heritage is stalling. Large national museums are at times refusing to repatriate—and rematriate—objects to their rightful custodians.

To get any preservation work done at all, some archivists tactically avoid working with politically delicate or controversial material for fear of souring already brittle relationships with national governments.

Contrarily, archivists are sometimes forced to refuse government funding because it is the only way to maintain an archive's social legitimacy in the eyes of the public.

Bureaucratic vagaries, visa restrictions, and the whims of embassies and other organs that regulate travel are obstructing international exchange and attendance at trainings and conferences.

Regulatory red tape—often a vestige of colonial institutional structures—hinders day-to-day work. Simple acts of solidarity, such as sending an unused machine to a partner archive, can be hampered by arcane rules.

Environmental and infrastructural instabilities, such as power outages or poor cooling systems, continue to make preservation work more difficult than it should be.

In some regions of the world, the low cultural status of archiving has resulted in a lack of professionalism and a passive attitude among archivists.

There simply is not enough money.

However, another ongoing theme was that even though these daunting challenges currently define the global audiovisual archives field, all is not lost.

Despite this grim outlook, there are genuine reasons to stay hopeful, and real progress is being made. International training programs *are* working. Internships, traineeships, and mentorships *are* working. Knowledge and skill exchange *is* happening. Machines do successfully make their way to archives where they are needed, and they are being operated by a new generation of knowledgeable experts. Many endangered records are ending up in safe hands and are being cataloged and made accessible. New cinemas—*real* cinemas—are being founded, and they occasionally turn into "accidental" archives (to borrow Didi Cheeka's expression). Those archives are succeeding in mobilizing audiences and volunteers, as we heard in the panel about the Cimatheque Cairo. Despite introducing their own administrative challenges, regulatory reforms have enabled some film archives, for example, in Thailand, to mature into healthy, functioning organizations.

We have seen ample proof that communities and individuals do care about historical audiovisual material. Artists, filmmakers, researchers, and students are willing and able to help out and can be fruitfully included in assessment, cataloging, preservation, or digitization efforts. Problems are never-ending, but workable solutions are being developed. Those solutions may not always conform to ways of doing sanctioned by guidelines and recommendations issued by AMIA, the International Federation of Film Archives, or the International Association of Sound and Audiovisual Archives. But they work. And that's the point.

In fact, if I had to pin down one message that resonated the strongest throughout the entire event, it would be this: we need to change how we think and speak of "global" audiovisual archiving. First, we need new concepts to replace the monikers "Global North" and "Global South," which were problematized repeatedly and historicized by Pedro Félix and Ilse Assmann. These labels are imprecise and do not map onto actual archival geographies of power. Materials in the North are not necessarily receiving better care, nor are they necessarily cataloged or stored properly.

Second, we need to reframe partnerships between well-funded and underserved archives. There is a tendency to interpret them in terms like "help" and "support," which imply unidirectional flows of resources or services from a benefactor to a beneficiary—usually from North to South, from national to Indigenous, from established to informal. Again, such language does not reflect the reality of such relationships and is, in fact, often indicative of what multiple presenters have called "toxic care"—practices that perpetuate patronizing or colonial hierarchies. The debates make clear that exchanges between archives always benefit both parties. Even well-trained archivists gain new knowledge from the adaptation to new circumstances; they benefit from the training and accumulate social capital around the "more experienced" institution's reputation and esteem.

Third, we need to take seriously the archival expertise and practices developed outside the traditional centers of knowledge. Archives all around the world possess skills and experience that institutions in Europe and North America do not. They are experts in dealing with very degraded material, with obsolete machines that are out of circulation elsewhere, with climatic conditions and chemical phenomena not encountered in higher latitudes, and with challenges that require nonstandard fixes. Recognizing this expertise—"intensifying local and regional solutions," as Marco Dreer put it—is a long-overdue step that professional associations must take if they truly want to represent the interests of all their global members. The community must acknowledge that existing "universal" preservation standards are anything but. Preservation ideals are often unrealistic, unsustainable, and impractical in contexts outside of well-funded European and North American cultural heritage institutions.

Instead, Carolina Cappa and many others appealed for standards that are local and expandable and grounded in sustainable paradigms of "good" rather than "best" practices. There is an urgent need to produce local technology, low-cost machines, and low-cost practices. Simpler and cheaper solutions need to be found, but, as Lila Foster has argued, in many cases, they already exist—they just need to be made widely available.

There are initiatives within formal professional organizations that are attempting to remedy the situation, such as the Minimum Viable Archiving project (FIAT/IFTA Technical Commission), a tool kit with easy-to-implement solutions for archives with limited resources. But as presenters Caroline Fournier and Camille Blot-Wellens acknowledged, the overrepresentation of European archivists in the Technical Commission remains an issue. Again, herein resonates one of the central themes of the conference: definitions and guidelines are often grounded in social, legal, and epistemological structures, habits, environments, and institutions of the North.

Alternatives can be found, however, and we do not need to look far for inspiration. The history of cinema offers many unexpected alliances, surprising migrations, and inventive forms of solidarity. Some of them were explored in "Cross-Continental Connections," a particularly vibrant panel that investigated the enigmas of a mislabeled Ottoman-era film from the Eye Collection (Asli Özgen), exchanges between Mozambican and Czechoslovakian film production and distribution (Klára Trsková), and the small but hugely fascinating Tokyo Palestine Film Collection (Mohanad Yaqubi).

We have seen an inspiring selection of collaborative and community-centered projects in various stages, some of them in their tenth iteration (New York University's APEX program) and some just taking off as prototypes (a matchmaking Tinder-like app for ar-

chives and archivists, for instance). A number of cataloging and database projects (such as *In Frame,* presented by Kate Dollenmayer and May Hong HaDuong) and experimental digitization centers (Jonathan Larcher) served as examples of ongoing local preservation efforts and raised discussions about the politics of cataloging and categorization. Novel types of partnerships were discussed in both formal and informal contexts. Rita Tjien Fooh and Arnoud Goos from the National Archives of Suriname and the Netherlands Institute for Sound and Vision, respectively, discussed their tenancy partnership, which allows one archive to use the digital infrastructure of another without giving up ownership of the collection.

Tentative shimmers of new archival possibilities emerged in presentations that tried to reimagine precariousness as potential (Débora Butruce) and archival inaction as a refusal of the colonial gaze (Jennifer Blaylock). In her search for the physically and bureaucratically inaccessible visual memory of the United Arab Emirates, Hind Mezaina asked, what is a filmography of a place, and how is it dictated?

Mohanad Yaqubi, Jonathan Larcher, and others convincingly showed the great importance of individual collectors and nonprofessional collective curatorial efforts in preserving audiovisual heritage. However, as Gabriel Menotti emphasized, informal and noninstitutional practices can also represent points of failure. Another risk affecting global audiovisual heritage is the fragmentation of collections, a truly global problem that equally affects the Indigenous cinemas of Latin America (as heard in Amalia Cordova's contribution), the countries of former Yugoslavia (Karla Crnčević), and the former Soviet Transcaucasian republics (Anri Vartanov).

Calls to action voiced at the conference included the need to recognize the role of language, for example, in translations of documents and guidelines, but also in cataloging projects that deal with collections that include local, minor, diasporic, or Indigenous languages. The importance of open source tools was also pointed out repeatedly (Sami Meddeb, Erica Carter), as was the need for shared resources and knowledge. Presenters and the audience debated thorny questions: Who should pay for the restitution of heritage in situations of unclear legal ownership? How do we document informal networks of circulation, from smuggled VHS tapes to itinerant flash drives and social media platforms?

I was especially grateful for several panels that addressed the productive role that universities can play in supporting preservation work, in circulating audiovisual heritage, and, as emphasized by Sonia Campanini, also in decolonizing knowledge structures. One example was the roundtable on the fruitful ongoing exchanges between the University of Jos in Nigeria and various German and Italian institutions. Another example was the panel (and screening) on exiled Sudanese filmmaker Hussein Shariffe (1934–2005), which demonstrated how students—not necessarily only students of film preservation—can thoughtfully cocreate a future for our audiovisual past.

It may be that my own oblique position vis-à-vis the archive, as a scholar working in the comparatively stable environment of a university in the center of a former colonial empire, is filling me with more optimism than the situation warrants. But I left the conference with hope and a sincere sense that events like these are meaningful and necessary and do lead to concrete successes in small and big forms. The Eye conference and other similar events in recent years have established a baseline for discussion about the complexities of global audiovisual preservation and provided a platform from which we can survey some of the shared tasks. Despite everything, there is perseverance, passion, and joy, there is discovery, wonder, and accomplishment, there is a willingness to collaborate as well as solidarity, friendship, resourcefulness, and learning.

But many questions remain. Where do we move from here? How do we get politicians and policy makers to listen? How do we make archiving, as Judith Opoku-Boateng put it, a "sexy" profession in countries where it is not? Aboubakar Sanogo appealed that we should "let newness enter the world of archiving." Who will pay the salaries? How do we make filmmakers trust the archive in places where they don't? How do we change film production culture and encourage filmmakers to value preservation as much as storytelling and profit? How do we change financing structures to encourage collaboration? Who needs to be lobbied, and who has to do the lobbying? How do we deal with visa restrictions that prevent people from attending these and similar events? How do we make standards realistic, inclusive, and environmentally responsible? How do we ensure that a training program or digitization project does not shut down once its funding cycle ends? As Floris Paalman asked in his closing words, how do we create financial sustainability and build viable archive economies?

I look forward to conferences that tackle this next set of questions—perhaps also elsewhere, in all the global localities to the north, south, east, and west of Amsterdam.

Marek Jancovic is assistant professor of media studies at the Vrije Universiteit Amsterdam. His current research is centered around the materialities of the moving image, film preservation practices, media and the environment, and format studies. He is the author of *A Media Epigraphy of Video Compression: Reading Traces of Decay* (Palgrave Macmillan, forthcoming) and, together with Axel Volmar and Alexandra Schneider, the editor of *Format Matters: Standards, Practices, and Politics in Media Cultures* (Meson Press, 2020).

NOTE

1. https://www.eyefilm.nl/en/programme/eye-international-conference-2022/563352.

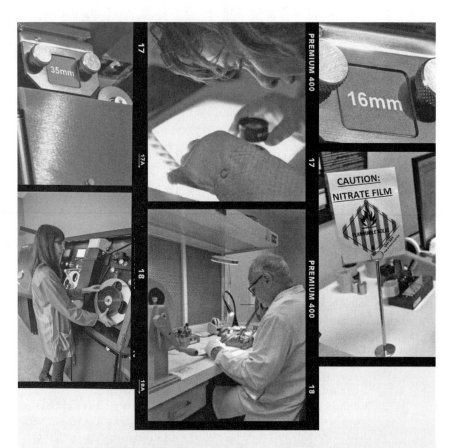

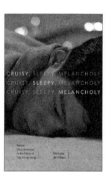

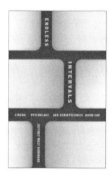